ABOUT THE AUTHOR

Daughter and granddaughter of nurses, Kelly Critcher qualified in 2007 and went into Acute Medicine. Following a moving encounter with a dying patient, she moved into palliative care. In March 2020, as Covid-19 took hold, Kelly put her years of acute and palliative nursing experience to use on the hospital's Covid wards, seeing the best and worst of the crisis first-hand.

A Matter of
LIFE &
DEATH

COURAGE, COMPASSION
and the fight against
CORONAVIRUS
on the front line

KELLY CRITCHER

JB

First published in the UK by John Blake Publishing
an imprint of Bonnier Books UK
The Plaza,
535 Kings Road,
London SW10 0SZ
Owned by Bonnier Books
Sveavägen 56, Stockholm, Sweden

www.facebook.com/johnblakebooks ⦿
twitter.com/jblakebooks ◘

First published in paperback in 2021

Paperback ISBN: 978-1-78946-441-2
Ebook ISBN: 978-1-78946-449-8
Audio Digital Download ISBN: 978-1-78946-446-7

British Library Cataloguing-in-Publication Data:

A catalogue record for this book is available from the British Library.

Design by www.envydesign.co.uk

Printed and bound in Great Britain by Clays Ltd, Elcograf S.p.A.

1 3 5 7 9 10 8 6 4 2

John Blake Publishing is an imprint of Bonnier Books UK
www.bonnierbooks.co.uk

*In memory of India and all the patients and families
I have had the privilege to care for – you have all been a
huge part of my life and my story.*

*With special thanks to Mark, for being my best friend
and for supporting me always. And to our children, Ellie, Livvie
and Ronnie – you make us so proud. Follow your dreams –
be the best you can be.*

AUTHOR'S NOTE

Although this book is based on actual events, some names have been changed to protect the identity and privacy of those who form part of the narrative.

Contents

Part Two
AFTER

'To be taken into the heart of the front line in this book is harrowing, yet it is rewarding to share the honesty and dedication of those people saving lives and working so hard. I feel inspired, and safe, to be able to read this book and feel very much in the hands of angels.'

Chris Difford, singer/songwriter, Squeeze, and curator of *The NHS Album*

Introduction

This book is an insight into my life and my work. I have no agenda other than to tell my story. I mean no offence to anyone, so please don't take any.

Have you, or has anyone you know, ever been called into hospital to have 'the conversation'? The one that goes something like... 'I'm sorry, we've tried everything possible, but things are not looking good.' Lives change during those conversations. Hearts break. Worlds fall apart.

Have you ever wondered what it might be like to have those conversations day in, day out?

I would like to show you a little of my world and what it's like to be a part of someone's life at the most difficult time, when it becomes numbered in days, weeks or months. For me, dying is just another phase of life, arguably the most important... our last chance to do things we want to do, say things we want to say. But to do this, we rely on the bravery of healthcare professionals to fight their own fears and be honest with us, telling us painful truths, even if this means causing upset.

I realised a few years ago that I had stopped coming home and relaying my extraordinary experiences to my family. What had started as extraordinary had become ordinary. Yet the things I see and do on a daily basis are fascinating. I was afraid that stories would go untold, lost forever as my memories fade. Some stories need to be captured, and I hope this book gives some insight into what ordinary NHS staff do on a daily basis. For reasons of privacy, some names and details have necessarily been changed. But all the stories are true.

I've been a nurse for seventeen years. Having first gained a degree in business management, I realised that my heart lay elsewhere. It took me a while to get there, but once I did, I never looked back. As a student nurse, I was asked to visualise and draw what nursing meant to me. So I drew (badly) an apple core – to signify that nursing is at the centre of everything I do, everything I see and everything I feel. I love being a nurse. I love my job.

Starting my career in the acute sector, I was like a sponge, absorbing every bit of knowledge I possibly could; seeing patients at their most vulnerable, watching lives being saved on a daily basis, witnessing medicine at its best, in all its glory. Yet alongside the treatable, the curable, the 'survivors' are those patients whose needs often get pushed aside. The patients who won't get better, cannot be cured, will not survive – the 'palliative' and the 'dying'. I felt they deserved better and the more I saw, the stronger my feelings became.

Eventually, I took a giant leap in the world of healthcare – from acute to palliative nursing. Little did I know it then, but in March 2020 this combination of nursing specialities would come to the fore in the battle against Covid-19, a dangerous and fast-spreading virus that took the world by surprise and brought some areas of the NHS to its knees.

In my book I take you into the world of Northwick Park, a major general hospital in Greater London. From my first days on the ward as a student nurse through to the recent coronavirus pandemic, there has never been a dull day. It is a place full of hustle and bustle – hosting a never-ending flow of people from all walks of life. Staff, visitors, patients, relatives, carers, police officers, ambulance technicians, porters, nurses, doctors, physiotherapists, domestic staff, adults, children, mums in labour. The happy, the sad, the new parents, the recently bereaved. All joined together, experiencing the best and the worst of the healthcare system. Each with their own story to tell about our magnificent NHS, of which I am hugely proud to be a part.

This is my story.

Part One

BEFORE

Chapter 1

Mum always thought I should do something 'in health'. From time to time during my childhood and teenage years she'd mention nursing, but when she saw it wasn't having much of an impact she'd talk about a career in occupational therapy. 'You'll be able to use your caring side doing that,' she'd say.

At the time I wasn't interested. I didn't really know what I wanted to do, to be honest, but as far as I was concerned it didn't involve nursing. I studied human biology at sixth form in Shrewsbury, where I grew up, but did embarrassingly badly at it. And yet, I was aware that nursing was in my blood. My mum, Jan, had been a nurse before starting a new career as a fitness instructor, my maternal grandmother was a nurse and her husband (my grandfather) had worked as a medical attendant in a silver and platinum factory in London, where he dealt regularly with gruesome burns and severed fingers. Mum and both her parents were members of the Red Cross, forever doing demos and talks, overseeing first-aid courses, civil defence manoeuvres and drills in preparation for emergencies.

Mum remembers how many of their fellow residents on the council estate in which they lived would call round to have minor emergencies treated. Bicycle crashes, roller-skating accidents, cuts, grazes, sprained ankles, sore throats, toothache – whatever the problem, Nan and Granddad appeared to be able to deal with it, thanks to their knowledge and a good stock of essential first-aid items kept in a kitchen cupboard, including aspirin, Anadin, Friars' Balsam, menthol and eucalyptus oils, calamine lotion (which, in her early years, she referred to as 'Caroline Ocean'), Contusol (a green, smelly liquid, always liberally applied to bruises), kaolin poultice for aches, pains and swellings, iodine, cloves, scissors of various sizes, tweezers and needles for splinters, tongue depressors, butterfly sutures, crepe bandages, cotton bandages, gauze swabs, Vaseline, non-stick dressings, slings and stockinette tubing of different sizes, along with the applicators necessary to wrestle them onto damaged digits… To say it was a well-stocked cupboard is an understatement!

Unlike me, Mum recognised early on that work in a caring role was her calling and despite her fears about her working-class background and strong London accent, she was accepted on a four-year combined children's and general nursing course at Great Ormond Street Hospital. She battled to get on the course, as most of the other trainees had A-levels and she needed to pass five O-levels, including a science. This took her a while but she persisted and in March 1970 her training began. She moved into a large house in Hampstead, along with twenty-six other trainees, and although she was conscious that she stood out from the rest, was determined to make her mark.

'I wore a pink-and-white candy stripe nurses uniform to the knee with a detachable white starched collar and apron,' she told me, 'plus a white starched hat that we picked up flat from a shelf in the uniform cupboard and made up ourselves.

'To this was added black tights and black lace-up shoes, and heaven help you if your hair was seen touching a collar. I had no problem with this but some nurses looked as though they'd let a two-year-old do it for them and never, ever managed to look smart.'

The start of Mum's life as a nurse (surprisingly, by today's standards) didn't involve patients. Days were spent emptying dozens of bins and scrubbing them clean with Chemico paste. Mum and the other trainees had to boil bedpans, jugs, kidney dishes, etc. in the steriliser before getting children's clothes ready for either that night or the following day. Then they bathed and fed the older children before putting them to bed.

Gradually, Mum was given increasing amounts of responsibility as the training rolled out. These were the days of formidable matrons and mostly male doctors that everyone was expected to bow down to, and the training was very exacting. Quite often they were left alone because of short-staffing (some things don't change…) and Mum and her colleagues would find themselves looking after numerous babies and children single-handedly at night. Sometimes these nights passed uneventfully; others didn't:

'I was on my own,' she remembered, 'sat down at the desk to start writing the Kardex [record for each patient]. I went to turn on the desk light and received an almighty electric shock, which threw me crashing back into the French window like a cartoon cat being splattered against a wall, before I curled into a ball on the floor. I managed to recover enough to call a night sister who, when she arrived, said I'd be OK in a bit and she'd send an agency nurse to help. I can still remember the startling effects of the shock, but it was worth it to get some help…'

From Great Ormond Street, Mum went to the London Hospital for her general nurse training. Having been in paediatrics, there was a lot she didn't know about adult conditions, but soon she gained knowledge of areas including orthopaedic, general surgery and medical patients. However, there was still a lot to learn….

'One night, when working on the female side of a cardiac ward, a man had been admitted to the side room as there was no bed on the male ward,' she told me. 'I saw him through the night, went back next day and he'd been moved to the male main ward – all fine.

'Early in the morning, I went round to the male ward and I saw the patient from the previous evening sleeping peacefully propped quite high on pillows. I thought how much better he looked than the previous evening.

'My friend Penny was on the male side of the ward, so when she came to my ward asking for the death certificate book a short while later, I was surprised to find it was for my patient – who I thought was asleep but must have been dead. My observation skills were still being honed!'

It was while she was nursing that Mum first met Dad. She and a friend were in a pub in Southgate and at the back of the crowded bar she spotted an attractive guy holding what to Mum was an unusual concoction – Pernod and lemonade. At the time she was on a diet and only drinking slimline orange juice, so this stranger and his drink must've seemed quite exotic.

She got talking to him, discovered his name was Derrick and that he was a dentist. To see if he was telling the truth, she promptly opened her mouth and asked him what fillings she had. 'I was very impressed that he knew the answer,' she said.

Dad was being a bit economic with the truth. Actually, he was a dental technician, and although originally from Aberystwyth was living and working in London at the time he met Mum. However, he didn't tell her that. He said he was only in the city that weekend to see an Arsenal match, giving him the chance to disappear if he and Mum didn't hit it off. Luckily for me, they clicked. Dad asked Mum for her number and rang her a few days later. They started going out and quite quickly it got serious.

'Soon after we met, Derrick's grandmother died,' Mum recalled. 'She lived in Shrewsbury, and as we were getting along so well, I suggested that I could accompany him on the train there, lose myself in the town while he went to the funeral and we could travel back together later in the day. Great idea.

'We set off from London in the morning. I was dressed in purple loon pants, yellow cerise chiffon shirt and red tank top. What we did not expect was that Derrick's mum and sister would be on Shrewsbury station to meet him. I take my hat off to them for the fact that they didn't bat an eyelid at the way I was dressed and even assumed that I was going to the funeral. When I told them of my plan, they wouldn't hear of it and insisted that I go to "the house" with them all. The way I was dressed seemed in no way to bother them and so I found myself in with this family of Welsh people who were treating me like one of them. I felt very out of place among the soberly dressed attendees, but what could I do?'

The same could not be said, however, of her first visit to Aberystwyth: 'I don't think any of Derrick's friends liked me and were all disappointed that their lovely Derrick had been hooked by some Cockney bird!'

I assume the disappointment among his friends didn't last long, because Mum and Dad stayed together, eventually marrying in Aberystwyth in 1975. Both were quite hippy in their ways and Mum insisted on making her own wedding dress, a flowery affair complete with Alice band. They didn't have a honeymoon because they'd previously travelled around Jamaica for six weeks. There was a plan to stay for a year and find work but for whatever reason, they decided to come home early and get on with their lives.

Mum and Dad decided that their married life would begin outside of London, so they moved to Shrewsbury – a kind of 'midway' between Mum's family in London and Dad's parents in Aberystwyth. They found new employment around the town (both eventually changed jobs: Mum became a fitness instructor and Dad started as a postman after he was made redundant from his dental technician's job) and lived in a semi on a council estate before mortgaging themselves to the hilt and moving into the four-bedroom house with a huge garden where they still live and I still call 'home'.

The move was prompted by the fact that by the early 1980s they had a young family: Lee, my elder brother, born in 1977; myself, born in 1979; and Ian, who came along in 1981. We were a happy family; I have fond memories of adventures in the garden; making go karts, scaling rope ladders, tree climbing and roller-skating. There was lots of laughing and plenty of arguing. We had the largest garden in the street and so all of the local kids (one of whom is now my lovely sister-in-law) could be found there with us most days, playing hide and seek and having gooseberry fights, and we would often shop-errands for the elderly neighbours.

We enjoyed caravan holidays in places like Saundersfoot and Lowestoft, along with days out to local National Trust parks and open spaces, complete with a homemade picnic. My favourite memories are of day trips to visit Gran in Aberystwyth. At least one of us would be car sick on the way there, usually me or Ian, but after a long journey we would drive over the bridge next to Gran's house, shouting, 'Put the kettle on, Gran.' She would make us tea and biscuits on arrival (I never found out why her custard creams tasted so much better than any others) followed by a day on the promenade, in the arcade and being blown away on the beach.

There wasn't a lot of money around – actually, there was very little – but Mum always insisted we ate healthily. When she was 10 she weighed 10 stone and really battled with her weight in her late teens and early twenties. Becoming a fitness instructor was part of this, I think, so we were on the carrot sticks and Thousand Island dip long before any of that became fashionable.

As is usual with middle children, I was the peacekeeper and the one who always seemed to care about what was going on around me. It's a complicated position. You have to take the knocks and the criticism from the older one while taking responsibility for and protecting the younger one. Mum says I was a good kid, if quite stubborn and opinionated, and I was very sporty, having spent most of my childhood outdoors. I was a tomboy and fearless with it. I loved playing hockey and I took part in Sports Acrobatics – this was like gymnastics but working in pairs or trios, with lots of throwing around and somersaulting. Needless to say, there were more than a few injuries.

I remember my training partner, Andy, breaking his ankle during a training session at Lilleshall (later, an FA Centre of Excellence). He had just performed a double back somersault when his foot landed in between two crash mats, with the result that his foot stayed on the crash mat and his ankle was forced down into the gap. My stomach still turns with the clear memory of what it looked like. An ear-piercing scream from Andy was quickly followed by a variety of reactions from the rest of us and it was obvious that this was a horrendous injury. Our coach was quick to usher us away, while making sure that her assistant coach went to call an ambulance. I was equally horrified and fascinated, feeling the need to keep looking over at Andy's inversely broken ankle. He passed out a couple of times due to the pain and shock. When the ambulance technicians arrived, they immediately gave him nitrous oxide – what we know as 'laughing gas'. It is perfectly named: he laughed his way out of the sports hall to great relief for those of us who witnessed our friend in so much pain and distress. Andy spent about two weeks in hospital having had surgery and pins inserted and a long period of recovery with further surgery months after. I remember watching him leave on the stretcher and being in awe of those looking after him, wondering and wanting to be a part of what would happen next. Maybe this was when the seeds were planted for my future nursing career.

Sports Acrobatics was my life for many years. Andy and I were great together. He was older and strong, therefore a perfect 'base'. I was small for my age but strong and fearless. Together, we entered many competitions and won plenty of medals. Andy was my hero – I loved being with him and being part of the Sports Acro 'family'. We travelled all over the country, even representing Great Britain in a competition in Wexford, Ireland.

But things started to change when Andy stopped coming to the same training sessions as me. Our coach gave excuses but I knew something wasn't right. Then one day I found out – he had another training partner. She was smaller and more flexible than me (flexibility was my weakness) and I was totally devastated. I was eleven years old and I felt that my world had fallen apart. That evening, I went to bed but couldn't sleep. It was summer, Mum was at work teaching an aerobics class, and Dad was outside watering the garden. It took me a long time to find the courage to go to him as I didn't want to show how upset I was, but I did, and he took me in his arms and hugged me tight. I cried and cried until I had no tears left. I carried on with Sports Acro, but it was never the same and as life as a teenager became more important, I left the sport behind aged thirteen.

Academically I was OK. I'd be the one who was average at most things. The kind of kid who could come out of school with As and Bs if they worked hard, but would generally make do with Bs and Cs. I never excelled at any one thing but could hold my own, where necessary. For me, school was something you just had to get on with, and while I was in the 'popular group', I always felt that I couldn't quite be myself once I was inside the school gates. There were too many situations you needed to fit into, too many occasions that demanded you become a certain person. I struggled with that, and also with the need to throw myself into conflict if I wanted to stand out. As I've mentioned, I was always the peacemaker who would do anything to avoid an argument. I'm still like that, but in the nursing profession avoiding conflict is just about impossible, so on occasions I've had to get stuck in. But more on that later…

When I was child and a teenager I wasn't one for a huge gang of friends, preferring a few close mates I could spend time with and confide in. One of these from my Shrewsbury days was Will. He and his family lived on the other side of the railway line to us and we had great times hanging out together. His mum and dad were very laid-back and he and his four siblings were given pretty much a free rein, including being allowed to keep creatures including iguanas and snakes in his bedroom. As teenagers we'd get drunk on his grandma's homemade potato wine and go looking around his garden for frogs we could feed to his snakes. He was, and still is, one of those people who always seem to make things happen, no matter where they are or who they're with. He's now a single dad with three girls and whenever I visit his house I'm reminded of our childhood days – kids and animals running around everywhere in a lovely, semi-feral atmosphere.

At the age of fifteen, I got together with Gavin, a bolshie, ginger, rugby-crazy Welsh boy who had moved to Shrewsbury from Carmarthen and with whom I stayed until finally having the courage to break up with him when I moved to university. For me, a relief – for Gav, devastation, but I'm sure he thanks me for it now as he is happily married with two lovely children.

As the end of my schooldays approached my parents were keen for me to continue studying with the thought of maybe going to university. Lee, my older brother, wasn't interested in being a student and at eighteen had joined West Mercia Police. He'd had an isolated childhood in some ways and wasn't the most sociable of people, very much wanting things to go his way.

He seemed angry at the world and I grew up feeling he hated me for coming along two years after him and grabbing all the attention. However, much of that anger went into developing his physical fitness and, despite not being the tallest, he is most definitely the strongest person I know and if anyone upset me at school, he was down on them like a ton of bricks.

At this point in time, my younger brother, Ian, was about fourteen and most definitely running with the wrong crowd. It was the usual teenage-boy stuff, but he wasn't trying at all at school and causing our parents a great deal of worry. He wasn't rude or unpleasant to them but he was getting into bits of trouble. For the moment, it didn't seem likely he'd achieve any kind of academic success so I felt it was down to me to live up to my parents' ambitions for us.

But what to study? Like a lot of young people, at sixteen I hadn't a clue what to do. The caring professions had been mentioned, of course, but at this stage they didn't appeal. I opted to study A-levels in English language, sociology and human biology at Shrewsbury College, and enjoyed a couple of years in an atmosphere that was definitely more relaxed and more 'me' than school ever had been. As ever, I did OK, scraping through the exams to earn a place at the then Cheltenham and Gloucester College of Higher Education (now part of the University of Gloucestershire) to study a degree in business management, specialising in human resources and marketing. Why I chose this, I have no idea. Perhaps I thought I'd enjoy the 'human' side of HR. Anyway, I'd made up my mind and in September 1997, I set off for Cheltenham full of excitement and anticipation about what lay in store.

When I arrived, I realised that I was going to enjoy living away from home and meeting new people. My halls of residence was a beautiful old house with high ceilings, and kitchens just built for partying in. There were people from all over the country, and from so many different backgrounds. I loved the freedom and I enjoyed Cheltenham as a place to live, with its many green spaces and beautiful buildings. Apart from attending lectures there were no demands made on us and I quickly got to bond with a circle of friends who were just as happy staying at home watching TV together as they were going for big nights out.

I didn't come home much during that period and I didn't really keep in touch with the friends I'd made from school and sixth form, apart from Will. I think they wondered what had happened to me, but I must admit that I'm a bit like that. I'm always happy with the friends I have at any moment, but when a situation has finished – the end of sixth form or leaving university, for example – I don't tend to hang around reliving the past or being particularly nostalgic. I just move on, and that's always been my way in life.

Part of my course was the requirement to attend a work-experience placement for a year. I was lucky: I was presented with an amazing opportunity to work in the HR department of the Gap clothing company in London. Even better, it was a paid placement and I was able to move into a maisonette in Northolt, west London, with some girls from my course. On paper, you'd think I had the dream placement that might one day turn into a real job, well paid and perhaps with the opportunity to travel. There was just one problem – I hated it.

For a start, I really missed Cheltenham and the life I'd been having there. But Cheltenham isn't far from London and I could've gone back there at weekends if I'd wanted. So that wasn't really the issue. The bigger difficulty was that I hated being in an office; I felt claustrophobic and bored. Sitting at a desk all day just staring into a computer completely threw me. Before I went into the HR office I'd done a week or so on the shop floor just to get an idea of how the brand worked, but even that bored me. I had no passion whatsoever for any of it and, sitting in the park one day eating my lunch, I realised that I would never last the year.

Also, I hated being away from Cheltenham because I missed Stuart, a boyfriend who was probably the first guy I thought I might end up marrying. However, he had ended our relationship while I was living in London on my placement and I was heartbroken.

So after a couple of months, I apologised, quit, and returned to Cheltenham, where I took up a job in a call centre. It wasn't really related to business management but somehow I persuaded my course tutors to sign it off as an appropriate placement, which they did, bless them. On my first night back in Cheltenham, having moved in with two friends, Elaine and Kristy, I spent the whole night crying about Stuart and my failed placement in London. They were great, got me through and introduced me to their group of friends, and we spent the next two years living together, having the best time.

I can't say I enjoyed the call centre job much either, but at least I was back in Cheltenham among my friends and the work wasn't too mentally taxing. I was processing insurance claims and dealing with enquiries, so it was just a case of getting the work done before going home or meeting friends in the park or the pub. The office was populated with people my age and there was always good banter and camaraderie around.

That time passed in a flash and before I knew it, it was June 2001 and I was graduating. And I still didn't know what I wanted to do. Like many students before and after me, I drifted back home with the vague idea that something would turn up that I enjoyed doing. I hated the thought of having to go back home and I felt so low at the thought of leaving my friends and all the fun that went with my life in Cheltenham. My parents came to collect me in a van they had borrowed and I cried all the way home.

I took a temporary job with the local council as a community development officer. My task was to see what kind of recreation provision there was for young people around the area and, after talking with kids from youth clubs and their workers, come up with creative solutions. If I'm honest, I found this hard going. I couldn't think creatively about what we could do to help the young people and I had no team around to support me. It was quite a lonely job and I didn't enjoy this solitary aspect. By February 2002 I'd quit, and once again I was looking round for something to occupy my time.

Like a lot of young people, my thoughts turned to taking time out and going travelling. As kids we hadn't been much further than Majorca and the more the idea cemented in my mind, the more I looked forward to seeing something of the world. I asked a friend if she fancied coming with me, and she did – except that as our plans were taking shape she was offered a job and decided to go with that. Undaunted, I quickly found someone else and the plans were in progress when the same thing happened. *Right,* I thought. *If I can't rely on anyone else I'll go alone. I really want to do this and I won't be put off or scared.*

All I needed to do now was let my parents know of my plans…

Chapter 2

'I really don't think that's a great idea, Kelly,' said Mum, when I told her and Dad about my plans. 'On your own? It's one thing to go wandering around the world with a mate, but by yourself? I don't think so.'

Dad nodded in agreement. 'Are you sure you can't find anyone else to come with you?' he said. 'There must be someone, surely?'

Again, I explained that people were accepting jobs and starting their careers. They were in no position to accompany me. Anyway, I'd be fine. What could possibly go wrong?

'We're just not happy about it, Kelly,' Mum said. 'If you go off on your own, I don't think I'll sleep for a year.'

Mum can be incredibly stubborn when she wants to but I was determined to take this time out travelling, even if it meant going on my own. I hoped they wouldn't try to stop me because I felt I needed to do this. Even so, I was aware they weren't happy.

A couple of days later, Mum and Dad asked me down for a chat. Mum was smiling. 'We've come up with a solution to the travelling thing,' she said brightly. 'We know someone who'll go with you.'

'We think this will work brilliantly,' Dad added.

'Go on…' I said.

'Ian. Take Ian!'

I looked at them in shock. 'You're not serious,' I said. Still smiling, they nodded in reply.

Yes, they were serious. Deadly serious about me taking along my younger brother. The 6ft 3in lump, now twenty-one, who, while generally good-natured and easy-going, had a nose for getting into trouble when drink was involved. Mum really thought he was turning into what she described as a 'lager lout' with a temper to match. There always seemed to be some incident or another happening when he was out in town, and from their point of view, a spell away with the sensible sister might do him the world of good. He was drifting. He had a job in McDonald's and seemed to have little ambition other than to earn enough money to live it up at the weekends. But what about me? How did I feel about looking after a silly boy only just out of his teens? This was my idea, my trip. I might never do anything like this again. Why did I have to take my little brother?

I said all this and they listened, but I knew their minds were already made up. If I were to go with their blessing, I'd have to take Ian. Really, there was no choice. My brother had obviously been primed for this and he came into the room beaming and full of enthusiasm for the trip.

'It's gonna be amazing!' he shouted. 'I can't wait. Kelly, we're going to have an excellent time. Where do you reckon we should go?'

'Where would you like to go?'

'Dunno,' he replied. 'You decide…'

Somehow, I knew that would be his response.

For a day or two I weighed up the options. I could just go alone but I'd never hear the end of it, and by the time I was ready to leave, I'd probably not feel like going at all. Ian and I got on well, generally, and he was big enough to see off any trouble. But would he get into trouble of his own making, me spending valuable travelling time bailing him out? I didn't want our adventure to be spoiled by having to pull him drunk out of various bars.

All that said, Ian being absent from home for a year would be respite for Mum and Dad and I felt he might behave differently if it was just the two of us and he was away from Shrewsbury. So it was decided – we'd go together and take responsibility for each other, whenever and wherever. I went into town, bought a selection of travel guides and spent evenings poring over them, working out where we'd go and how we'd get there.

September 2002 came around quickly and before we knew it, we were at the airport, saying our goodbyes. Mum, being her usual self, was in tears, but I'm not sure the gravity of travelling to the other side of the world on our own had hit me until this moment. I turned around and saw Dad start to cry and I was genuinely shocked. I'd only ever seen him cry once before, when our first family dog died. What an emotional goodbye – Mum and Dad waving off two of their three children into the unknown. Despite feeling my own doubts for the first time, we reassured them that all would be well, we were going together, yes, we would look after each other, no, we wouldn't split up, and yes, I would make sure Ian didn't get into any trouble. Meanwhile, I was rooting in my hand luggage for passports, visas, flight numbers, etc. Notice that I've used the plural... Ian, of course, had done little to no preparation and had quite clearly left me to take care of all the admin and planning.

Our first stop was Singapore, where we spent a few days finding our feet and getting used to the traveller's way of life. After that we headed for Malaysia, and to a cousin of Dad's who lived out there. We stayed with him for a while before heading off to explore the rest of the country and at one point, probably three weeks into the trip, I recall throwing the guidebook at Ian while we were on a sleeper train and telling him he could bloody well decide where we were going next! I suppose, on reflection, that I have always taken the role of decision-maker and those around me are used to that. Poor Ian was probably thinking he was doing the right thing by going along with my plans when along comes the *Lonely Planet* thrown full force in his direction.

After Malaysia we headed for Thailand and the island of Koh Samui. For me, this is where the travelling experience truly began. It was nothing less than heavenly and I loved the dreamy quality of the island and its laid-back, friendly people. We lived in a hut on the beach, rented scooters to explore the island and enjoyed swimming in the clear turquoise waters. I even found time for a holiday romance – a guy from Scotland called Dave who, with a friend, Mark, was on his way home after travelling for several months. We met on the boat home from a Full Moon Party, infamous in Thailand and supposed to be great fun. I'm sure it would have been – had I not spent the whole night either asleep or being sick. Despite my worries about Ian, it was he who ended up looking after me that night. Dave and Mark brightened the mood though, with plenty of tales. We would often spend nights together, chatting and laughing, dancing and riding around on street bikes or mopeds, getting food such as beautiful spicy chicken and delicious seafood kebabs from the local street vendors. When I arrived in Koh Samui, I was a vegetarian, but when I left, I was a reformed meat eater. The guys were great company and spent time telling us where they'd been and what they'd done. However, if only we had taken heed of their warning to 'beware of the scammers'…

Once back in Bangkok, we must have been like sitting ducks for the locals. Two naïve young travellers, already running out of money, not used to city life. Scams change over the years but the principles remain the same: they're believable, well tested and devastating to those being scammed. It was so well rehearsed – you get taken on a tuk-tuk ride around the city, the driver talks to you about precious jewels in the local area and how they are generating lots of interest. Then you arrive at one of the Buddhist temples, wander around and overhear a conversation between a few people about the same stones the tuk-tuk driver talked about. Is it coincidence?

The next stop is a jewellery shop. Surely the penny must be dropping now, but the naïvety is in full force and I am cringing just writing this. We were taken into the jewellery store, shown the beautiful blue stones and then sold a story about how much we could buy them right then and how they will then be worth double in Australia. What can I say? We fell for it – hook, line and sinker. Not only did we believe them and hand over our money, we also believed the bit about having to pay tax on them if we took them through the airport, so they would send them to a PO Box address in Australia for us.

Almost as soon as we arrived back in our dingy room, I picked up my *Lonely Planet* guide, which had a chapter on scams, and didn't even have to read it. The words 'precious gemstone scam' jumped out at me and I sank onto the bed. I showed it to Ian, who was immediately full of rage. We went and found a phone box to call home, and I remember saying to Mum, 'We're going back to find them and tell the local police what has happened.' She later recalls telling me how after that phone call she expected never to see us again, predicting the news headlines 'Brother and sister missing in Thailand' as she had visions of Ian finding the scammers and taking his own revenge.

Needless to say, the local police were not a bit interested and by the time we found the jewellery store the next day it was all boarded up. I wonder if they managed to fool any other travellers that day?

When we did eventually call home, Mum was so relieved to hear from me that she cried and told me she loved us both. This was quite a shock as we aren't a family who says, 'I love you', not even during emotional goodbyes at the airport. Luckily, our parents felt sorry for us and despite having little money themselves, somehow bailed us out and we continued our adventures. Personally speaking, I'm incredibly lucky that they helped; had we been forced to return home it's possible that I'd never have become a nurse and this book wouldn't have been written.

Putting the past behind us, our next stop was Perth, Western

Australia. While exploring this remotest of cities we met up with a group of young travellers who were planning to drive in convoy to Sydney over a period of eight weeks. We figured this would be an amazing way to see a good chunk of Australia and we decided to tag along with them. There were eight of us – six boys and two girls – in three different vehicles and we had a whale of a time crossing the big barren interior of the country and having all sorts of adventures.

When we finally arrived in Sydney, Ian and I had little money left and we knew it was time to get jobs. Ian found work in a posh restaurant as a kitchen-hand while I ended up serving drinks at the World Bar, a travellers' hangout in the King's Cross area of the city. I loved it. I met people from all over the globe and we both fell in love with the city itself – such a vibrant, warm and interesting place, especially when you're young. Ian thought he might only stay a month or two in Sydney before flying home, but it wasn't difficult to persuade him to stay on longer. He was making many great friends and his happy, easy-going side was really beginning to shine.

That said, now we'd semi-settled in Sydney, we decided to go our separate ways for a while and enjoy a bit of independence from each other. He moved in with some friends while I shared a place with a guy I'd met. He and I travelled up the East Coast for a short while but he turned out to be something of an idiot, so I decided to head back to Sydney and pick up where I'd left off in the World Bar. Friendships were rekindled and partying picked up on. We really did have the best time in Sydney – meeting friends who we would stay in touch with for many years – Colin, Graham, Anna, Gav. All now with families of their own – back then, completely wild and free.

It seemed the World Bar's boss had missed me because a few days after I returned, I was offered the job as bar manager. I would be sponsored for a visa and it seemed I'd arrived at one of those pivotal moments in life: the crossroads that indicates a big life change if you take the path that is offered. I thought and thought about it, wondering whether a life spent in Sydney, Australia, would be for me. I enjoyed managing the bar but I knew it wouldn't really be forever. However, I was still young, and any number of possibilities might come up for me if I stayed on.

Not long after the offer I was walking towards the bar for another shift when a thought came out of nowhere.

I want to be a nurse.

I almost stopped in my tracks. Suddenly, the path I wanted to follow had opened up to me. It was as clear as the sunlight bouncing off Sydney's skyscrapers. I wanted to be a nurse. That's what I'd do, and I would go back to England to start my training.

To this day, I've no idea where that thought came from. As I've mentioned, the idea had been planted way back, but I'd taken little to no notice of it and hadn't thought about it again until that moment. Now, it seemed obvious and I decided to act on it immediately.

'You've decided to do WHAT?' shouted Mum when I'd eventually found a phone box and got through to her at God knows what time in the UK.

'I've decided to become a nurse,' I repeated. 'Don't ask me why, but that's what I'm going to do.'

To say she was delighted is an understatement. She said she'd always known I'd go into something that would bring out my caring side, and she was burbling ideas about where I might train and what I should specialise in. 'Hang on, Mum,' I said, 'I'm still abroad. I don't think I'll be able to start until next year.'

'Yes, but you need to apply now, Kelly, otherwise you might miss your chance.'

We agreed that we'd both start looking for training places straight away and on my next day off I'd find the nearest internet café and see what was going. Between the two of us we decided that Thames Valley University looked to be the best option. Their Advanced Diploma in Adult Nursing course would begin in February 2004, giving me enough time to apply. In those days there was no online application; the forms would have to be sent to Shrewsbury, then on to a Post Office Box in Sydney. I decided to hang on until they arrived and I could post them back safely. Also, Ian and I were having such a good time we didn't want to leave, and although New Zealand was our next destination, we kept putting off the departure date.

Finally, the day came when there was no choice but to leave. Our visas were running out and we had to go. Our friends accompanied us to the airport to see us off, amid many tears and beers. We hung on for so long that we had the experience of a Tannoy announcement demanding that 'Kelly and Ian Phillips make their way to Departure Gate 21 immediately. Final call for Ian and Kelly Phillips.' We grabbed our bags, said our hurried final tearful goodbyes (mental note to self: do not allow anyone you love to escort you to the airport for an emotional farewell ever again) and made the plane by the skin of our teeth, earning ourselves some unpleasant looks when we got on.

Although a very different experience to Australia, New Zealand was beautiful. We toured the South Island, taking in some of the most breathtaking sights. We were fortunate enough to hike up the Franz Josef Glacier when it was still mostly ice. Sadly, due to global warming, you now have to take a helicopter ride to get to the ice, which I'm sure we wouldn't have been able to afford. The hostels in NZ were much classier than Oz, as most of them had hot tubs – a lovely experience when the ground is covered in snow and you are lying in a bubbling 40 degrees, gazing up at the stunning night sky. New Zealand was and still is a very sparsely populated country, and at the time of our travels there were about 1 million sheep per person. Quite a statistic…

After a few weeks in this beautiful country, touring the South Island by bus, we made for Fiji, our final destination. Again we were short of money and although we'd been told that the place was best seen from the little island, our budget could only stretch to the more touristy main island. It was awful, like a glorified Blackpool, but we hung on in there for a couple of weeks, trying not to think about going home. Although I'd decided where my future lay, I felt sad that the trip was over. My heart wanted to go straight back to Australia, and I wondered whether I might be able to train as a nurse in Sydney and what the cost might be. I remember being on the plane home and crying, wanting so much to be back there. I think I felt my heart 'ache' for the first time, feeling homesick for a place that wasn't my home and knowing I couldn't yet go back.

Eventually I accepted the inevitable and, in August 2003, we arrived home in Shrewsbury. I'd been accepted on the course for the following February, so I whiled away the next few months in a series of part-time jobs. One of these was in a pub in the middle of the town. One evening after the pub was closed,

I was driving home in Mum's car with a couple of bouncers I was giving a lift to. Shrewsbury centre is a one-way system but there is a particular junction which, if you make a sneaky turn right, means avoiding a long trip right around the system. It was late, there was no one around and I decided to make the turn.

Within seconds my rear-view mirror was lit up with blue flashing lights. I'd been spotted making the illegal manoeuvre, so I pulled over and waited for the knock on the window. When it came, I wound the window down and was confronted by a familiar face in police uniform. My brother Lee…

'Why have you stopped me?' I said. 'You must've seen it was Mum's car.'

'I did see it,' he said, 'but my sergeant's in the van. We both saw what you did. He wants me to give you a ticket.'

I knew that Lee was a stickler for the rules. 'Alright then,' I said, 'give me the ticket. I don't want you to get into trouble.'

He paused, weighing up the situation. 'Go on then,' he said finally. 'I'll let you off this time. Don't do it again.'

I drove off with relief, wondering if my law-abiding brother was finally mellowing!

The months passed quickly without further law-breaking and in early spring 2004, I moved down south to take up my place at Thames Valley University, which was based in Ealing. I was to move in with my cousin Mel in Rickmansworth, Hertfordshire, and like most students, I would need to find a part-time job to tide me over financially for the next few years.

By the end of the first day as a trainee nurse I knew I'd done the right thing. I couldn't wait to get stuck into the training and I was really looking forward to time spent on the wards during the placement element of the course. There was an air of excitement and anticipation. Ealing was a bit of a rundown hole, but that didn't matter to me. I met friends on the first day who I would remain with throughout the entire course. Gillian was from the Republic of Ireland and we hit it off straight away, stopping at the pub on the way home for a few too many Budweisers. I also met Tara, from Northern Ireland, on the first day, and I ended up moving in with her the following year.

Our student nursing placements were meant to be as varied as possible within the realms of adult nursing, so we'd be visiting surgical and post-operative care wards, as well as general admissions, geriatric and maternity. There was even a placement scheduled in a care home.

I was surprised by the fact that I was one of the youngest on the course. I'd just turned twenty-five and fully expected to be in the 'mature student' category. Not so. There were all ages, and all backgrounds too, particularly from the Caribbean, Indian and Irish communities. A lot of the female students were married with kids and were looking for a new career alongside the raising of children. Over a period of four weeks, which was classroom-based, we came to know each other as friends and colleagues, and no matter what our age or background we were all facing the same long, challenging journey on the path to becoming fully qualified nurses.

That first four weeks was an intense period of learning the basics of the human body and how it works. Academically, it was demanding but I coped with it well enough. In fact, it seemed easier than some aspects of my business management course. Maybe that was because I was enjoying it more, and felt naturally inclined towards it. Of course, some of it was boring or difficult to get your head around – particularly around ethics and human rights – and didn't make much sense until later in my career as a nurse when I was able to understand it all in context. A great deal of the classroom learning was about the NMC (Nursing and Midwifery Council) Code of Professional Conduct, now called The Code, setting professional standards that nurses and midwives must follow to be registered to practise in the UK. We needed to know it off by heart.

It was an incredible thrill to know that soon I would be undertaking my first placement on the wards of a nearby hospital, Northwick Park in Harrow. My first location would be the Ear, Nose and Throat (ENT) ward and when the day came, I was incredibly excited to put on my nurse's uniform for the first time. It was almost forty years – and, thankfully, a radical change in cut and style – since Mum had first worn her pink-and-white candy-stripe outfit, starched white hat, and belt, but across the decades we were united in our sense of pride in that uniform and what it represented. Although I was still a long way from the end of the course, and had a huge amount to learn, I will never forget stepping on to the ward that first time, and feeling like the NHS nurse I so hoped I would become.

Chapter 3

A trainee nurse on the wards of a busy hospital is in an unusual, somewhat awkward position. You're there, in a uniform, looking like you might have been walking the corridors for years. Yet you're still very much the rookie, with an awful lot to learn about the business of caring for people, both in terms of medical knowledge and your approach to the sick. 'Real' nurses and doctors – those qualified, with years of experience – tend to view you in several different ways: you're either treated with respect and understanding, or you're there as a cheap pair of hands, required to do all the dirty stuff and expected to get on with it. Or at best you're ignored and at worst treated as a downright nuisance.

This very much depends on the individual you're dealing with, and the institution you're working in. Some medical staff are much more positively inclined towards trainees than others, going out of their way to demonstrate best practice while taking into consideration your newness to the whole situation. Others are like the kind of motorist who's stuck behind a learner driver, becoming exasperated and irritated by the trainee's fumbling lack of progress. I've met both kinds and fortunately the latter are in a minority, though they're still very much around. During my surgical placement, I was fortunate enough to be observing a planned hip replacement procedure. The orthopaedic surgeon performing the operation realised I was a student and asked me if I would like a front row seat. Of course I jumped at the chance. While everyone else got busy scrubbing up, he asked one of the scrub nurses to help me get 'gowned up'. He instructed her to put the gown on backwards, which sounded strange to me but soon made sense. The gown came up to my neck and completely covered me, arms and all. This meant I didn't need to scrub up and I would be able to observe the surgery close up. The surgeon let me stand right next to him throughout the whole procedure, which I have to say was completely brutal. At times it was like watching a carpenter, complete with hammer and chisel. This was by far the most interesting part of my surgical placement and I will never forget the kindness of that surgeon.

I was lucky to have some great mentors during my training. One of them, Catriona, was excellent at nursing people as human beings and not just bed numbers. She completely understood how the personal touch made a big difference, and taught me that very often it was the little things that counted for so much, like making sure patients had enough toilet breaks and that they were eating properly and regularly. One day I was on the head and neck ward when a patient right down the end of the corridor rang their bell to summon assistance.

'Aren't you going to do something about that?' asked Catriona, when it was obvious I wasn't going to answer the call.

'Oh,' I replied, 'it's right at the far end. It's not one of ours.'

She glared at me. 'Every patient in this ward is ours,' she said. 'Now go and answer that call.'

I did as I was told, and I learned an important lesson – that patients are not numbers. Neither are they nuisances, even when it might feel that way. I realised that while this was going to be a busy, demanding and sometimes maddeningly frustrating job, patient care should always come first. Most healthcare professionals know this instinctively but, as we'll see, there are those who need reminding now and again.

The ENT ward contained a lot of people with tracheostomies and quite quickly I learned that while I had no problem with blood (which is as well, because I wouldn't have lasted long otherwise), I did, and still do, come over rather queasy at the sight of phlegm. As you might imagine, working on ENT involves a fair amount of this, particularly when suctioning a tracheostomy. The first few times I observed the procedure I had to take a few deep breaths, but eventually I got there, learning to put my revulsion aside. As a nurse you get used to anything and everything…

I surprised myself with how well I seemed to tolerate the sights and smells experienced daily. I have never been one for fainting and I've never passed out, though I came close one morning during my first placement, on the head and neck ward. A guy in his fifties was being treated for a head and neck cancer that was literally eating away at his skin. He had no skin left on the entire right-hand side of his neck down to the top of his chest. The nurse removed the dressing to clean the wound. You could see all of the veins and blood vessels, a huge area of open flesh. I started to regret the few glasses of wine I'd drunk the night before. I came over all flushed, beads of sweat formed on my forehead and I started to go deaf on one side. My legs were like jelly but I managed to will them to get me out of there. I nipped through the curtains and into the nearby toilet, where I sat down and put my head between my legs until I slowly started to feel normal again. This was the only time anything like that has happened, despite seeing all kinds of stomach-turning sights – blood, pus, phlegm, faeces, infected ulcers, snot, lice… the list goes on.

In those first few weeks I was in awe of what went on in the ward. I watched a doctor perform an emergency tracheostomy on a patient who had gone into sudden respiratory distress and couldn't breathe. It was a matter of life or death, and with only a pair of scissors to hand, the doctor just got in there, cut the opening and got a tube into the patient's airway, allowing him to breathe again and no doubt saving his life.

Another patient, a guy called Horace, was brought in following a drink-fuelled argument with his girlfriend. During the row she'd lunged at his face with a knife, stabbing him through the chin and into his tongue. The wound was horrendous, but he was fixed up and stitched up and everything seemed OK. A few days post-surgery, there was a sudden commotion from Horace's bedside, the stitches burst and he began haemorrhaging. If there was ever a time to faint at the sight of blood, this was it. As they pushed his bed at speed to theatre, blood was gushing out of his neck and mouth like a waterfall. I'd never seen anything like it, and as the bed disappeared around the corner, I wondered how someone could survive such a catastrophic loss of blood. Yet not four weeks later, having been operated on and discharged home, Horace came back to visit us on the ward, thanking everyone for saving his life. The staff were pleased to see him – it's always nice when a patient gives us recognition for what we've done – but for us it was all in a day's work. As the weeks progressed I began to see how for nursing staff, the extraordinary quickly becomes the ordinary, the routine, the everyday. This isn't to say nurses take everything for granted – far from it – but always remember that if you're feeling unwell and you're embarrassed about something, please don't worry about telling a nurse about it. If they're experienced enough, they have seen literally everything.

After the ENT placement it was a return to the classroom. This was fine, though I felt – and still feel – that the real business of learning to be a nurse takes place on the wards and I couldn't wait to get back out there again. My next placement was on a general medical ward at Central Middlesex Hospital in the Park Royal area of west London. At the time it struck me as a grim old place and subsequently most of it has been knocked down and rebuilt. Additionally, the area in which it was located was a largely deprived one. There were a lot of patients in for drug and alcohol problems, and people from care homes who were in a really bad way. That upset me a lot – I found it hard to understand how older people could be so neglected.

I sat with an older man who was suffering from a fungating cancerous tumour (one that grows from inside and breaks through the surface of the skin) that had eaten away most of his ear. Somehow, a fly had laid its eggs in the crevices of what was left of it and it had become infested with maggots. It was like something out of the Middle Ages – it was hard to believe a situation like this could exist in twenty-first-century Britain.

But there it was, and it needed dealing with. I found a pair of surgical tweezers and spent the next hour picking maggots from the poor man's ear while we chatted. He was so relieved to be free of his unwanted guests and although it was a horrible sight, I was pleased to be able to give him that relief and it was actually rather satisfying.

It was a tough hospital, with the result that many of the nurses had a resilient sense of humour, particularly those of Caribbean origin. They were excellent nurses but they gave little ground and took no prisoners, particularly among us students. Later, I'd come to know and appreciate their sense of fun. One morning I started my shift by asking one of these nurses where a certain elderly patient I'd seen the day before was.

'Oh,' she said casually, 'she's gone upstairs.'

'Right...' I replied. 'But I thought we were on the top floor here?'

The nurse looked at me and began to laugh, a deep rumble followed by a high-pitched chuckle.

'No!' she said, wiping her eyes and rolling them upwards. 'Not up the stairs. She's "upstairs upstairs". Know what I mean?'

Finally, the penny dropped. The poor old lady had died in the night and this was the nurse's way of telling me that. I could've crawled away in embarrassment, as the nurse looked at me in pity. *That girl has a long way to go*, I could almost hear her thinking.

After Central Middlesex it was a stint in the classroom followed by another placement in Northwick Park, this time on the respiratory ward. I was glad to be back at this hospital, which might seem a strange thing to say, given that it's a huge, rambling, anonymous place that has definitely seen better days and has obviously suffered from chronic underfunding over the decades. It serves one of the most ethnically diverse populations in London – there must be well over a hundred languages spoken in the place at any one time – yet it is overlooked by the famous Harrow public school, located in a beautiful and leafy park on a nearby hill. The contrast between that seat of learning and the day-to-day life of Northwick Park couldn't be sharper, and I think it's fair to say that of all the patients we treat, very few, if any, are Harrow pupils or their parents.

Yet despite its ugliness and general air of neglect, Northwick Park was (and remains) a vibrant, energetic place to work. You can feel the purposeful atmosphere as you walk down the shabby corridors or haul yourself up the concrete steps, worn down into hollows by generations of medical and non-medical feet, to the various wards. It's not a pretty place, far from it, but it has a certain 'something' that you often don't find in modern, hi-tech and newly built hospitals. Those places, while shiny and efficient, often feel sterile. They're too quiet. Give me a bustling, busy place any day, with the air of something always happening, and people communicating. Northwick Park is far from perfect, but perhaps it's those imperfections which give it its unique energy and drive.

The respiratory ward was run by Sister Fay, a formidable nurse from Jamaica. She knew everything you ever needed to know about nursing, and about patients too. She was more than willing to share this information with us students, but if she thought you were slacking, you were in trouble. She wasn't a person to get on the wrong side of but I think she liked me because I worked hard and showed willing. I had (and still have) a reputation for being late for everything but I made sure that while working under Sister Fay, I always got up extra early to make sure I was there on time.

And in the sister's presence you had to know your stuff. If you went on a ward round with her, she would not allow you to give a patient any medicine, not even aspirin, if you couldn't tell her exactly what it was, why you were giving it and how frequently the patient could have it. If you got it wrong, you'd get 'the look' from her, sending you scuttling home after your shift to dig out your textbook for the right answer. And yet, I frequently saw Sister Fay's humanitarian, empathic side. One of the respiratory ward's 'regulars' was a man from the local travelling community with recurrent chest problems. Whenever he felt unwell he didn't bother to check in at A&E – accompanied by various members of his family he'd simply come straight up to Respiratory to be examined. As we know, this isn't the usual way of things in the NHS, the four-hour wait being the usual option, but whenever he and the clan arrived, Sister Fay never batted an eyelid. She simply admitted him to the ward, greeting him like an old friend, and the respect shown to her by the man's family was absolute.

Then there was the care-home placement in Harrow. From beginning to end, I hated this experience, mostly because the care of the residents seemed to be far below even minimal standards. There was also the fact that, as a student nurse, I was treated as a complete dogsbody with little opportunity to learn anything positive.

The residents had little to no life in there. Occasionally someone would come along and have a sing-song with them, but other than that, it just felt like they were plonked in front of the TV from dawn to dusk and left to get on with it.

The staff seemed unhappy and neglected too, and I think this impacted on the way they cared for the patients. One member of staff told me she'd seen a colleague slapping one of the residents, an elderly woman, across the face. I couldn't believe anyone could treat a vulnerable person this way and although I'd not personally witnessed it, nonetheless I reported it to the nurse in charge. Result? Nothing happened.

The minor cruelties that went on in there really upset me. Each day, I'd help one old lady to get dressed as she'd recently undergone an amputation to her leg. We chatted, and I always made sure she knew that she could take her time. All she looked forward to each day was a fried egg for breakfast. One morning, as I was dressing her, she told me that she wouldn't be having any more fried eggs.

'I'm told they're bad for me,' she said sadly. 'But I've been having them all my life…'

'Who told you?' I asked.

'One of the nurses. Too much fat in them, she said.'

After I dressed her, I went straight down to the kitchen and asked if this was true.

'Yep,' came the terse reply. 'Too many calories.'

'Oh, come on,' I said. 'She's in her eighties. What harm can a fried egg do now? It's about quality of life, isn't it?'

In response, the cook just shrugged. 'New guidelines,' she said. 'Nothing to do with me.'

I was furious. There was no reason to treat individuals this way, guidelines or no guidelines. People aren't numbers. Everyone is a person in their own right, and should be treated as such, especially those whose sole source of daily pleasure was a fried egg.

Over time, I realised I could try my best, but would make little difference to the way the place was run. Everyone was institutionalised, staff and residents, and that seemed to be just how it was. I hated it so much there were days I simply didn't turn up for a shift, ticking myself in the following day. No one seemed to care if I was present or not. Back then I was a smoker and one evening, I was outside having a cigarette when a nurse passed me on the steps as she went into work.

'Those things will kill you,' she commented. 'You should give them up.'

'Do you know what?' I said. 'I'd rather die from these early than end up in a place like this.'

She looked shocked, but I meant every word of it. If working in the care home taught me anything, it was that everyone deserves to be treated with dignity and respect. Yes, you might be in a care facility with advanced dementia and not even know your own name, but that doesn't mean you're not a human being. It was a lesson I would take forward as my nursing career progressed.

Then there was Dickens ward, back at Northwick Park. One of the most demanding placements I undertook while a student nurse. The energy, the adrenaline, the pure chaos of a medical-assessment unit (MAU) combined with a high-dependency unit (HDU). The ward comprised thirty-four beds – four bays of six, one bay of four and six side rooms, which were used for patients with infection, those being protected in isolation (having no immune system) and for those recognised as dying.

I loved Dickens ward from the first day I stepped foot through its doors. The atmosphere was palpable, and I knew that this was where I wanted to be. As a student nurse, you get at least one emergency medical placement. Some get A&E (which I'd really wanted), some get ITU (intensive therapy unit; scary but my second choice after A&E) and others are given MAU on Dickens. I initially felt short-changed when I received my allocation; I wanted to be where all the drama was, imagining myself as one of the heroes on *Casualty*. But I soon realised that the learning opportunities on MAU far outweighed the others. The vast range of health conditions, both acute and chronic, allowed me the chance to develop my learning, skills and knowledge at a rapid rate.

The culture of wards depends on many, many factors, one of the most important being whether the ward is mainly nurse- or doctor-led. It tends to be much more nurse-led in more acute and specialist areas because difficult life-changing decisions need to be made constantly and there is not always a doctor on hand. Nurses need to become confident and proficient at assessing a patient and quickly making decisions about treatments and interventions, many of which can mean the difference between life and death. Dickens was such a ward. Strong, dynamic leaders; experienced ward sisters; and charge nurses oozing confidence and often outspoken, direct and a great comfort when you are newly qualified. There was always someone I could go to, someone to ask questions or just to reassure me that I was doing OK.

There was a complete mix of nationalities within the team on Dickens. Nurses and carers from the Philippines, Jamaica, India, Ireland, Zimbabwe, Nigeria and many more places. It was a healthcare assistant (HCA) from the Philippines, Elmer, who taught me the importance of basic care during my placement on Dickens ward. He was so kind to the patients and knew the importance of giving a good wash. Nursing a bay of dependent patients is physically demanding. No sooner have you finished washing Mrs Smith in bed C2, the familiar smell hits your nostrils and you just know that another patient also needs a wash. Elmer taught me the essential skills needed to wash people well but efficiently and quickly – how to roll the clean pads under the patient, avoiding the dirty pads and sheets – managing to roll the patient from side to side and ensuring they end up clean and comfortable. Basic training, perhaps, but absolutely essential.

Chapter 4

Only a few months into my training I decided to move out of Mel's place in Rickmansworth and in with a set of friends I'd made on my course. I needed to go – I jumped before I was pushed after several arguments caused by Mel feeling I'd brought my partying ways to her door, while I felt she was expecting too much from me and trying to act like my mother. Anyway, it was time to move on.

Around then I'd got a bar stewarding job at a local social club in Rickmansworth, along with two of my housemates. It was a part-time role I juggled with my studies and hospital placements. The social club's clientele was mainly older men, dropping in for a pint and a game of darts. However, there was a younger crowd among the club's regulars and we soon got to know them. We enjoyed having a bit of banter with them and I think we brought a bit of life to the old place. Among this crowd was a guy called Mark. He was in the darts team with a group of friends and they would be in most Monday nights for darts matches, as well as Friday, Saturday and Sunday evenings for drinks. There were so many nights of fun. At the time, smoking was still allowed inside and lock-ins were standard; I would often not get home until two or three in the morning, stinking of cigarette smoke. Most of the guys had been friends since school and are still best friends to this day. Mark and I hit it off from the start, spending hours chatting away about anything and everything. He went through a tough time when his marriage broke down and his ex-wife moved to Kent with his two daughters, Ellie and Livvie. It was a heartbreaking time for him, only seeing the girls every other weekend. Supporting him through this brought us closer to each other and in the summer of 2005, we finally got together. Even then, we both knew this was more than just a fleeting romance. Much later, in 2011, Livvie would come to live with us while Ellie stayed with her mum in Kent.

Meanwhile, back on Dickens ward I was coming towards the end of my placement. I wasn't sure what would happen to me after my training was finished but I knew I enjoyed and thrived on the fast-paced environment of the acute medical environment. Luckily, I seemed to have made a good impression on the ward, because I was called in to my manager's office just before my placement finished and offered a job.

I was over the moon. I couldn't have been more delighted. I felt as though I'd drifted since I left school, not really sure which way to turn, and now I had my dream career in the area of nursing I really wanted. All I had to do now was pass my exams, so I got my head down, studied hard and by February 2007, I was a fully qualified nurse, ready to start a demanding but wholly rewarding job.

Dickens ward comprised five bays: A, B, C, D and E. A and B were closest to the main door and were for very sick patients. In C, D and E, patients were less acutely unwell, so there you'd find the more elderly patients, people in with general medical problems, those with dementia, infections – a real mix. Dickens was predominantly older people – as is the case in most hospital wards – but we had younger people too, many coming in with drug and alcohol problems, or poorly controlled type 1 diabetes and so acutely unwell on admission that risk of death was high. We also had a contingent of homeless people coming in with general problems, commonly complaining of chest pain as they knew it meant a night in hospital, which meant the safety and warmth of a bed along with at least a couple of free meals.

On one of my shifts, a young man was admitted, barely responsive and with a worryingly slow breathing rate. There was no obvious sign of injury. It took many hours of tests, investigations and even an urgent review by ITU before we managed to establish what the problem was – he'd taken too much ketamine. He was in what is called a 'K-hole'. He had accidentally overdosed on the drug, which is known as a horse tranquiliser, used as an anaesthetic and to relieve pain, but is often abused for its stimulant and psychedelic effects. Imagine all of the money, time and resources wasted that night. Lucky for him that he recovered, and that we have free healthcare. I'm sure his bill would have been in the tens of thousands otherwise.

Another time, during a summer heatwave, a young girl in her late teens was admitted with ongoing seizures. The seizures had started suddenly that afternoon with no previous medical history and no family history of such problems. Her blood tests revealed that she was dangerously low on sodium – a chemical element essential in maintaining the electrolyte balance in your body. Due to the extreme heat, she had been drinking water – litres of it. In hot weather many of us are concerned about not drinking enough water, but it can be dangerous and even fatal to drink too much. The opposite of dehydration, overhydration is when the electrolytes in your system become too diluted, causing sodium levels to drop. Side effects of low sodium include seizures, muscle cramps and weakness, loss of consciousness, which can lead to coma.

Her dad stayed by her bedside the whole time and was so relieved when she woke up and was told what had caused her seizures, realising this was a one-off incident, not a life-changing diagnosis.

Night shifts were intense but sometimes good fun. You always knew from the rota who you were working with, which nurses and healthcare assistants (HCAs), and that would give you an idea of what your night was going to be like. However, it was always an anticipatory wait to see which doctors were on duty. This was akin to going out to the local pub in the evening and not knowing who will be there. When you get there and see one of your best mates – well, that was what it was like seeing one of the doctors who you got on with really well; someone who would be good fun but also confident and could be relied on during a crisis. The alternative scenario, which can be compared to walking into the pub and seeing no one but that annoying person you'd much rather avoid, was like working with the kind of doctor who talks the talk but is hopeless in a crisis. Unfortunately, there were a few of this sort of doctor: ones who had the bravado, but not the knowledge or experience to match.

For example, on one night shift, I was with a doctor who certainly talked the talk. But that night a patient became very unwell. Mrs Pritchard was a seventy-four-year-old lady being nursed in one of the non-monitored beds. She was being treated for a severe chest infection which had developed into pneumonia. Initially, Mrs Pritchard had responded well to treatment of antibiotics and fluids. To treat pneumonia, intravenous (IV) antibiotics will be given for a few days and if the patient improves, they are switched to oral antibiotics. The day team had switched to orals following the morning ward round, but Mrs Pritchard deteriorated quite quickly from the start of the night shift.

Frankly, I was worried. There are many ways to tell when a patient is deteriorating. Vital signs indicate stability of the cardiovascular system: blood pressure, heart rate, respiratory rate, temperature, oxygen saturation and urine output. When acutely unwell, blood pressure changes, usually dropping. The heart rate also changes – usually rising. The breathing is a big sign, and one of the most important things to look for when you are worried about someone. The change in the breathing will depend on the cause for sudden deterioration. For a chest infection, breathing will become more rapid and the patient will visibly be working harder to breathe, all signs of what we call 'respiratory distress'. Think about your own breathing at rest – gentle, calm breaths that mostly go unnoticed. You cannot fail to notice someone in respiratory distress. Mrs Pritchard was awake but drowsy. She was flushed in the face and clammy to the touch. Her rate of breathing was high and she was using all her available muscles to help get the air in and push it out again.

A normal respiratory rate is 12–20 per minute. Mrs Pritchard had a respiratory rate of 35 per minute. Her heart rate was more than 100 beats per minute and her blood pressure had dropped to 90/40. Oxygen saturations were 94 per cent (normally 98–100 per cent). Her urine output was very low – another worrying sign that someone is deteriorating.

Put all of this together and the picture is grim. Lying in front of me was a very poorly seventy-four-year-old who, if left untreated, would die. I decided to 'bleep' the doctor to let him know the urgency of the situation.

'I'm just on Hardy ward with a patient,' he replied. 'I can be there in ten minutes.'

'I'm really worried about this lady,' I said. 'I really need you to assess her urgently.'

'I'll be there as soon as I can. If she has fluids prescribed, put them up and do hourly obs.'

He didn't mention the oxygen but I started oxygen therapy anyway, knowing that this would help. She did have a bag of fluids prescribed, so I put them up and asked the HCA to help me with regular obs ('observations' – nurses' shorthand for measuring vital signs, such as blood pressure, heart rate and respiratory rate) and to keep a generally close eye on our sick patient. Although I was still only newly qualified, I had seven other patients to look after, meaning seven lots of medications and seven lots of observations to take and record. In addition, at least five of these were dependent on us for their personal care needs, equating to five washes and pad changes to do before they went to sleep. In short, I was very busy indeed, but ten minutes had flown by and there was still no sign of the junior doctor. I bleeped again.

'Sorry, I got caught up with this patient,' he said. 'I'm on my way down.'

I reeled off the latest vital signs readings, which were getting worse each time we recorded them. I was increasingly worried now and my other patients had to be put on the backburner. Unfortunately, soiled pads would have to wait. All I could offer for the moment were my apologies to all those patients whose dignity had been neglected at the expense of another.

The junior doctor arrived shortly after this second bleep but I could tell his confidence was lacking. Bravado was replaced by uncertainty. He was the one looking for guidance from me – the newly qualified me. I remembered that he was newly qualified too and with much less 'hands-on' experience in his seven years of medical school than my three years of nurse training. Now, I had to think on my feet.

'We need to get her to a monitored bed,' I said. 'She needs blood cultures (these can identify which antibiotics target the specific infection in the body), aggressive fluids, and we need to do a blood gas.' (This final procedure takes blood from the artery – usually the radial artery in the wrist – and checks for levels including oxygen and carbon dioxide in the blood. Essentially, it measures the pH of the blood, letting us know in an instant exactly how unwell the patient is.)

Silently, we worked together. Mrs Pritchard was transferred to a monitored bed in A bay. Fluids were commenced and after blood cultures were taken, a broad-spectrum antibiotic was given intravenously. We increased her oxygen and gave paracetamol for her fever. Slowly, over the next few hours, her breathing slowed to a more normal rate. Her urine output increased, as did her blood pressure.

By now it was 2am. One patient was saved, but seven others now needed tending to. I finally got my break at 4am – eight and a half hours after the start of my shift. The junior doctor did show his gratitude by recognising my input but wasn't given much of a reprieve as his bleeper went off and he disappeared to another ward, and another round of life-or-death decisions to face.

Although I'd never forgotten the lesson I was taught when I didn't rush to answer a patient's bell, I soon became aware that as in life, there are hospital patients who seem to exist solely to test your patience. 'Nurse, can you pass me my water?' (When you know full well they can reach their own water.) 'Nurse, can you help me get out of bed?' (While knowing full well that after all the effort of getting them out, five minutes later you'll be asked, 'Nurse, can you put me back to bed?')

Then there were the serial bell ringers. I have tinnitus and I have to confess that I've always hated the sound of a patient's bell ringing, but I've never ignored it. In fact, I'm often first there so I can find out the problem and turn off the annoying noise. Even so, it's amazing how so many ward staff can turn a deaf ear to the sound of that bell. In all my years of nursing, this remains one of my frustrations. How can they just let it ring and ring? How do they know it's not someone in trouble? What if someone is bleeding or has fallen in the toilet? If there was a record for answering call bells, I think I would have broken it in my first year of nursing. However, even I would get fed up with the serial ringers – the patients who would feel the need to ring their bell as soon as you'd stepped foot outside their door. Believe it or not, there were even those who would ring their bell while you were still in their room or bay. This happened frequently, and as much as I tried to be kind and compassionate and understanding, at the end of a busy shift the kindness was often replaced by a whole world of tiredness and a short temper shorter than most.

It was difficult then not to snap and sometimes I did. 'Could you please stop ringing that bell?' I'd say through gritted teeth, while trying to sound polite and measured. 'I am here in the room with you, I have been here most of the night, my other patients have hardly seen me. We might need to treat your thumb for repetitive strain injury soon. So please, just leave the bell alone unless it's an emergency. Please?'

Naturally, there was the guilt that followed such an outburst but sometimes it did the trick. As I became more experienced, I realised that usually this type of behaviour is due to the patient being scared or lonely and ideally they would have someone sitting with them all day and night. This is just not possible and so we learn to deal with the constant bells. That said, I am aware there were times when ward staff simply unplugged the call bell. This was hugely frowned upon, as you can imagine, but it was also easy to imagine what had driven someone to these lengths, as you'd usually discover when you 'did the right thing' and plugged the bell back in.

As I've mentioned, the ward was largely full of elderly people, many of them coming towards the end of their lives. As time passed on Dickens ward I began to notice that while treatment for the elderly was given to the best of the staff's ability, it wasn't always wholly appropriate in the circumstances. Let me explain… When we become nurses and doctors, we all sign up to saving lives. This goes without saying, and it is our paramount responsibility to get people better. But very often, people don't get better. We might give everything a go, medically speaking, to turn around a patient's condition and get them back on track but eventually find that it doesn't work. At this point, an ethical dilemma sets in. Do you persist in trying, even when the treatment can be invasive, distressing and possibly painful? Or, having accepted that the person isn't going to get better, do you stop treating them and instead make them as comfortable as possible, managing their journey towards death with as much care and compassion as you can give?

Mrs Shah was a case in point. She was ninety-two-year-old lady admitted to Dickens ward after deteriorating at home – becoming weaker, less responsive, more confused, eating and drinking less. At her age this isn't uncommon and she also had a significant past medical history, including type 2 diabetes, hypertension (high blood pressure) and vascular dementia. When she was admitted she was diagnosed with hypernatremia – raised sodium levels in the blood – usually caused by dehydration, especially in the elderly. If left untreated, it can cause symptoms such as muscle twitching, confusion, seizures, and can result in death.

Hypernatremia is fairly easy to treat by means of giving slow intravenous fluids. However, we know that when elderly people are reaching end of life, they gradually eat and drink less. This is part of the natural process of dying. We often try whatever we possibly can in healthcare to reverse this process and, as a nurse, it can be very distressing to watch. I knew from handover that Mrs Shah was very unwell. I also knew from looking at her more recent history that she'd had multiple admissions to hospital in the last few months, all with similar presentations: dehydration; urine infection; not eating and drinking; becoming less responsive. Her 'baseline' (the normal level of function/ability) was being housebound. She spent most of the day in bed, needing assistance to transfer from bed to chair and for washing and dressing. Plus, she was doubly incontinent, of both urine and faeces. She lived at home with her son, daughter-in-law and grandchildren and had carers visiting four times each day to assist with her personal care needs.

In short, I saw a very elderly lady with severe frailty, multiple co-morbidities (a medical term for pre-existing health conditions), globally deteriorating and likely to be approaching end of life. But it appeared that the treating consultant clearly saw something different to me. When I looked at the plan of care, I saw that the team had requested six-hourly blood tests to monitor the sodium levels. Now, don't get me wrong, I do fully understand that hypernatremia can cause death, and with very high levels there are other symptoms it can cause, too. What I failed to understand was how a consultant couldn't see the implications of these interventions for the lady lying in the bed. Blood tests are horrible at the best of times. In a frail patient with dehydration and, added to that, advanced dementia, taking blood felt nothing less than cruel. It made no sense to me. The established treatment plan was slow IV fluids. Checking her sodium levels every six hours would not change this plan – so why were we doing it?

It didn't take me long on Dickens ward to realise that I was the patient's voice. Families are often happy to go along with a plan set by a consultant, not always realising the consequences for their loved one. Some families want survival at all costs, which means that we're in the strange situation of being the patient's advocate against their own relatives. I had not met Mrs Shah's family but I knew from the documentation that even the 'Do Not Resuscitate' conversation was a difficult one, so my guess was they hadn't argued about the intensive and aggressive treatment.

But I did. I felt that what was about to happen to this poor woman was unfair, and I was not about to spend half of my shift digging needles in this frail lady just for the sake of numbers. Oh, how we love 'the numbers' in the medical world! Blood test results show a whole list of numbers; these help to diagnose medical conditions such as infection and indicate how well the body's organs, such as liver and kidneys, are working. Repeating blood tests will indicate whether the body is improving with treatment or not. You might hear doctors say, 'Things are going in the right direction' and often this is based on the 'numbers' – the blood results.

At this point the consultant wasn't around, but his junior was. I explained my concerns to her.

She gave me a sympathetic look. 'I know,' she said. 'This doesn't seem right at all. We shouldn't be doing it – not to her. But what can I do?'

We nurses have our gripes about them, usually on a daily or even hourly basis, but life for junior doctors is hard in so many ways and one of them is in this area. They will commonly have to push aside their own views and opinions in the way patients are cared for. Challenging a consultant is still taboo. With very few exceptions, consultants do not like being challenged by their juniors. It is seen as rude, interfering and 'jumped up', and juniors face being humiliated in front of their peers if they even try.

'I think what we can do is take the bloods every twelve hours instead of six,' I said. 'As far as I'm concerned it's still too many but we'll just have to make do for the moment.'

The junior doctor agreed, hoping that further evidence as time went on might help to change her consultant's mind. I wasn't so sure. Even though I was still newly qualified I'd had enough experience to know that it could be the devil's own job to try to influence a consultant.

So, here's how my shift went: Checking on Mrs Shah at least every hour. Answering questions from her family members all day long. Watching her recorded observations of vital signs get worse and seeing her getting visibly frailer as the day went on. She was barely responsive, but the family were celebrating every time she blinked. It is amazing what people will hold on to when someone is dying – although that hadn't been mentioned to this family yet because we were still trying to work miracles and reverse the dying process. Every time I looked in on Mrs Shah, I became increasingly concerned. By the time of the afternoon ward round with the consultant, I was feeling brave.

'I think this lady is dying,' I said to him, noticing that he flinched a little when I mentioned the unmentionable; I was convinced I saw a little flinch as I said the 'D' word.

'What are her latest blood results?' he asked, addressing the junior doctor. She then read out the numbers, which had actually improved. This isn't unusual by any means. Blood results will often improve with treatments but are only one part of the bigger picture.

'But overall, things aren't great,' she added quickly. I watched with interest as she took a nanosecond's pause before continuing.

'Mrs Shah's blood pressure is dropping,' she said, 'and her oxygen requirements are increasing. She hasn't been responsive for most of the day, and hasn't been awake enough to eat anything. Generally, we are quite worried.'

I was pleased the junior had managed to give her opinion, albeit in a less forthright way than I might have done. But just as the consultant was about to reply, members of Mrs Shah's family ambushed the ward round, desperate to hear some good news. It's often the case that families only want to speak to the consultant as they feel anyone lower down the medical order doesn't count. However, it's also true that such people often aren't afraid to challenge anyone, even the consultants.

Unflustered by their interruption, and knowing they were hanging on his every word, he turned to them and spoke kindly.

'Well, my junior doctor here tells me that your mother's numbers have improved, so that's excellent news,' he said.

There was a collective sigh of relief from the family and smiles all round.

'However,' the consultant continued, 'we are still rather worried about your mother and I'm afraid to say that things at this moment are critical.'

'What does this mean?' asked the eldest son. 'Critical? Will she die, doctor?'

The consultant proceeded with caution. 'She has been severely dehydrated,' he said, 'and because she is so frail, we are concerned she might not recover.'

The smiles now turned to frowns of disappointment.

'But she's alive, right?' said the son. 'So this means we can carry on the treatment. What happens next?'

'There must be other things you can do for her,' piped up a

younger woman who might've been a granddaughter. 'What's the plan?'

The consultant was in a double bind. He was fully aware how sick Mrs Shah was. Yet he had his duty of care to contend with, plus relatives clamouring for answers and action. By the end of the consultation there was a plan of care in place, which I remained unhappy with but the relatives seemed appeased by: two-hourly observations, daily blood tests and IV fluids to run at a rate of one litre every eight hours. IV fluids are used as part of many treatment plans but even in my limited experience as a nurse back then, I knew what three litres of fluid a day could do to a frail, elderly, dying person. The fluids cause oedema – the collection of fluid in the body's tissue – commonly in the hands and arms and the feet, creeping up to the knees, hips and even to the abdomen. It causes uncomfortable swelling. It can be distressing for the patient but for relatives it offers a line of hope – at least she won't be dehydrated, right?

After a particularly long and challenging day the shift ended and I left the hospital completely frustrated and exhausted. The drive home allowed me the time to wind down and by the time I'd pulled into my driveway, I was less tense. The frustration had faded and I looked forward to doing an evening of very little, knowing I was back on shift the following day and could see what had happened to Mrs Shah overnight.

She died.

A frail, elderly lady died with fluids running through her and being disturbed every two hours to have her blood pressure taken. But at least her family were with her, and for them, she died with them 'fighting' for her all the way. How could I criticise that? They'd done all they could for their mother and grandmother, but it wasn't to be. I just hoped that their 'fight', their way of treating her to the end, would reflect what she would have wanted. Even at this early stage in my career I knew there had to be a better way, but as time passed there would be many more Mrs Shahs and many more battles lay ahead.

Chapter 5

My manager Catherine, the Dickens ward matron, was a hard-working and inspirational person. She set her standards high and newly qualified nurses like me were expected to live up to those standards. Quite right too, and I worked to the best of my ability to maintain the level of professionalism demonstrated by dedicated staff like Catherine.

She always wore a distinctive perfume, Aromatics Elixir, by Clinique, and in quantities so generous you could very often smell her before you saw her. This was a sign to get busy – if you weren't already – and make sure you were prepared to answer Catherine's taxing questions fully.

Oh, but those night shifts could be tough. Unless you've worked nights, it's hard to describe the effect they have on body and mind. I didn't complain because it's just part of the job, but there were times when tiredness would completely overwhelm me and I'd have to take a nap in the staffroom during my break. We weren't supposed to but we all did, dragging out bedsheets 'borrowed' from the linen cupboard and curling up in them for twenty, thirty minutes, or as long as we could get away with. And when that distinctive whiff of perfume floated on to the ward, someone would knock loudly on the staffroom door to wake everyone up before Catherine discovered us.

Within my first year of being qualified I'd gone from a band 5 to a band 6, which meant that often I would be given responsibility for the ward, especially on night duty. If you're in charge, you're not only responsible for the patients but also for the staff in there. So you have constant pressure from senior managers who want to know what's happening at any given moment, who's going home (and who isn't), how many empty beds there are, who's doing what, where, when and how. It's a lot of responsibility, especially for someone recently qualified, and there were many times I stepped on that ward feeling I was risking my 'pin number' – the number given to all newly qualified nurses giving you permission to nurse professionally, and which must be renewed every three years.

Nurses are very quick to pick up mistakes made by other nurses, which helps to fuel the 'stab-you-in-the-back' blame culture which can exist in hospitals right across the NHS. It's hard to know where this comes from – perhaps it's too many managers and too many targets to hit, or years of overwork and underpayment. Whatever the cause, there does seem to be a jealousy among some nurses, particularly towards those colleagues who've worked their way up the ladder quickly, causing resentment and a determination to make life hard for that individual.

In short, we nurses seem to hunker down and protect ourselves, sometimes at the expense of others. This looms in the forefront of your mind every time you are worried about giving a certain medication or carrying out a risky procedure. It makes you want to second check everything, having worked so hard as a student nurse through all manner of placements and completing module after module of theory. It's like getting into a car for the first time on your own after you pass your driving test – suddenly no one is there with you to guide you and reassure you that everything is OK. You are alone with your pin number and effectively with people's lives in your hands.

I remember clearly my first drug error on Dickens ward; I drew up five times too much intravenous heparin for an infusion. Heparin thins the blood and for this patient was used after he suffered a heart attack/myocardial infarction. Giving IV medications requires the checking and signature of two nurses, the role of the second nurse being to check the prescription, review any allergies noted on the chart, check the drug is in date and – importantly – double-check the dose. Each nurse should separately check their calculation (the dose you want divided by dose available, multiplied by volume) and when both nurses are happy with the dose, it is drawn up and checked again by the second nurse.

This was a night shift. My second nurse was a sister, more senior than me, and she loved to chat. We were nattering away, and I don't think she even checked the dose at all. Now, it is common in the nursing world to realise mistakes hours after your shift when you are in a deep sleep, waking suddenly in a full-on sweat as the vision of the error is revealed. That is exactly what happened to me. I went home from my night shift just as the patient on the heparin infusion was transferred to the cardiology ward for further treatment, the infusion still running. As usual, I drove home with the windows down and the car radio blasting away to keep me awake. After a quick shower I tumbled into bed, exhausted. Unlike many nurses, I sleep very well indeed after a night shift – unless, of course, one of those sudden thoughts interrupts my almost unconscious state.

I jerked bolt upright as my subconscious shoved a vision into my conscious brain: 'You got the dose wrong… Kelly… you got the dose wrong.' The creeping horror of the situation seemed to crawl down from my brain into the rest of my body, paralysing it with fear. Oh my God. I got the dose wrong. I seemed to be staring at myself, asking how I'd managed to do such a stupid thing. *And what the hell should I do now?* I thought, and thought… and thought some more. I did not go back to sleep. As soon as I could, I called the ward sister who had checked the drug with me. I was so newly qualified, the thought of losing everything was unbearable. As I was trying to get through to her, I looked up possible effects of a heparin overdose. It didn't make for happy reading, involving as it did haemorrhage and life-threatening blood loss.

Finally, my call was put through and my colleague answered. She was very calm and collected, telling me not to worry and that she would make an immediate call to the cardiology ward. This was an antidote to my feeling that some nurses were out for themselves. Immediately she made me feel better, and that I didn't have to go through this alone. These days we are very hot on 'incident reporting' and have a system called Datix, in which we are encouraged to report everything from serious incidents to near misses. Back then, this was less so. The ward sister spoke to one of the junior doctors, who told her they would document and monitor the patient, but it was not likely to have serious implications.

No serious implications? I was not convinced. Fear and paranoia had me in a tight grip. So much so that the day after my night shift I called the ward and pretended to be a relative of the patient. Yes, I know… this looks deceptive and cowardly. But I was just too afraid to say, 'Oh hi, I'm the nurse that overdosed the patient on heparin – how is he?'

Luckily, he was fine. His stenting procedure post-heart attack was slightly postponed, but he had it and recovered to leave the hospital. For him, this was a near miss; for me, it was a huge wake-up call. This stuff just got real. Literally, people's lives in my hands, and all for the grand salary of £21,000.

There was a graduation ceremony for us trainees in the October of 2007, but a lot didn't attend and it was very low-key. The ceremony itself was held at the Barbican in London and Mark's mum attended with me because my own parents were on holiday. To be honest, that's about as much as I remember of the day, other than I was constantly being sick, even having to get off the Tube ride into town several times to find a place to throw up. To my surprise, I'd just recently found out I was pregnant.

It was early into my career, of course, but as prospective new parents, Mark and I were delighted. The morning sickness was unbearable but I was lucky: it only lasted about four weeks. I don't know how women cope when they have it all the way through pregnancy and I don't know why it's called 'morning sickness' because I felt overwhelming, relentless nausea day and night. I resorted to asking my GP to sign me off work for two weeks after a horrendous night shift during which I felt sick all night long. I couldn't eat anything and could barely tolerate sips of water without dashing to the bathroom to be sick. By 5am, I was completely exhausted. The nurse in charge sent me on a break and I managed to eat half a Rich Tea biscuit and drink a small cup of cold milk. No sooner had I taken the last mouthful than I knew I was going to be sick. It was so sudden that I didn't even make it to the bathroom. I had to open the staffroom bin and use that, then tie it up and do the walk of shame down the corridor with the bin bag. Mark came and collected me from work that day as I was too weak and tired to drive home. We got through the door of our flat and off I went to be sick once more. I don't think Mark had realised how bad things were until that moment when he heard me being so violently ill.

At the time we discovered we were to be new parents, Mark and I were planning a lovely wedding in Kefalonia for the summer of 2008, inviting family and close friends. However, shortly after all of the guests had paid their deposit I learned I was pregnant, which threw something of a spanner into the works. We were due to fly on 20 July and my due date was 24 June. Not ones to let people down, we decided to carry on with our plans and worry about any issues later, the main one being that if I went two weeks over my due date, I would not be at my own wedding. Taking after me from day one, Ronnie was just a few days late, being born on 27 June, so the wedding plans were still on. There was no post-baby relaxing for me – I spent the next few weeks getting Ronnie's passport and travel documents sorted and all of the relevant information translated officially now that we knew the wedding was going ahead. Some people thought we were mad, taking a newborn baby on holiday to a hot country in the middle of summer, but as my mum said, 'They have babies in Greece!' As it turned out, it couldn't have been better. It was a brilliant holiday, the wedding was great fun and with so many friends and family, I had a never-ending supply of babysitters.

I worked up until June 2008, when I took maternity leave and was off for ten months. Being part of the NHS has its perks and the fact of being able to take this length of time without having to worry was incredibly helpful. My whole experience of the NHS through pregnancy and birth was fantastic. Despite an eighteen-hour labour and ventouse delivery, we were discharged home after just one night in hospital and I can't fault the care we received. My midwife was really great and even stayed beyond her shift to make sure my baby arrived safely.

I loved being a new mum and did as much as I could with our new son, who we named Ronnie. I knew that this time was short and that I should make the most of it, because the return to work would be no picnic.

As every nurse who has become a parent knows, the adjustment from new-baby bliss to night shifts, day shifts, weekends and the rest is very hard indeed. You might do two long days on, or several nights in a row, then have a day off before returning to the series of long days or nights. The day off is meant to be 'R&R time' but with a new baby, it's anything but. I admit I was pretty useless on my days off. I'd lie on our bed, completely exhausted from the previous days or nights of work, drifting in and out of consciousness while Ronnie crawled over me and pulled at my hair. Thankfully he was a good sleeper, only waking up once in the night for a feed before settling back down until a respectable hour of the morning.

It was a difficult transition back to work but to make things worse, Mark was made redundant. This was really frightening as a new parent. He still wanted to continue paying child maintenance as he didn't want his daughters to suffer, though I felt we compromised our own lives to make sure the girls were always OK financially and sometimes that was hard to swallow. I recall going to the local council offices to ask about any benefits we might be entitled to, even just a reduction in council tax, but there was nothing. They even suggested that we would be better off financially and have access to more benefits if I didn't have a job. *How could this be right?* I asked myself. Mark had joined the army at sixteen and had never been unemployed or claimed any benefits, paying into the system for his whole working life, but when we needed help the most there was nothing. It seemed so unfair. Luckily my parents were able to help, lending us enough for Mark to start his own business in the property maintenance and construction industry, but we suffered for many months, at times barely able to cover our rent and always living in the overdraft.

At work I still gave everything my 100 per cent. I was like that then and I'm still like that. But perhaps I should've been a bit easier on myself during those new-mum days. Now, I see how nurses, doctors and healthcare workers carefully manage their energy levels, making sure they don't reach the point of burnout, which is easy in demanding NHS jobs. I didn't look after mine at all. I was 100 miles an hour, day or night, and foolishly exhausting myself to the point where I felt I was no longer being a good mum. From being someone who embraced motherhood, I was now no longer enjoying it and this became an issue. I was so much less patient with Ronnie and would snap at Mark over the smallest of things. During my maternity leave I would cook lovely fresh dinners every day and was so careful about what I fed Ronnie; now I was taking the easy option with everything as I was always so tired. Fast, easy meals like beans on toast or even takeaways. If Mark was around on my days off he'd take Ronnie while I lay collapsed on the bed, feeling that it was all too much.

Around this time the Government target of a maximum four-hour wait in A&E was installed and this had a huge impact on what we were doing. Care for the sick became a conveyor belt system of patients on trolleys along corridors, whisked out of A&E so the target could be achieved. It was ridiculous, and of course it had a knock-on effect right through hospitals including Northwick Park and we felt ourselves getting busier and busier. The pressure was on and I was using up all my energy at work. Some days you'd be short-staffed and be looking after two bays of patients single-handedly. For example, I might be responsible for A bay, with six people, and a couple of side rooms with patients on continuous positive airway pressure (CPAP) machines that help people struggling to breathe, or some on cardiac monitoring devices which need checking every hour. If I was lucky, I'd have a healthcare assistant to help; if I wasn't, it was down to me, and that became exhausting.

Something had to give. We had a childminder, Trisha, who was an absolute blessing, and Mark was able to look after Ronnie at weekends, but I knew I needed to spend more time with my son. I think my final moment of realisation came when I collected Ronnie from Trisha's late one morning after I had slept for a few hours following a night shift. I strapped him into his car seat and as he wriggled around in the excitement of seeing me, I dropped the keys into the footwell. In my tired state, I didn't bother to reach over and get them, I thought I would just get them from the other side. But as the passenger door slammed shut, a horrible thought crossed my mind. I had heard the doors lock as I dropped the keys, and it was a one-touch key fob.

I took a deep breath and tried to open the door. It was locked and Ronnie was trapped inside. The panic was rising and my tired brain wasn't helping. Ronnie had clearly picked up on my fear and although he was too young to realise what was happening, he started screaming. I burst into tears. Disturbed by the sudden commotion, Trisha came outside. She was so calm. 'Come inside,' she told me. Initially I was absolutely horrified at her for suggesting I should leave my son all alone locked in the car. 'He will cry more if he can see you,' she reassured me. Trisha put the kettle on while I called my friend who had a spare key to the house, inside which was the spare car key. I kept looking over at the car and could see Ronnie's chubby little legs moving about, but I didn't dare go outside and risk him seeing me again. Within twenty minutes my friend was at Trisha's with the spare key and I was a whole lot calmer. I was even more relieved when I got to the car door and saw that Ronnie had fallen asleep. 'I told you he would be fine,' Trisha said.

Soon after this incident, I reduced my hours to two long days a week and the difference I felt in my own well-being was immediate. I'd still be knackered after the long shifts had finished but at least I knew I wouldn't have to go back in straight after my rest day and I carried on this way for around six months, until I felt ready to go back full-time again.

Meanwhile, the high-speed nature of Dickens ward continued

unabated. Once, at the start of a night shift, I was leaning over a patient's bed at the far end of a bay when something large and almost formless hurtled past the window, followed by a sickening thud. An on-call doctor working in the same bay had seen it too and immediately he sprang into action, summoning colleagues to what was obviously a very serious situation on the ground below.

A woman had jumped from the eighth floor. She was withdrawing from alcohol, but clearly had had enough of this notoriously difficult battle. Whoever reached the terrible scene on the ground had started cardiopulmonary resuscitation (better known as CPR) on the poor woman. The rules about CPR mean that once it's been started it has to continue until such time as it becomes obvious that it isn't going to work, so although this lady was clearly dead, the doctors at the scene had a professional responsibility to continue until the full cardiac arrest team arrived and a senior doctor could officially cease the CPR efforts and confirm the time and death of the casualty.

But sometimes miracles can happen and the dead can come back to life. Or so it seemed, as a couple of us stood around the bed of a very elderly lady one afternoon.

'I think she's Cheyne-Stoking,' said one of the healthcare assistants. 'Do you think she's dying?'

'Cheyne-Stoking' or Cheyne-Stokes breathing is when a person's breathing slows down and becomes irregular. It may stop for a while, then pick up again before pausing for a longer period. Eventually the breathing stops. It's a classic sign of a person at the end of their life and when I first listened to this lady's breathing, I was ready to agree with the healthcare assistant.

'I think we'd better get the family in,' I said, and the health-care assistant went off to make that difficult but necessary phone call.

I sat by the old lady's bed and held her hand. Her pulse seemed to be slowing and she was going blue in colour. But the Cheyne-Stoking had stopped, to be replaced by a rattling sound that certainly wasn't the famed 'death rattle' you hear in patients who are about to die.

Gently I opened her mouth, and was horrified to see that far from slipping peacefully into death, she was actually choking on her dentures, which were right at the back of her throat. I shouted out for a pair of forceps and quickly pulled the offending items clear of her airways. Immediately she started to look perky again and while she didn't have the best baseline to begin with, she certainly returned to it once her dentures were back in the glass of water by the side of her bed. Meanwhile, we had the somewhat embarrassing task of telling the family, who'd just arrived at the hospital in a mad dash, that their relative was now sitting upright and having a cup of tea, not much the worse for her experience.

Some patients, however, never quite recover from their sufferings. During one shift I looked after a young man in his thirties, Nasim. He was from Iraq and had made it to the UK as an asylum seeker. I didn't get to know Nasim's full story and I should probably be grateful for this. He had scars all over his young body after being tortured by his own people under the Saddam Hussein regime. But worse than the physical scars were the mental ones. During the visiting hours, Nasim asked me to help him as his wife could not find her way to the ward. After establishing where she was in the hospital, I asked her to wait there and walked with Nasim to find her. We needed to walk down some stairs but as soon as I opened the door to the stairwell, Nasim froze. He fell to his knees as they buckled underneath him, a look of sheer terror on his face. It took me a while to help him up and for him to recover enough to tell me what was happening, explaining that one of the places they were taken to be tortured was a stairwell. Nasim had been left with mental scars that, like the physical ones, would remain forever.

Chapter 6

As time went by and Ronnie grew from a baby into a toddler I began to understand that the general busyness and constant stress of Dickens ward was, in the long term, not going to be for me. Aside from my responsibilities at home as a mum, I felt I wanted to do more for each patient I looked after, even just spend a little longer with them if possible. On a ward like Dickens, where the emphasis was on getting people better and getting them out, this just wasn't possible. I still enjoyed the buzz of the ward and liked the team working on it, but increasingly I felt it was time to broaden my experience.

I began to wonder if and where I might be of use in other areas of nursing around the hospital. One role which appealed to me was that of palliative care. There was a small team of specialist palliative care nurses and consultants in Northwick Park and they were frequent visitors to Dickens ward. I watched as they took their time with patients, even the sickest ones, talking to them and their families and assessing their individual needs. These needs weren't necessarily medical. In fact, quite a bit of the team's work seemed to be around making sure the patient was comfortable and that whatever they were facing, they weren't alone.

Like a lot of people, medical professionals or not, my first perception of palliative care was that it was something to do with dying. We've all heard the phrases, 'It's not looking good for X – they've called in palliative care' or 'There's nothing more they can do for Y, other than palliative care'. To some extent these words speak a truth, but as I began to talk to members of the palliative team during shifts or on breaks, I began to see that it was about a whole lot more than just dealing with the 'D' word.

Palliative care, I learned, is about looking after people with life-limiting illnesses whose quality of life has become more important than its length. It's helping someone live as well as possible while they're alive, enabling and assisting them to make decisions for themselves, and for the families they will leave behind. It's about dignity, respect and understanding. And the more I saw the palliative team at work, the more I was in awe of what they did.

The act of spending time with people to make sure they had everything they needed, and that they were clean and comfortable, really chimed with me. Although we often worked miracles on Dickens ward there were times, as I've described, when I felt we weren't looking at the situation holistically enough. Why were we prolonging painful and undignified treatment to those who were clearly dying? The answer, of course, is that's what we do – but was it appropriate in every circumstance, or could we look at the situation a bit more closely with regards to the individual? Those were certainly my feelings, but not everyone shared them. Least of all some consultants who would stop at nothing to keep people alive, even when all hope was gone. They were doing this for the right reasons – but were those reasons 'right' for that particular patient?

Those were the questions spinning around my head as I watched Dickens ward become ever busier. It was like a conveyor belt – people came in, we'd fix them up as best we could, then send them on to another ward. There were times when there were patients waiting in the corridor to occupy a bed before it had even been vacated. And when people died on Dickens ward, they died in hectic, noisy, busy and stressful surroundings. Increasingly, this didn't feel right to me. I thought that people at the end of their lives deserved better than this.

I knew I was reaching a turning point and it came during a busy night shift. I was allocated A bay and two side rooms to look after eight very sick patients. Three were hooked up to cardiac monitors so that we could constantly check their vital signs and they would emit an alarm if the heart rate went too high or the oxygen levels dropped. One of these was on a type of ventilation called BiPAP (bilevel positive airway pressure). Similar to CPAP, it helps patients who are struggling with their breathing. BiPAP is used when people are experiencing what we call type two respiratory failure. This means their oxygen levels are dangerously low and their carbon dioxide levels are too high – essentially, they are not able to perform effective breathing. BiPAP involves wearing a restrictive, tight face mask, which is very uncomfortable and difficult to tolerate, and often patients try to remove it. Patients receiving BiPAP require close observation. This patient had an arterial line in place, similar to a canula inserted to deliver intravenous medication, a line inserted directly into the artery so that the arterial pressures of the blood can be constantly monitored and blood can quickly and easily be withdrawn to check oxygen, carbon dioxide and, vitally, the pH levels of the blood. I was in for a busy night.

At the far side of the bay, next to the window, was Mr Jeffries. He had been admitted two days previously with a gastrointestinal (GI) bleed. Symptoms of GI bleeding vary in presentation and severity depending on the cause. The GI tract starts at the mouth and ends at the anus, with bleeding possible throughout. A bleed higher up will often cause vomiting of blood whereas a lower bleed will result in blood in the stool. Sometimes this is mild and causes the stool to appear dark and it will be sticky and tar-like, called melaena. In severe cases, blood, leaks from the rectum at a continuous and uncontrollable rate. Patients experiencing this will be urgently assessed by the medical team and usually undergo a scoping procedure where a camera is pushed down the throat into the stomach or inserted into the anus to try and find the source of the bleeding. If found, the bleeding can usually be stopped or at least slowed while further investigations take place. People suffering continuous bleeding will be given blood transfusions to try to replace what is lost.

Mr Jeffries had undergone a scoping procedure (in which a tiny camera attached to a flexible tube is put down the throat to try to locate the source of the bleed), but attempts to stop the bleeding had been unsuccessful. He had received multiple units of blood, but he continued to deteriorate. Due to multiple co-morbidities, he was not deemed fit to undergo further investigations or surgical procedures because he was not likely to survive the anaesthetic. Essentially, he was now dying from an untreatable bleed – he would haemorrhage to death.

As mentioned previously, a strong stomach is essential for nursing. But ask any nurse – melaena is up there amongst the worst of the worst for offensive smells. If a patient on the ward is having melaena, the whole ward knows about it. You smell it when you walk through the doors and sometimes you are smelling it for many hours after your shift has ended.

This makes it even worse for the poor patient. Even those who are normally able to control their bowels are not able to hold in the blood. It pours out and the stench is unbearable. The flimsy bedside curtains do as much to stop smells from travelling as they do the 'private' conversations held behind them; in other words, nothing. It is undignified, embarrassing and unstoppable. Mr Jeffries had no family who could easily travel to the hospital, no wife to be by his side holding his hand and no siblings or children to comfort him. He was going to die alone. And that is just what happened.

Despite my best efforts to be there with him when he died, I wasn't. I checked on him just after two o'clock in the morning while my healthcare assistant was on his break. I was alone and Mr Jeffries had died alone. I wanted to cry. But instead I went to his bedside, held his hand and whispered a silent apology, promising Mr Jeffries that I would do my best never to let this happen again. Then I got everything I needed to give him the best after-death care possible. Shower gel, clean sheets, soft washcloths. As if dying this way wasn't terrible enough, the blood doesn't stop after death. As much as I wiped it away, more blood would trickle down. I had to pack the anus with gauze, which felt like the final insult to this elderly gentleman, but was the only thing I could do to stop the blood. Eventually, after rolling him side to side many times (apologising to him as I went), Mr Jeffries was clean. At last, he looked peaceful and settled but it came at a cost – both to him and me. For Mr Jeffries, a far-from-perfect death, and for me, the final straw.

That experience made up my mind. I wanted to use all the skills I'd learned over seven years of training and ward experience to try to ensure that patients in a similar situation to Mr Jeffries never had to endure such indignity at the end of their lives. At the time, my thoughts about such people coincided with a national incentive to improve end-of-life care across the NHS. The determination to treat, treat, treat, with little understanding that a dying person might need a different kind of approach, was certainly not confined to my hospital.

Towards the end of the 1990s a scheme called the Liverpool Care Pathway (LCP) was developed at – surprise, surprise – a hospital in Liverpool, together with the Marie Curie Palliative Care Institute. It was based on approaches and techniques developed in hospices and intended for use in more general care settings, including large hospitals. In short, its aim was to ensure a dignified and peaceful death in which issues including further medication and intervention, keeping patients comfortable and acknowledging religious needs had all been considered and discussed by healthcare professionals, patients and their families.

There were issues, of course, not least around consent and the decision-making process that judged someone to be dying and 'beyond all hope'. These issues would become prominent later on, when a number of media outlets reported that families had not been told their relatives were on the LCP, describing it as a 'controversial pathway to death'. Others said their relatives had been placed on it inappropriately. However, despite a small number of individual cases where standards obviously weren't met, the LCP was a humane and dignified approach to end-of-life care and, to my mind at least, was certainly better than the one-size-fits-all way of treating dying people I'd frequently witnessed. The LCP certainly wasn't meant to replace medical knowledge or expertise; rather, it was an aid to good decision-making in busy, pressurised situations.

I was in my third or fourth year of working on Dickens ward when the LCP arrived at Northwick Park and there was an appeal for volunteers among nursing staff to be trained to train others in its use. I didn't have to think twice. I applied immediately and was accepted for training, so that I could become a 'link nurse' (i.e. one who specialises in a certain area while continuing to work on general or acute wards) in palliative care and pass on my knowledge of the LCP to the staff on Dickens ward. It meant I could spend time with the nurses and doctors from the palliative team when they were on Dickens ward and I started to experience the poor understanding of and resistance to palliative care. Nurses, doctors, patients and families alike would often worry as soon as they heard the words 'palliative care' or even 'dying'. On top of this, there were challenges getting ward staff on board with using the document. In a fast-flowing environment such as Dickens ward, the introduction of a new twenty-plus-page document to complete is not an easy sell. This meant that the LCP was often not completed properly, even among those I'd trained.

Still, I persisted, spending as much time as I could with the palliative care team. I learned about the importance of family involvement and true holistic care. One of the consultants from the team, Dr Charles Daniels, invited me to join him during a family meeting for a patient who was thought to be dying. I was shocked to hear that it would take place at the bedside – surely these sensitive discussions would be too upsetting for the patient? (a commonly-held belief). But I soon realised from this fascinating consultation that it's hugely important for the patient and their family to hear the same messages. I had been introduced to a new world of care.

The more I became involved, even indirectly, in palliative care, the more I realised that this branch of nursing was truly for me. It's hard to say why. Like most people, I'd gone into nursing to make people better. When people die, even when it is wholly expected, it's common for nurses to feel a sense of failure, and I guess the same goes for doctors. Like pretty much any other healthcare professional working in a busy hospital, I'd seen people die and I'd also felt that disappointment and self-recrimination that I couldn't do more for the person.

However, I'd also experienced another feeling – that of privilege. And of love, too. Anyone who has been with a person at the very end of their life will know that it's a surreal experience, full of wildly varying emotions. My reaction to the situation is one of a deep well of feeling, knowing that it is an honour to be with someone at this moment. We will all die, and ideally we'd all like to die to a pain-free way, surrounded by care and love. Sadly, it doesn't always happen this way, but if the circumstances are right, the moment of 'passing' is exceptionally precious and – although I'm not religious in any sense – deeply spiritual.

What happens when you see someone die? I've seen it many,

many times now and while each occasion is always different, the love and privilege I feel is exactly the same. Nevertheless, there are a few elements to the dying process that seem to be more common than others, and I think it's worth sharing these because a) no one ever seems to, and b) it can bring comfort to those who might wonder what their loved ones have been through.

So...a dying person in the last hours of their life will quite possibly show some signs of distress and will usually be in a comatose or semi-comatose state, so they are not able to express what they are feeling. Experience allows you to assess in other ways and to look for signs of pain or distress, such as facial grimacing. Not all symptoms at the end of life need medicating but facial grimacing may indicate pain, which should not be left untreated. Many people experience agitation (what we call 'terminal restlessness') and this is upsetting for relatives to see. It can be controlled with medication, keeping the patient calm and comfortable. The most noticeable feature of dying is the change in breathing. Regular, rhythmic breathing patterns are replaced by erratic breaths, sometimes rapid and shallow, at other times deep and laboured. Some people will develop the noisy secretions in the chest and throat known as 'the death rattle'. This too can be upsetting for the family but the patient isn't thought to be suffering – the noise just means that the muscles are now so weak that they are unable to clear any secretions.

The patient is also likely to be 'cyanosed' – in other words, developing a blue tinge, especially around the lips and tongue, and in the fingers. This is due to a lack of oxygen in the blood, and it can also cause a certain coldness in the hands, which, of course, continues after death.

Then the breathing becomes slower and shallower and, as

the lungs are emptying of the last breaths of air, you very often see the previous signs of distress disappear. Sometimes you will notice the breathing seemingly stop, then start up again for a few seconds, which is probably a last-ditch effort by the heart to get the blood pumping and the lungs working again. Then there is the final outbreath as the last particles of air leave the lungs, and at that moment there is often an immediate look of peace on the patient's face.

I've never been a midwife (or even had much training in maternity), but I imagine the experience of seeing a human being born is quite close to seeing someone die. An amazing, privileged event to witness and be part of, which is why I wanted my career to progress in this direction. Some might say it's weird, or morbid, or even terrifying, but I would say that to 'die well' should be the right of everyone, and I knew I wanted to be part of this vital process.

Having seen the palliative team at work around Northwick Park, and having helped to introduce the LCP on Dickens ward, I now felt that my future lay in this direction. At that time there were no vacancies within the palliative team, and in any case I felt I needed more experience in an environment where dying was not only recognised but prioritised. So in early 2010 I began to work some bank shifts in a local hospice, the Peace Hospice in Watford, going in on my days off from my regular job, and on Saturdays when Mark could look after Ronnie.

The hospice had a great reputation locally and a couple of the older crowd at the social club had heart-warming stories about family or friends who had died there. It had become a lot closer to our own hearts when in 2007, the wife of one of Mark's best friends died at The Peace. Louise was only forty, leaving behind her husband Martin and their three children, all under the age of ten. The Peace Hospice supported Martin and his family through their darkest days and the thought that I would now be a part of this team was a true privilege to me.

Despite being a relatively small organisation, the Peace Hospice serves all of south-west Hertfordshire and when I first started working there, the hospice comprised an in-patient unit of twelve beds. Most of these were in single rooms but a couple contained two beds. There was a day-care unit, where people being treated at home went for respite care or for a planned intervention like a blood transfusion, or a session of physiotherapy or complementary therapy.

As well as patient-centred services the Peace Hospice also housed a large fundraising team on its third floor, vital for the upkeep of the hospice, which relied on charitable donations to keep it going. There was also a Hospice At Home team (HAH), mostly made up of registered nurses with several healthcare assistants. As the name suggests, this team went out into the community to visit terminally ill patients who had opted to be looked after in their own homes.

In a similar way to how I felt on my first days as a student nurse, I knew from the moment I stepped foot into the hospice that this was where I wanted to be. Things could not have been more different from the chaotic life on Dickens ward. There was an overwhelming sense of calm and the patient was at the centre of everything – decisions, care plans, discharge planning, and the rest. All of this was done involving the patient and those closest to them. Individual, holistic care was on show everywhere.

I would be working in the inpatient unit, and with this

calmer and quieter place of work came a different breed of nurse. Many were older in years, winding down after decades on hospital wards or years spent as busy district nurses and now seeking a slower pace of life. The patient-to-nurse ratio was much lower: usually each nurse would have three or four patients to care for. I couldn't quite believe that, after my ward experience. Still, at times some would moan that it was busy, which I always found laughable, and I often thought to myself that some of the hospice nurses could have done with a night shift on Dickens every now and again to remind themselves how lucky they were.

Being allocated fewer patients meant you could spend more time with each one. I would sit and read to people once my medication round was done, or spend time listening to someone's fascinating life history. Distraction is sometimes better than any analgesia on the market, allowing a person to become lost in their thoughts and memories as they tell their story. If I had a confused or agitated patient to care for, I could be the one by their side, instead of relying on a healthcare assistant or student nurse.

The hospice was a home from home for patients. It had wooden flooring throughout, with French doors in every room opening on to a beautifully kept garden. Beds could be wheeled into the garden so even the sickest people didn't miss out on one of life's most valuable commodities – fresh air. There was a television for every person and even one for relatives in a communal area hosting a small kitchen and children's play area. The hospice was kept alive with volunteers in every department – gardeners, catering staff, chaplains, drivers – all giving up their time to make it such a unique place to be.

I would sometimes be on a bank shift when a patient was admitted to the hospice from the local hospital, Watford General. As people arrived through the doors of the hospice, you could almost see the relief wash over them. Peace at last.

Eventually I was offered a full-time job with the Peace Hospice, working with the HAH team. I left Northwick Park in December 2010, saying goodbye to my colleagues with a poem and a few lines of thanks…

Communicate, initiate, support and dedicate
your time to listening to your workmates.
Play not alone but as a team, results are better
shared – so are problems.
Speak up, be heard, make a difference.
Remind them that our patients are people, not numbers.
Never forget but never be afraid to move on.

To all those in this little staffroom eating, drinking,
laughing, moaning, story-telling, listening, sleeping –
I will miss you.

Thank you to all those who have shown me kindness, passed
on knowledge and experience, listened to me, understood me,
comforted me, laughed with me and taught me. Thank you.

To all the domestics, caterers, care assistants, nurses, doctors,
housekeepers, volunteers and peers whose blood, sweat and
tears go unrewarded – I salute you!
Your friend, Kelly C

Chapter 7

Going from Dickens ward to the Hospice At Home team was like stepping out of a Formula One car after twenty laps of the track and doing the whole thing again in a horse and cart. I'd been so used to doing things at 100mph that initially I found it hard to adjust to this slower pace of working. Luckily, I was helped and supported by Fodeen and Shanti, both ex-district nurses, among five registered nurses working on the HAH team. They were old school and I appreciated them teaching me that while I was now working at a different pace, there would be no relaxation of standards, or the general thoroughness expected of nurses in whatever branch of medicine.

In fact, it was this increased attention to detail that was to become one of the main aspects of the job. The care we'd give to people in their homes would vary – anything from a basic wash and help to get dressed to regular injections and the renewal of syringe pumps to those who needed it. We would also assist during regular visits from district nurses whose workload, even a decade ago, was starting to become stretched very thinly. I can't imagine what it must be like for them now, although I can make a good guess.

My initial impressions of HAH was that people were more relaxed and comfortable at home. I suppose this goes almost without saying, but the other aspect was that they had already been given the news that they were going to die, and while it can't be said that everyone involved was particularly comfortable with that, the stage of raw grief that I'd seen when patients had been given such devastating news in hospital was no longer there. That extremely difficult conversation had already taken place and the person in question had now chosen to stay at home and undergo treatment from their own bed.

Which is why basic care, such as washing, becomes particularly important. Fodeen and Shanti taught me that where terminal patients are concerned, a wash isn't just a wash. When you're helping someone bedbound to wash, you're learning which parts of their body hurt, where they are uncomfortable or where they may be developing pressure sores. By assisting in such an intimate experience you're also helping to build up trust between you, so the patient understands that you're aiming to respect and maintain their dignity in the midst of an extremely difficult situation. In a hospital ward you don't have much time to build rapport, never mind respect dignity. A wash is very often a rapid sequence of events that can leave a patient feeling self-conscious, exposed and vulnerable. Nonetheless, you just have to get on with it. In a hospice or home-nursing environment the experience is far less pressured and much more patient-centred. For example, if you're cleaning someone's bottom half, you maintain dignity by leaving their top half of clothing on, and vice versa. You also aim to use the patient's own shower gels, soaps and moisturisers, which means they have the comfortable feeling of familiarity. And you don't rush. If it takes time, it takes time, and it is time that can be used to build trust and listen to your patient's fears, worries, concerns, joys and memories of better days.

In the early days with HAH, I expected that my reactions to very sick and dying people would be pretty much the same as it was on the wards, in that you'd obviously feel empathy for the patient, and some sadness when they died, but you also knew you had a job to do and you couldn't let your emotions get in the way of that. Little did I realise then how much my emotions would quite often get the better of me in this type of work.

One of my earliest visits was to a woman in her mid-thirties called Rachael, who was diagnosed with ovarian cancer and was initially treated at the Royal Marsden Hospital, one of the world's foremost cancer treatment centres, based in London. At that time, there was hope that her treatment would provide a cure, but eventually the cancer was shown to have progressed to the point where no further treatment was available.

After Rachael was given the devastating news she opted to return to her childhood home in the Elstree area of north-west London. It was in this beautiful house, complete with an enormous garden that she could see from her bedroom window, that I first met her. Rachael was a handful of years older than me but we hit it off straight away and had a lot in common. She knew she was going to die, but despite that huge elephant in the room we'd have chats about anything and everything.

It wasn't long before her condition worsened. There came a time when she needed to be moved from her own double bed into a hospital bed at home that could be raised or lowered so carers could assist her more easily. I visited on the day she was due to be moved. She looked absolutely awful, and in no state to undergo the disruption that a move from one bed to another would bring.

With hindsight, had I been more experienced I'd have somehow vetoed the move. It was obvious Rachael only had hours to live and while installing a hospital bed is a health and safety requirement on behalf of the carers, I think I'd have bent the rules in Rachael's favour. Unfortunately, the care package had been established and there was little I could do at that stage to stop the move going ahead.

The bed arrived and with the help of a healthcare assistant we inched her from her own comfortable bed and on to the hospital contraption with its levers and pulleys. Rachael grimaced, then cried out in pain.

'I can't do this,' she said. 'It's too much…'

I saw the fear in her eyes and could almost feel the pain wracking her body as we gently slid her on to the new bed.

'I'm really sorry, Rachael,' I said. 'I hate to have to do this. But once you're comfortable we can show you how it all works and it will make things a bit easier.'

As I spoke, I knew I was reassuring only myself. Rachael just wanted to stay where she was and it took us an age to get her comfortable. Finally, she seemed calm and settled, and I motioned to the healthcare assistant that it was time to leave.

'I'll be back tomorrow, Rachael,' I said, 'but in the meantime if there are any problems or anything you need, just ask your mum or dad to call the hospice. OK?'

Rachael didn't reply. Her eyes were closed. But just before

I turned to leave I heard something. A slight change in the rhythm of her breathing. I leaned closer to her and listened. Yes, there was a definite change, an unmistakable slow, shallow sound that could only mean one thing.

The healthcare assistant looked at me. 'She's dying, isn't she?' she whispered in my ear.

I nodded. We stared at each other for a split second, thinking the same thought. Downstairs, Rachael's poor parents were waiting in the living room. They were lovely, good people and my heart went out to them. They were in their sixties, maybe seventies, and like all parents with a terminally ill child, had the look of those who never expect to witness the death of a daughter or son. Also with them was Rachael's heavily pregnant sister.

'I think I should go and talk to them now,' I whispered to the assistant. 'You stay here and keep an eye on Rachael.'

I made my way downstairs and with every step the feeling in my stomach became heavier and heavier. As I entered the large living room its three occupants turned to me as one, expecting to hear that Rachael had been moved and that she was now comfortable. They wanted to know that the night would pass quietly, and that tomorrow would be another day.

'I'm sorry to have to tell you this,' I said, 'but Rachael's breathing has changed and it isn't a good sign. I think you should go upstairs to her now.'

'Oh no,' said Rachael's mum. 'Is this it, Kelly? Is this the end?'

I could hardly open my mouth to speak. Instead I just nodded and without another word they passed me and trooped upstairs. I followed them up but then, on the landing between the two flights of stairs, I stopped. We'd established a great relationship and the sadness I felt was quite overwhelming. Despite everything she had been through, Rachael showed no anger, no regrets. With dignity, humility and courage she'd accepted the situation she was in.

The tears were coming, and they were unstoppable. I huddled in a corner of the landing and silently cried my eyes out. After five minutes, maybe ten, I calmed down, found the bathroom, washed my face, took a deep breath and went into Rachael's bedroom, where there were more tears. Many more. Just to make the situation more emotional, Rachael's sister was holding an envelope. They had not wanted to know the sex of the baby as they wanted it to be a surprise, hoping that Rachael would live to meet the new arrival. But they had prepared for the worst and promised her that she would die knowing whether she would be aunty to a niece or nephew. Everyone else left the room so her sister could open the envelope and quietly whisper to Rachael the gender of the baby who would never meet her.

This time I bit my lip, knowing the family would need me in the immediate aftermath of Rachael's death. They were Jewish, and in keeping with their religious traditions the body would need to be buried within twenty-four hours. The healthcare assistant went off to phone the GP so the death could be confirmed and registered while we contacted the funeral director.

Rachael's mum looked at me and smiled. 'You did everything you could for her, Kelly,' she said, touching my arm. 'She's at peace now. Let's think about her that way.'

The lump in my throat felt the size of a cricket ball. I could hardly reply, I felt such a fool. My barriers had dropped and they wouldn't be coming back up anytime soon, not in this house. But again I composed myself, smiled and got on with my work.

I learned a lot that day. I learned that, if necessary, it is fine to overrule officialdom if it means that a dying person isn't made uncomfortable or distressed as a result. I also mastered resilience in the face of overwhelming emotion and in time, whenever I was present at a death, I would learn to be just a little bit steely, despite my feelings. But more importantly, I would also learn that it is OK to shed a tear. In fact, it is positively healthy because it means that you never lose your sense of compassion, which you need in spades if palliative care is your chosen career.

And it wasn't always the deaths of younger people that would get to me. I nursed a man in his eighties by the name of Jack, who lived near Watford and in his younger days had been a professional jazz saxophonist. He had terminal lung cancer, perhaps the result of spending so many years playing in smoky clubs, and because of that I never heard him play 'live'. But during our visits he'd often play the records he'd been part of and talk about his career. There were black and white photos of him all over his room looking smart and snappy as he posed with members of various jazz bands.

I'd sit with him for hours, listening to this lovely man's tales, while his wife, Ruth, went out for a bit of respite time. He'd had a good life and although he knew it was approaching, he didn't fear death. One afternoon, myself and Sarah, a healthcare assistant who worked with us, were re-priming Jack's syringe pump when, with little warning, he deteriorated and died within minutes. Sarah and I were both quite taken aback and it was a really emotional moment. When Ruth, Jack's wife, came home from her trip to the shops and saw what had happened she gave us both a huge hug. At that moment, both Sarah and I started crying – to this day we look back and cringe…

'It's OK, Kelly,' she said, squeezing me tight.

This is all wrong, I thought. *It should be me hugging her!* We did manage to have a little laugh with Ruth about our emotional state and stayed to help her make the relevant phone calls, etc. We said our goodbyes to her – for the last time – and set off to our next call, taking some time out first to reflect on what we'd just experienced.

Unlike in my previous role at Northwick Park, there was always time between patients to take a breath and settle your mind before the next visit. As I've said, it took me some months to get used to the change of pace, and because of the area we covered the journeys between patients could be long. There was also the detailed note-taking to contend with. Back in the hospital, working twelve-hour shifts, I might scribble a few lines down after each interaction with a patient, but that was it – there was little time for anything longer. With the HAH team, however, there seemed to be enough time to write an essay, and initially I was surprised at the length and detail of the write-ups that Fodeen and Shanti produced following each visit. They were doing the right thing, of course, but you'd have to type up everything you'd written later on and I found that very time-consuming.

Managing patients' GPs could be stressful at times. There were some fabulous doctors out there who understood us and the need for our services, and offered no end of support. But there is no getting away from the fact that we struggled with others. One time I was looking after a man with a large extended family, who initially found it hard to accept that he was dying. We had to have many careful conversations around the subject until they started to accept what was happening.

The family were adamant that their relative would be treated at home until he died and of course we were fine about this. As a matter of routine I asked the patient's GP for a 'Do Not Attempt Cardiopulmonary resuscitation' (DNACPR) form so that if the man had to go into hospital, this could be taken with him in the ambulance.

'Oh yes,' said the receptionist at the GP surgery, 'we've filled out the form. But the doctor has decided to keep it here in the surgery in case it upsets the family.'

I groaned. There wasn't a whole lot of point having a DNACPR notice locked away in a surgery if it might be needed immediately. It was what the family wanted. But in this case, the doctor considered he knew best. In other cases, we'd ask for a certain medication from a GP, only for them to refuse to prescribe it because they didn't agree with it.

However, overall my gripes about the job were very minor compared to the benefits I was getting from it. Despite the obvious challenges posed by the nature of this work, I would go home after every shift feeling energised and fulfilled. I felt that I had more to give, to my family as well as my patients, and rarely had the feeling of flopping through my front door in a state of exhaustion, totally wrung out by the day's events. Friends and family wondered (and still wonder) how I do what I do every day, but if you're not pushed for time you can have the most amazing, positive visits in which you are able to sit and chat to the patient and have a good discussion about their thoughts, feelings, worries and concerns. Or you may talk to a husband or wife struggling with their partner's illness and be able to offer support and advice.

In one way or another I came out of every single visit I ever made feeling rewarded, even when the visit itself was challenging. Visiting deprived parts of Watford or Borehamwood made me upset about the difficult circumstances some people lived in, never mind all the problems they were facing with a terminally ill person in the house. It would sadden me to walk into houses where people had nothing, not even a carpet on the floor, and kids were running around everywhere. The noise and chaos of such situations weren't really conducive to the calm, quiet conditions that people need when they're dying and this was sometimes made even worse if there was a drug user in the house. In those situations you weren't able to leave certain medications in the home, so a discussion would be needed with the family to install a safe that could only be opened by healthcare professionals. If this couldn't be achieved, there was no choice but to take the medications away and call an out-of-hours GP if injections were needed. Hardly an ideal situation, but sometimes it was the only choice.

All that said, I noticed that it was the least well off in our society who dealt with a devastating, life-limiting diagnosis the best. I don't know why – maybe because they have to put up with a whole lot of shit in their lives and this is just one more thing. As a medical professional, poorer people seem to trust and accept what you're saying far more than the wealthy, who often consider they know better, demand a second opinion, cannot accept that they have been diagnosed with this or that, etc. For some people, money has bought them out of every difficult situation in the past, so they often find it hard to accept that diseases like cancer don't speak the language of money. But cancer has a way of ignoring your financial worth…

I remember visiting a lady called Catherine, who lived towards Potters Bar. She was married, and she and her husband were real high-fliers. They wanted for nothing, and the trappings of their enviable lifestyle were everywhere. Their house was evidently expensive and luxurious. Yet she was suffering from a cancerous brain tumour that was incurable. She'd had radiotherapy, which meant she'd lost her hair, the steroids she was on had caused her to become bloated and gain weight. If all that wasn't bad enough, early on she'd developed hemiplegia, a condition connected to brain damage that causes paralysis down one side of the body.

We saw her almost every day for eight months until she died, and got to know her very well. I felt for her; here was a woman who'd gone from being slim, glamorous and attractive into someone even her own husband didn't particularly want to see. Whenever we saw him, he treated her like she was an embarrassment that had to be hidden away. He seemed to feel very guilty that we were doing most of the caring, yet the minute we'd arrive he'd be waiting on the doorstep for us, poised to get in his car and zip away for a game of golf or tennis.

Catherine was aware that in her present state she embarrassed him. What made this worse was that the tumour on her brain was right by the centre, which controls emotions, and the pressure on it would cause her to suddenly start crying. You'd be having a normal conversation with her and she'd just break down in tears without knowing why, although she knew she felt sad. It's a horrible side effect and we did our best to keep conversations light and chatty. We used to take her into the garden – her husband refused to have a wheelchair because he didn't want to be seen pushing her about – and let her enjoy an hour or so in the sun before he returned, looking shamefaced and sheepish.

There were times when you felt privileged people were living in a totally different world. We were dealing with a patient at home in the most beautiful house I think I've ever been in, a converted barn with the most gorgeous entrance hall and balcony right around the top. We needed a bowl in which to put water to wash the patient and I asked if they had anything suitable.

'You know, like a washing-up bowl,' I said, as we stood in their enormous kitchen, 'a plastic washing-up bowl.'

There were puzzled looks all round. I noticed several grand Belfast sinks, none of which would've sat very comfortably alongside a £3 yellow plastic washing-up bowl from ASDA.

'I'm afraid we don't have anything like that,' said the man of the house. 'But we'll see what we can do.'

We went upstairs to the patient's bedroom to make our preparations. Twenty minutes later, there was a knock on the door.

'This is really all I could find,' said the patient's husband. 'I'm afraid we don't cook much…'

In his hand was a lasagne dish with a depth of about two inches. He looked genuinely sorry that he hadn't been able to provide us with anything else.

'It's fine,' I said. 'We'll manage.' And we did, despite having to fill the thing up about twenty times just to provide one wash.

Then you would find those who stay in your memory because they were absolute beacons of courage and resilience. The youngest person I looked after during my time at HAH was a guy in his early twenties called Sam, who lived in Borehamwood.

Sam had been diagnosed with melanoma seven years previously. Melanoma is a cancer of the skin and is often caused by UV damage, but a rarer type of melanoma is not caused by sun damage, rather a genetic mutation, and this is the type Sam was diagnosed with. By the time we met him, he had endured more than twenty operations, chemotherapy, radiotherapy, gamma knife brain radiotherapy (radical technology that delivers many small gamma rays to deliver a precise dose of radiotherapy to a target such as a tumour) and several trial melanoma drugs. When he realised the disease was progressing, he had proposed to his fiancée, Ali, and they married shortly after.

The cancer had now spread to the tissue under the skin, causing painful swollen lumps all over his body, and these caused Sam a great deal of distress. Some had started to fungate, making them even more unbearable. It was a horrible condition and he was in the most terrible pain. He was on the highest level of painkiller I'd ever known. We had set up a syringe driver, a machine about the size of a paperback book connected to the body via a small butterfly needle which delivers a continuous infusion of medications. At one point in his syringe driver he had 120mg of alfentanil, which is thirty times stronger than morphine. And yet, he would do his best to get up and about, getting himself to the bathroom when he could and generally being considerate and thoughtful to everyone around him. The unfairness of his situation was in direct contrast to his kind, accepting nature, but he was lucky to have an equally amazing wife and supportive family.

At times like this, it was a real blessing working with the HAH team. There was such a mix of people in the team, all with something different to offer. Sara, one of the nurses, and

Ros, an HCA, both had such a great sense of humour and an ability to read a situation before adding just the right amount of comedy. Ros would rarely leave a visit, even the most challenging ones, without having made patients and families laugh out loud. Never afraid to make fun of herself, she had a beautiful way of distracting patients away from their world of horror and into her world of fun. She was like this with Sam, as was Sara, and I would have given anything to be a fly on the wall during one of their joint visits. They brought life to situations where death was looming, and for Sam and his family this was always so important.

Gradually Sam deteriorated until he was no longer responsive. This was a truly awful time for his family and young wife. They were constantly holding out hope that he would wake up and open his eyes once more – anything to have another opportunity to say their goodbyes. It would never have been enough. How could it? He died peacefully at home, surrounded by those he loved the most.

About eighteen months on, Sara bumped into Sam's wife, Ali, who, incredibly, was pregnant. It turned out that Sam had opted to have his sperm frozen prior to starting chemotherapy and his wife had chosen, with the family's blessing and full support, to have Sam's baby. Even in the depths of darkness, there is always a ray of hope.

Sam's family have since set up the Sam Keen Foundation, which has raised more than half a million pounds for the Royal Marsden Hospital. The Foundation has also sponsored two research fellows, who published a groundbreaking paper introducing aspects of immunology to fight cancer, which are now part of mainstream cancer treatment.

Chapter 8

One of the most important aspects of the Peace Hospice's outreach work was learning to observe and listen. After my experience on the wards I was used to leading the agenda, finding prescriptive solutions to problems and doing things according to the book. Which is exactly what you need to operate in a busy environment. In hospital there just isn't time to do everything your way – you just go with the demands of the moment.

Hospice At Home was far different. Building trusting, genuine relationships with patients and their families was everything. Nursing at home means you are being allowed into people's lives at a critical time, and given you can sometimes be there three times a day, you almost need to become part of the furniture, for however long or short the amount of time is.

So you talk, and you listen. You talk about the weather, or the TV, or what's going on with your family, what's happening within theirs. Then you listen. You listen to fears, hopes, concerns, grumbles, memories, sorrows, joys. And by listening, you pick up on clues to what's really going on for the patient, because those might not always be immediately obvious.

I've already mentioned the elephant in the room and even though the patient has received a terminal diagnosis, and even though hospice staff have been called in to help, that elephant often looms large over everything. There have been times when I've picked up the phone to introduce myself before my first visit, to be told, 'Oh, I'm dying, am I?' You can hear the defensiveness provoked by fear in their tone of voice and it's vital not to get off on the wrong foot.

'OK,' I'll reply, 'do you think you're dying?'

'Well…no. Not yet anyway.'

'Then I don't think you're dying either. What I'm trying to do is see if you need some extra support, so I'm hoping we can have a meet-up and a chat, then maybe we can find a way of making things better for you at home.'

And from there you visit the person, start to get to know them and, using your eyes, ears and instinct, assess the situation from their point of view. From the beginning they may be happy to talk about their illness in the fullest and frankest terms. Quite often, that isn't the case at all and you need to instigate conversations to explore what feels safe, and what doesn't. And to do that you need them to set the agenda, not the other way round. So, for example, if someone flinches while I'm giving them a wash, I might say something like, 'I notice you're getting a bit of pain in that area. Do you worry about what's causing that?'

If they say 'yes', you might then take the conversation a little further, saying, 'Do you feel the pain is getting worse?' Again, you're allowing the person to make up their mind about how they reply, and whether they feel strong enough to keep the conversation going. If they shut you down and won't 'go there', then there is no pressure to continue and the elephant stays for a while longer until the patient is ready to talk.

Being mindful of cultural issues is also a big part of the job. When you step into someone's home you also step into their world, their values, their beliefs. You get to understand which cultures are comfortable talking about dying and which aren't. Which cultures have specified rituals for those who have just died, and who is allowed to attend (or not attend) in the immediate aftermath. Attitude towards food is also an element to be aware of. When patients stop eating or drinking, which is common, particularly with cancer, it can be extremely hard for relatives to accept that their loved one is refusing nourishment. Sometimes I've seen a daughter or daughter-in-law blamed for this, simply because they've assumed responsibility of care for their husband's parents and now they're doing the majority of the cooking. In this scenario, you have to explain that loss of appetite is no one's fault, and that it's just a natural reaction to this horrible illness.

There were more than a few patients who ended up dying in hospital because the family could no longer manage the issue of eating and drinking. They would see it as something that needed investigating and fixing, rather than a natural symptom of dying. For many families, back then and now, they see not eating and drinking as the cause of their loved one deteriorating.

'Of course he's getting weaker, he's not eating anything,' a patient's son once said to me. It didn't matter how much I tried to get him to reverse his thinking, he just couldn't go there.

'His cancer is getting worse', I would say. 'It's because of the cancer that he is getting weaker, he has less energy, less demand for food.'

But my words were never enough. The son, convinced he was doing the right thing and that his dad was not trying hard enough, would constantly be pushing food in front of him. Every time I visited, there was food there. It got to the point where his dad, Hitesh, would practically beg us to stop the food coming. In advanced cancer, there are many changes to the body and plenty of reasons for the appetite to diminish. As the body starts to shut down, the digestion process shuts down too. Eating and drinking even small amounts can cause nausea, sickness and feeling uncomfortably full. Cancer treatments often change people's smell and taste, so foods they once enjoyed become unpalatable. Medications can affect the appetite as well as symptoms such as pain and breathlessness. Cachexia (extreme weight loss and muscle wasting in chronic illness) is common in advanced disease and is exceptionally hard for families to cope with. Most other symptoms we can manage, but when the appetite goes, there is little we can do apart from giving support and reassurance, especially to the family. It is a symptom that distresses the family more often than the patient.

Hitesh was one of our patients who ended up in hospital. Once there, people become a number, a statistic, a sitting duck for every test and investigation under the sun. Luckily for Hitesh, we were able to liaise with the palliative care team at Watford General, who worked with the medical team and Hitesh and his family to reiterate the messages we were giving them at home. They helped to discharge him home with a care plan reflecting his wish to die there and not to be readmitted to hospital. We help patients create these plans when they are approaching the end of their lives, to reflect their wishes and preferences about their care. The aim is to achieve better outcomes for patients so those caring for them understand what is important to them. The care plan, completed with input from Hitesh, included helpful advice for the family on how and when to offer food, with a focus on aspects of life Hitesh was still able to enjoy, rather than focusing on what was no longer achievable.

Attitudes to pain can also vary. Some cultures are wary of using pain relief, seeing pain and suffering as a clear route to a better afterlife for the sufferer. Obviously, that can be a difficult position to work with. I'll not forget dealing with one man who belonged to an African fundamentalist Christian Church who was in a terrible pain, almost screaming out with it, but he and his family wouldn't even allow us to talk about dying, and painkillers were most certainly not an option. Those visits were particularly difficult for me.

If we knew our outreach shifts were going to be quiet we'd often volunteer our services to the Peace Hospice's in-patient unit, or even do a full bank shift there. Again, compared to life on the ward of a mainstream hospital I felt the pace of work within the hospice was slow. A large number of the staff had been there for many years and were used to doing things in a certain way. Sometimes I found this to be restrictive and I didn't always enjoy the feeling of having to do things because 'that's the way we've always done it'. Even after two years working with HAH, I was still being told to slow down!

That said, it was mostly a pleasure to work there. For a nurse it was a great job, in which you were well looked after, you worked at a good pace and you weren't expected to do things out of your remit. The environment was a good one, for staff, patients and families, and by and large, it was a lovely and relaxed workplace.

Coming to terms with a life-limiting illness is challenging for most of us, but it is particularly difficult for younger people, especially those with a young family. During one shift when I was helping out on the in-patient unit, I was caring for a lady in her late thirties, Karen, who had been admitted for terminal care. Karen was married to Mike and they had two young children: Scarlet, aged nine, and Max, just six years old. I don't think you ever get used to seeing other people's devastation but sometimes it smacks you in the face so hard you just want to run the other way. Of course, running away is not an option, so you carry on – doing the best you can to make even the slightest difference.

Karen had been battling a rare peritoneal cancer, complicated by a delayed diagnosis and progressing through multiple lines of chemotherapy. Her most recent chemotherapy was given only a few weeks before I met her, now in her last days of life. Perhaps it could be argued that the chemotherapy shouldn't have been given, she was already too unwell, but how do you tell a thirty-eight-year-old mother and wife that there are no more treatments for the cancer? So she had the chemo and became acutely unwell one week later. Chemotherapy is an aggressive treatment, intended to kill the cancer cells, but it also kills off healthy cells, which is why it causes so many side effects. Karen's body was too weak for chemotherapy, her healthy cells too few, and it is highly likely that the chemotherapy actually shortened her life, despite being given in the hope of prolonging it.

Karen had been restless and agitated during the previous night and had required multiple doses of a sedative to relax her. Terminal agitation is a horrible symptom, which often becomes so hard to manage that the only option is to heavily sedate. This is hugely traumatic for families who are hoping to have that one last conversation, a few last coherent words with their dying loved one. Mike was beside her, a broken man sitting and watching his wife die. It's hard to know how much comfort to offer a grieving relative. Too much and they back away, not wanting the outpouring of sympathy. Too little and you risk denying them the opportunity to talk, to open up. I quietly approached him.

'Mike, is there anything I can get for you?' I waited, already feeling helpless.

When he didn't reply, I busied myself a little, brushing Karen's hair and wetting her lips with her favourite lemon squash by her bedside. I was about to leave when Mike spoke.

'How can I manage without her?' he asked pitifully.

I couldn't answer, I didn't need to answer as there were no words right at this point in time that would have possibly made him feel any better. Sometimes, it's better to let the emotions do the talking. He cried and cried and somehow it felt right just to allow that to happen.

Later on, towards the end of my shift, I saw Mike in the relatives' area. I sat with him and he started to talk. He told me how he had struggled with what to tell the children, how much to disclose to them, how honest to be with them. He talked about his friends: how supportive they had been and how he wouldn't have got through any of this without them. And he spoke about some thoughts that had really been troubling him: how he had wished over this past week that Karen would just die, because all he could see now was how much she was suffering; agitated, restless, horribly oedematous. Then the guilt that comes with thinking these thoughts. What a battle this poor man was going through, and for him it was only just beginning. He would soon be on his own with two young children and would no doubt be faced with many challenges.

Because we had days like this to deal with, it was important to be able to lift our mood and have some fun in between the death and dying, whilst working with HAH. There was always lots of laughter and with big characters in the team, plenty of banter. Sara and I were called out to support the family of a lady who had died at home during the night. They wanted her washed before the funeral directors came. So off we went. When we arrived, we did the usual dishing out of condolences before getting to work. We gathered everything needed – bowl (this was a 'normal' family home, so a plastic wash bowl was present!), shower gel, moisturiser, hairbrush, toothbrush, toothpaste, clean pyjamas. Sara and I looked at each other as the daughter handed us the pyjamas – beautiful dark green silk. Most pyjamas now are a nice mixed blend of cotton and synthetic materials, making them soft and stretchy. But not silk. The elderly lady lay peacefully in the bed and we soon realised that rigor mortis was well and truly established. Rigor mortis, which usually starts three to four hours after death, causes muscle stiffness and rigidity over the entire body due to chemical changes.

We started with the wash – talking to her as we went through our well-rehearsed routine. Now, remember when you were little at the dinner table and one of you got the giggles and despite being told to stop, you couldn't? As soon as we started trying to put this pair of beautiful pyjamas on, we knew this would be a 'dinner table' moment. Well, we laughed so much that tears were streaming down our faces, but we were trying not to make too much noise – how very inappropriate! No matter how many different ways we tried, we couldn't get both of the arms in, but we kept going, we were determined. Suddenly, we heard an almighty rip as the seam down one of the arms gave way. I think at this point we lost the plot entirely and had to fully compose ourselves before leaving the room – letting the family know that their mum was now fresh and clean but unfortunately, there was a 'small rip' in the pyjamas...

After more than two years working with HAH, I decided the time was right to progress my career again. I wanted to move up the nursing ladder, but because HAH was such a small team there was nowhere to go within it. Fiona, the manager who'd done a lot of work with our team to make it more efficient and dynamic, was a great source of inspiration and was regularly pushing me towards a specialist nursing role.

In the meantime, Sara, the nurse from the HAH team, had taken up a job to develop a referrals service in the hospice, triaging new referrals (allocating the workload to the team), liaising with the community team and making sure each patient was getting the right service. This was very much an office-type admin role and after about six months, Sara was keen to move back to HAH, simply because she missed that kind of work. However, she'd laid strong foundations and I decided that the referrals role might give me useful experience. Also, it was a band 7 grade, which meant I'd be bypassing band 6.

So I took it on, and spent the next eighteen months doing a job that was a complete change for me, to say the least. My nurse's uniform was put away and as this was a non-clinical role, I wore office clothes every day, which felt very odd. I looked after the referrals for all our services and I also took over the bed management for the in-patient unit, allocating spaces when patients were admitted. I had some input into discharge planning and I started a nurse-led assessment clinic for the outpatient services called The Starlight Centre. This was a huge learning curve for me, utilising a variety of skills. I organised appointments, decided how to market and promote the service and how to reach out to people who might benefit from the ever-expanding services. We deliberately sold it as 'The Starlight Centre' rather than 'The Peace Hospice' as we didn't want to scare people away. The Starlight Centre was offering physiotherapy, rehabilitation, complementary therapies, counselling and many more services to people affected by a life-limiting illness. Even those on a curative treatment path were able to access the services so, as you can imagine, many were put off by being based at the hospice. It was hard enough promoting the service to local healthcare professionals. Once through the doors, people were usually sold, but I would always dread the initial phone call.

It was a worthwhile and useful role, but for me it was stressful, lonely and sometimes thankless. I'd never wanted an office job in the first place and I wasn't much interested in strategic business meetings and all that kind of thing. The best part of my day was managing referrals to the in-patient unit, because at least then I was interacting with people. I was also managing an admin assistant with whom I had a few problems – lateness, phone calls in work-time, the usual thing. Perhaps the biggest problem I had was that I didn't want to be a manager and wasn't cut out for it. Whenever I raised my concerns, the admin assistant became defensive and I just couldn't deal with it. With hindsight, I'm pleased I learned early on that it's fine not to want to be a manager. I've seen this happen right across the NHS – perfectly capable clinical staff going into management and ending up hating their job because they don't have the qualities needed to be a good manager. That unhappiness filters down to the staff and so we have a no-win situation which could've been avoided had the person recognised their limitations in the first place.

By this time I'd pretty much decided – with Fiona's encouragement – that I wanted to be a full-time palliative care nurse. And, as opposed to working in the hospice or with the community palliative care team, I wanted to take the role back into the busy hospital environment. Why? Because I felt the need for such a service within such a setting was great. I'd been in awe of what the palliative care team did at Northwick Park and I considered that I'd be a useful addition to it. Also, I missed the hustle and bustle of a place like Northwick Park. I'd genuinely appreciated the calm and quiet that working with HAH had provided, but I'm an 'on-the-go' person by nature and I realised that I thrived on work that had a certain pace and energy.

As I carried on trying to be managerial, a vacancy came up with the palliative care team at Northwick Park. As ever, Fiona was supportive. 'This is where you need to be,' she said, encouraging me to apply. I did, and I got the job, thanks to all the experience and knowledge I'd gained at the Peace Hospice.

After several years dealing with sick and dying people, plus their relatives, I was extremely well equipped for my new job. I'd learned how to have difficult conversations with people and I knew how to read warning signs when things were deteriorating. I understood when I should intervene and, equally importantly, when I should back off. I realised that death – this difficult subject, this elephant in the room – had become an everyday part of my life and while it is no small subject, I felt less scared about it personally. I'd been able to talk to Mark whenever I'd had a particularly challenging day and he was always open to hearing my stories. I suppose the whole experience made me more aware of my own mortality but that didn't affect my ability to do my job and pursue the specialist work I'd come to love.

As is usual when I leave a workplace, I wrote a few lines of thanks to my colleagues.

Smile, always. Laugh every day. Cry only when necessary, but sometimes it is.
Love carefully. Listen intently. Ooze kindness. Shadow anger. Be yourself – be the best you can be.
Remind yourself what a difference you are making to the lives of people in turmoil. Bringing peace, tenderness, care and compassion to those who feel abandoned by life.
From fundraisers to front line staff, cleaners to cooks and to the army of volunteers, you all play a part in making this place amazing.
Thank you to all of you for sharing, teaching, listening, guiding, caring and supporting me.
Gratefully and humbly yours – Kelly C.

Chapter 9

As I walked down its crowded corridors and up the worn concrete steps to the Palliative Care department on my first few days back at Northwick Park in February 2015, I couldn't believe that I'd actually missed the old place. It's not a pretty hospital to work in, and by the time of my return it had its share of troubles for sure, but I was glad to be back in an environment that still felt vibrant and alive. It was like I'd never been away, especially when members of staff smiled or said 'Hi' to me as I walked past, not realising that they'd not seen me for a few years. Others would stop me and say, 'Oh my goodness, where have YOU been?' and I'd quickly fill them in on my HAH years before hurrying on.

One thing was for sure – I would now have to get used to that fast pace of life once again. It felt great to say I was part of the 'Palliative Care Team' and I wore my badge with pride. I was welcomed into the team (comprising four nurses, a team leader and consultants) and due to my palliative experience, was quickly up and running on my own. I was surprised at the numbers of referrals received and the variety of reasons for referral. It might be a straightforward referral to see a patient who was comfortably dying, or a referral to see someone with complex and troubling symptoms. We saw patients throughout the hospital, from A&E and ITU through to all of the medical and surgical wards, but we did not see children under the age of eighteen. It seemed in the majority to be a well-respected team, receiving warm welcomes in most areas of the hospital.

The hospital as a whole had seen some change but largely it was the same place I'd left at the end of 2010. However, there had been a lot of changes within the palliative care team and I didn't recognise anyone from the 'old days'. There had obviously been something of an exodus and we were a brand new team. Those starting with me included Claire Windsor and Kerry Wloskowicz, both of whom have become great friends of mine and at the time of writing are still in palliative care.

From the beginning I liked working with Claire and Kerry. Claire is a Belfast girl who trained to be a nurse in Glasgow before moving to England. She had years of palliative care experience in hospices and the community before coming to Northwick Park. She is a calm, collected and highly professional nurse whose whole focus is patient-centred. Kerry, who grew up just ten minutes from the hospital and is of Polish/French descent, is a passionate nurse with a background in oncology. She has high standards for herself and everyone else. She's quick-witted, funny and doesn't mind telling you exactly what she thinks. The three of us hit it off immediately and we're as strong today as we always were.

Our team leader was a woman called Anna. At the time, she seemed to be delighted we were there and was enthusiastic about managing a new team that would bring energy and vitality to the department. Anna was extremely friendly, constantly bigging us up as individuals and as a team, and I certainly thought we were in for a smooth ride.

I must admit that I'm not always the greatest judge of character and I'd not spotted that Anna was perhaps being a little over-friendly. I wasn't suspicious of her in any way, but Claire and Kerry had other ideas. Whereas I saw someone enthusiastic to the point of gushing, they saw a manipulative, controlling person who ran the department to the tune of her own agenda and would stop at nothing to get her own way.

They were right to be wary. After a few weeks, her enthusiasm for us seemed to dissipate, to be replaced by attempts to control and undermine us at every opportunity. One day you'd walk in and she'd be friendly and smiling. The next, she wouldn't even raise her head to acknowledge you. Any ideas we had for the way we worked were always shot down in flames and replaced by her own thoughts, which never quite seemed to work in practice. She was particularly good at demonstrating to her managers and very senior medical staff that she was an efficient manager of people whom she increasingly painted as troublesome and difficult. In other words, us!

Her divide-and-rule approach was most noticeable when we met her individually for one-to-one meetings. For example, she'd tell one of us that 'the other girls' thought she was over-confident with the patients. So you'd go away thinking your colleagues were ganging up on you behind your back. This wouldn't be an irrational thought – as I've mentioned, nursing can be a tough profession in which you sometimes need to watch your back carefully. Naturally, this ongoing suspicion caused problems between us nurses and it took us a long time to realise what was happening.

The department underwent a restructure and a manager was recruited who would be above Anna. This was Randall Jones, an Australian guy who'd been a specialist HIV/AIDS nurse in London for many years. We'd heard great things about him, but when he arrived, Anna wouldn't allow us to have any time with him. Instead, she got in there first and offloaded all the 'problems' she was apparently having with us on to him. As he says now, he was suddenly working with a team he felt was 'in freefall' and it took him a while to understand what was going on and get a grip on the situation.

Anna was a clever woman, covering everything she said and did with a trail of emails and making sure that whatever she said verbally wasn't replicated in a subsequent email, so we had little to no written evidence of whatever she'd said or done to upset us. This made Randall's job difficult and, as he says now, he only realised the extent of the difficulties we were experiencing when each of us came to him in turn and broke down in tears. My turn to cry was when I'd asked for a couple of hours off to attend Ronnie's Christmas play and she'd point-blank refused to give it me. It was hard to believe that someone could be so heartless; she knew we worked hard every day, and that we asked for little in return. I felt frustrated and trapped, and my reaction was to break down and cry at the unfairness of my situation and the uneasiness we were all experiencing as a result of Anna's management.

The final straw, Randall later said, was when the department's admin assistant came to him and started to cry. 'If someone has affected that many levels of staff there has to be something seriously wrong,' he said, and even he didn't feel capable of managing such a difficult situation.

So he called in an external psychologist by the name of Barbara Wren (the mention of whose name always got us nurses singing, 'Ba-ba-ba, Ba-ba-ba Wren', Beach Boys-style) and she did two sessions with us all, paid for by the Trust. That's how bad things had got, and it was telling that Anna didn't attend either of these sessions, despite being invited. However, a senior manager was invited and she listened in shock to what we had to say before apologising personally to us, saying that she'd had no idea of what had been going on. And why should she when Anna had covered her tracks so well?

It wasn't long after these meetings that Anna handed in her resignation and we all blew a large, collective sigh of relief. But as often happens in the NHS, especially in nursing, the problem wasn't solved. Instead, it was moved somewhere else because Anna found a job in another NHS Trust and, incredibly, was even promoted a level. At least, though, we didn't have to deal with her anymore and could get on with what we did best.

As I've mentioned, I felt well equipped to be in a palliative role at Northwick Park, having had both hospice and acute ward experience. Even so, in those first few weeks I often felt like I was back at nursing school. Palliative care seemed so different in the hospital compared to the hospice and I felt like I had so much to learn. I loved being on the wards again, even though the general hustle, bustle and busyness of the place meant that hospital patients couldn't get the amount of time or attention they perhaps needed. As ever, the priority was getting people better and getting them out of hospital – giving them a nice wash with their own toiletries while finding out how they were feeling wasn't high on the agenda. So at the beginning, that adjustment was hard and the three of us struggled with it. For example, you might see a patient who's incontinent and you know they have been lying in their own excrement for some time. And they might not have been able to reach their call bell to tell someone, or even get a drink of water to relieve their thirst. It was difficult not to get frustrated by sights like these – as nurses with plenty of experience we were passionate about basic standards of care and we were seeing too much of what shouldn't have been happening. Time taught us to be more helpful and understanding to younger, less-experienced nurses, so now we lead by example, saying that we'll help them out with the basic stuff and letting them know that just because we're specialist nurses we're never 'too posh to wash!' We want to build relationships, not destroy them, but busy and pressurised nurses can become defensive if we point out what we see as a lack of basic care. Yes, they're busy, but everyone working in a hospital like Northwick Park is in the same boat. It's not an excuse for poor care.

Another, more complex, challenge I noticed from the start was one I'd witnessed just as I was leaving Northwick Park for the Peace Hospice, and that was the frustration of seeing someone clearly dying – or at least at a very high risk of it – undergoing acute treatment and aggressive interventions in order to keep them alive for just that bit longer.

One of my first experiences of this in my new role was with a lovely man, a Caribbean guy in his seventies. He'd had a stroke and had been fitted with a nasogastric (NG) tube because he'd lost the ability to swallow and needed to be fed through this tube, which goes up the nose and into the stomach. A severe swallowing problem often means that a person aspirates on their own saliva, causing chest infections, and this is what was happening to this man.

He struggled with the NG tube, which isn't a comfortable experience at the best of times, and at one stage he even pulled it out. Eventually, a chest infection he contracted turned into pneumonia and when we saw him he had a high respiratory rate, looked very clammy and was in real distress. In fact, he looked close to dying.

His family were lovely, and accepting of the situation. We spoke to his grandson and granddaughter and while they were devastated, they understood what was happening and recognised that he'd suffered a lot. Between us, we decided he'd be more comfortable in a side room so they could spend time with him before he died. We put a plan in place, prescribing medication for his respiratory rate and to calm him down as he was becoming restless.

The following morning, Kerry and I went to see him and he was much more settled – a totally different person to the man we'd seen the previous day. He wasn't particularly responsive, just fluttering his eyes open now and again but he seemed calm and comfortable. As we were leaving, a consultant entered the room, accompanied by several junior doctors.

'He seems to be much more settled now,' I commented to the consultant as I made my way out of the door.

'Yes, absolutely,' he replied. 'He's definitely improved, so this morning we're going to take bloods from him, pop the NG tube back in and start IV antibiotics.'

'You're joking,' I said. Before I knew it, the words were out of my mouth. Here was a man clearly in the last stages of life, yet this consultant wanted to eke out the rest of his time by putting him through more uncomfortable procedures.

The consultant stared at me. It was like a switch had been flicked. I'd obviously rattled him by speaking out of turn in front of his juniors.

'No, I'm not joking,' he said testily. 'That's exactly what I'm doing. I've told you my plan for him. He's improved and he's going back to the bay.'

'Right,' I said. 'OK.' Judging by the consultant's brusque manner, clearly I wouldn't be able to influence him any further. Feeling devastated and helpless, Kerry and I walked off without another word. Back in our office we spoke to our colleagues, who wondered if one of our palliative consultants might have a word with him. But even they knew there would be little chance of success, if any.

The following day we discovered that the man had died during the night. As the consultant promised, he'd been moved back into the bay and the nursing team on the ward had tried multiple times to cannulate him (i.e. put a tube into him) so he could receive the IV antibiotics. They'd also tried, without success, to get the NG tube up his nose and down into his stomach. At 8pm this poor man had died with all this going on, and with no small level of discomfort. We were upset that we'd tried our best for this man, who was obviously dying, but we hadn't reckoned on a consultant determined to prove that he held superior knowledge.

Certainly, there was (and occasionally still is) an old-school attitude among some consultants that 'Doctor knows best'. I think this stems from a time when society put doctors on a pedestal and there was tremendous respect for their knowledge and authority. This isn't to say that such authority isn't well deserved – consultants are aware that when difficult life-changing decisions must be made it is they who have to make them, and the buck stops there. That is a responsibility we nurses don't have, generally, and I understand that it takes a person with a great deal of confidence (sometimes bordering on the arrogant) to make decisions of life and death.

That said, frustrations creep in when you feel your role as a palliative care nurse is undervalued, or not recognised at all. I recall one consultant who worked in care for the elderly who didn't understand palliative care and wouldn't take the time to learn about it. His catchphrase was, 'If they [the patients] aren't blue and mottling, why do we need palliative care?' It's hard to even challenge such an entrenched attitude, never mind change it. I was involved in the treatment of one elderly man who, in my opinion, was clearly dying. He was undergoing all sorts of interventions and he was extremely agitated and restless. Yet his basic care was being neglected; once I went to see him to find him covered in faeces. Immediately I asked a nurse on the ward whether she would be able to see to his personal care needs, but she replied that she'd only just done it and besides, she was busy. So instead of conducting a full-scale argument I did it myself and as I worked, I noticed more elements of the situation that convinced me this man was dying, albeit slowly.

Next time I saw the consultant I decided to say something.

'Oh,' he replied, raising his eyebrows, 'well, thank you very much for that. Thanks for your opinion, but I think I will decide who's dying and who isn't.' And with that, he walked off without another word, leaving me standing open-mouthed.

Sometimes difficult situations make me angry, sometimes I feel the need to write…

Fluids, needles, antibiotics… let's try one more course.
One more blood test, one more scan, let's just make sure.
Medicine works wonders but it has its flaws
And whose are these decisions to make, are they mine
 or are they yours?
You are the expert, doctor, you're guiding me.
But this is nature, right? What's meant to be…?
This is not a fight or battle that I can win or lose,
This is my path, my destiny… I cannot choose.
I have not 'given up', don't you say that to me.
This is nature, predetermined, can you not see?
I have lived my life, please leave me to rest.
Some respect and dignity, that's all I request.
'Bloods today for the lady in B1'
That's your plan, doctor, but what have you begun?

Thankfully, such situations don't happen often and in fact, one of the differences I noticed on re-joining Northwick Park was that many more consultants were open to being challenged, as long as it was done in the right way, i.e. with facts, not opinions. I learned to be a lot more on the ball with consultants as a result of our weekly Multi-Disciplinary Team Meetings (MDTMs), during which staff from different disciplines will get together to discuss patients' care, making sure we're doing the right thing and sharing ideas for other ways of working. It has become quite common for the consultants attached to the palliative care team to openly challenge us about what we've done and the decisions we've made. It's not a matter of trying to catch us out, more a case of challenging our thought processes, which I think is good for constant learning and certainly keeps you on your toes.

Learning to cope with such challenge gives you the confidence, as a nurse, to go head-to-head with consultants if you feel something needs to be said. You might say something like, 'I'm not sure about the decision-making process for Patient X – can you tell me a bit more?' Or, 'I see we're doing this for Patient Y, but is it also worth thinking about that?' You're careful how you phrase your questioning, but if you get that part right, very few consultants will refuse to engage with you, even if they're 100 per cent convinced they're right.

I've learned that an especially bad time to challenge a consultant is when they're with the junior doctors. As I've said before, consultants don't like losing face, particularly when there's an audience. That said, there are occasions when the only opportunity to challenge is when juniors are present, and it's interesting to watch their reactions when the challenge is on. Quite often, you'll feel them agreeing with you, perhaps because they're emerging from a more empathic generation of medical staff which has been given at least some (but not nearly enough) training in patient care, bedside manner and when the palliative approach is appropriate. Even so, while young heads might nod in agreement, it's very, very unlikely a junior would even express his or her support for your opinion, at least in front of the consultant. It simply isn't worth their while to create so much trouble for themselves, and this comes back to the strange, hierarchical set-up that still exists in medicine.

Personally, I think that's quite sad. From the start, the palliative team has generally got on well with junior doctors, who more often than not respect your seniority in terms of your experience and quite often seem to have a better handle on palliative care than their seniors.

That said, sometimes that relationship is strained when junior doctors don't quite get the idea of the service palliative care provides. For example, I got a call from a junior doctor on the cardiology ward. 'I've just put in a referral to you,' he said. 'We need support with a patient who we're going to withdraw treatment from this afternoon.'

Within the cardiology ward there's a coronary care unit (CCU), where patients go when they need constant monitoring and intervention. You might encounter patients on life-saving interventions like dopamine infusions for patients who can't maintain their own blood pressure because something's going on with their normal heart function. This particular patient, a lady in her eighties, was in CCU and had been on two lots of infusions to keep her blood pressure and her heart rate up. If these treatments stopped, she would die.

The call came at 2.15pm and I was working on triage. As most of our nurses finish at 4pm, mid-afternoon isn't the best time to be summoned, particularly when all our nurses had already been allocated. I asked the doctor for more information and he explained that they had spoken to the patient and the family the previous day.

'We've told them that we're trying everything we can,' he said, 'but there's really only one more thing we can have a go at. If that doesn't work, and we have very little hope that it will, we will have to withdraw treatment.'

I was pleased that the family had been involved and kept informed, but I was somewhat worried about how that approach had been made. Was it a bit too matter-of-fact and brutal?

'It might be really useful,' I said, treading carefully, 'to have involved us a bit earlier in the process so that we can help the family prepare and plan. It'd be good to find out what her wishes are and what her family feel. She might want to come home to die, and if so, we need to get everything in place for that to happen.'

'Oh,' said the doctor, 'we haven't really thought about all that. We haven't time. I just wanted someone to come down and help get this sorted ASAP.'

I explained that we are an advisory service, not rapid response. We're not like the cardiac arrest team who come straight away to see someone, doors flying open and staff running everywhere.

'In that case,' he said, 'maybe you need to reprioritise the patients you're seeing today. We need some help down here.'

I bristled, then took a deep breath. 'You're not really in a position to be telling me how to reprioritise my patients,' I said.

'I know,' he said, 'but I was just too busy yesterday evening to refer this lady, so that's why I'm doing it now. OK?'

Behind the confidence I detected a note of nervousness. If the plan was to withdraw treatment, we should've been told much earlier, and I'd no doubt that the junior's consultant might pick up on this and give his colleague a dressing-down. I recommended that he reconsider stopping the treatment now, in order to give this lady – who was still fully awake, alert and compos mentis – and her family a chance to adjust to the fact that they would be withdrawing the treatment and that she would die, allowing her more time with her family. And giving us a chance to support both her and them the following day.

'Right,' he said, clearly unimpressed, 'so you're not bothering to come today then?'

'It isn't a case of "not bothering",' I said, trying to keep my temper. I understand how difficult it is in an Acute Trust not to feel that everything needs a snap decision. The young doctor needed us to see this lady urgently, because to doctors on such wards everything is urgent. I didn't have the staff to send out and, besides, I didn't really see the need to rush things. I couldn't understand why treatment couldn't be prolonged for just a little longer while we did things properly.

The following day I discovered that the lady had died in the night. I learned that some of the treatment had been withdrawn as planned, but not all, and she'd died with some of the machines still running. I felt guilty, asking myself if I should've reprioritised, sending someone as a matter of urgency to assess the situation. But as it seemed so late in the day, treatment-wise, would it have made any difference? And would our team member have spent several hours there, trying to sort things out in rapid time, while another patient or patients missed out on visits that day? Who knows...

I didn't hear from the junior doctor that day, but I understood his stress. He should've put the referral in earlier but his priorities lay elsewhere and he'd simply forgotten. He was probably angry at himself and worried he'd get a rocket from the consultant, so he was trying to pass it down the line. Such is the life of a junior doctor in the NHS – not an easy one, by any means.

Chapter 10

A great deal of the work done in palliative care is taken up with family meetings. Such meetings are integral to our service because if palliative care is about anything, it's about establishing good relations with the family of a person at the end of their life so that crucial decisions can be made in good time and with the full knowledge and consent of everyone involved.

That, of course, is the theory. It's often said, right across departments in hospitals, that our lives as medical professionals would be much easier if we only had the patients to look after. But we don't, and increasingly we all recognise that families have an important role in the care of their loved ones, even if dealing with family members can, at times, be frustrating. To say the least.

As I mentioned in the last chapter, there is still a noticeably strong system of staff hierarchy in hospitals. However, in contrast to how things used to be, this pecking order is mostly ignored by the families of patients. Gone are the days when the word of medical staff was close to the word of God, to be obeyed without question. Now, families are much more vocal about the treatment their loved ones are getting, and they're not afraid to shout about it. Sometimes, quite literally.

All sorts of beliefs – cultural and religious, or those influenced by money, status, power or perceived knowledge – come through hospital doors with families on a daily basis. To be effective in dealing with such beliefs and expectations the nurse or doctor also needs to be a social worker/counsellor/diplomat. And, on occasions, police officer and nightclub bouncer, too. Some families will try to shout you down before you've even opened your mouth to speak. Others will throw themselves at your mercy in the hope you'll miraculously bring their dying relative back to life. There are the 'Googlers', too: the families who have spent hours on the internet, researching their loved one's condition and symptoms, and now know the best course of treatment and what the outcome ought to be. In the minds of such people, even as a professional your opinion is less important than the work they've put in at their computer, and it can be extremely difficult to persuade them otherwise.

What drives much or all of this is the fear and anxiety that families and patients have. People want their loved ones to get better, not die, and can act in irrational ways if they feel they're not getting the best treatment. In patients it can be fear of death itself, or that they haven't fully sorted out their affairs, which helps give them a sense of closure. If the hope of survival is fading, or gone, it can be extremely hard to redirect that hope, especially among cancer patients who've pinned everything on that last treatment working. Recently, the son of a patient I was assisting told me that: 'treatment is first, more treatment is second and palliative care is at the bottom.' I get that, but I was able to have a good conversation to help him understand that the palliative approach can work alongside treatment, because it is also about managing symptoms of the treatment itself.

Our job as a palliative team is to turn lost hope into something else: perhaps a return home for a while, or the opportunity to pass on some memories to loved ones. But all this takes time, and among family and patients there can be a great deal of anger to be released before acceptance takes place.

In a hospital like Northwick Park, where between patients and staff more than a hundred languages are spoken, you have to be incredibly careful that your own values and attitudes don't get in the way. For example, you might have an elderly Asian man with Parkinson's disease and pneumonia who keeps coming back and forth to hospital because his family will bring him if there's even the slightest chance of him getting better. The medical team treating him might think this is an utter waste of time, but we understand that for cultural or religious reasons, people believe that any moment spent alive is worth being alive for, even if others don't see it that way, including myself. So we have to say to the team, 'Allow him to be admitted and we will work towards getting the family to understand that there is dignity and respect in accepting that their loved one will die.' When the time comes that the team really can't do anything more for the patient, it's hoped we've laid enough groundwork that the family understands the reasons for this.

Yet, people will always surprise you. We get into the habit of assuming that because people are from a particular cultural or religious background it will be a difficult conversation, but that's not always true. And quite often, the most challenging times are when someone outlives their prognosis. That can be very distressing for patient and family, because people work towards a rough timeline, putting their affairs in order and saying final farewells – then they don't die when expected and the energy all that preparation took has to continue. Other difficulties occur when family members disagree about what is best for their dying relative, especially when the person dying has disagreements with family about his or her treatment. I've even known the dying person being made to feel guilty for expressing their wish to die without further medical intervention. There is this expectation that 'you can't give up' and the question, 'What will we do without you? Life will be hard for us.' Dying can be a complex business, with a lot of unexpected and unexplained emotions involved.

Some families get it straight away. 'My mother is ninety-five,' a son or daughter will say. 'She's had a great life, we know she's dying, and all we ask is that you make her as comfortable as possible.' Occasionally, we have families who will say, 'Can't you give him/her something that will get this over with now?' And they're serious, too. At the other end of the spectrum we have people who insist on continuing treatment, even if that is painful and the patient is in their eighties or nineties. Their parent might be lying unconscious and unable to eat, but they insist that a feeding tube goes in. It doesn't seem to matter that their mother or father is frail, has been deteriorating at home, is bedbound, has developed pressure sores, is not able to eat or drink, sleeps all day and has been admitted to hospital numerous times. That feeding tube must go in, regardless of the fact that all those symptoms, taken together, are sure signs someone is dying. If you try to explain the situation, even in the gentlest terms, you get a look on their faces that says, 'I'm just not going to accept anything that you offer me because I don't trust you.' Then the nurses are given a hard time, the doctors are given a hard time. Even the porters get a hard time. Such people are angry at the system and they take it out on everyone and anyone they can.

Naturally, this can be frustrating but 99 per cent of the time you keep those frustrations to yourself while trying to think of another way of saying the same thing. Only once have I lost my temper, which I felt terrible about, and which shocked my colleagues because they only ever see me composed – well, with patients and families at least. I was holding a family meeting with a brother and sister whose mother was dying. They were in their forties but they both still lived at home and both seemed to have lived a rather sheltered and mollycoddled life. Their mother, in her eighties, had been admitted to hospital with a severe stroke and wasn't expected to live long. As ever, my job was to work with the family to ensure that their mother's final days were as peaceful and comfortable as possible.

Right from the get-go, this obviously wasn't going to be the case. My colleagues, Kerry and Agnieszka, were present and I was trying to explain that it wasn't really appropriate to push a feeding tube down the throat of a frail and elderly lady who would not recover from her stroke. But every time I tried to explain the situation, my comments were thrown back in my face. 'Mummy wouldn't want that!' 'Mummy would want this!' 'You cannot do this to her!' 'You are making her die!' I tried all different approaches but seemed to fail every time. In the end, I lost it.

'This is ridiculous!' I said, my voice rising up a notch. 'You're not listening to a word I'm saying! We're trying our best to help but all you do is refuse to see how much your mum is suffering!'

The words were tumbling out of my mouth before I could even think and I could see Kerry and Agnieszka looking at me like I'd gone mad. Then the daughter jumped up and with a dramatic flourish, flounced out of the room. Then she lay on the floor of the corridor and had a full-on temper tantrum, just like a toddler might. Her brother followed her out, glowering at me in silence.

This is completely bizarre, I thought, realising that I hadn't added much to the situation by losing my shit, provoking some kind of child-like reaction in the daughter. Anyway, the result was that, despite all the best advice, the son and daughter ended up taking their mother home. This process took ages because they wanted everything in place, and did not want follow-up visits from us or anyone else. They seemed completely determined to do every single thing for their mother who, it appeared, had complete control over them, even in the state she was in.

We didn't hear any more until one afternoon several weeks later when the poor lady was admitted to hospital again, this time with a brain haemorrhage. Sadly, it led to her death – and not really the peaceful and comfortable one she might have wanted.

No one in the medical profession likes giving bad news. Who could possibly enjoy it? Often doctors get around it by saying things like, 'Your scan shows the cancer has become worse, but your bloods are better and you've got over the infection you had, so that's all good news.' Naturally, we want to put the best possible spin on a negative outcome, but in effect we're encouraging the patient to assume they're getting better. As palliative care nurses we have to unpick this situation slowly, taking the patient back a few steps to see what they understood about their condition before they came into hospital and how they view it now. You can talk about the good news element while steering the conversation gently round to the less welcome aspects of their illness. Some people might be ready to go there; others might need more encouragement and trust to get them to acknowledge the reality of their situation.

Occasionally, you'll meet someone whose no-nonsense approach to dying is as surprising as it is inspiring. I think of a patient called Phil, a guy from the north of England who was diagnosed with lung cancer. A tumour was pushing into his oesophagus, making it difficult for him to swallow. He and I spent a considerable amount of time talking about this, and the level of intervention he could tolerate. He knew he was going to die, and also knew that what was important to him was the quality of the time that remained. He wanted to be able to enjoy food but he couldn't swallow it down. He still felt hungry and was aiming to get home, so, after discussion, he agreed to us putting in a feeding tube (I know I've harped on about feeding tubes being used inappropriately, but if someone is not imminently dying and has a physical reason preventing them from eating, a feeding tube may be the right option). Phil was adamant he wanted to donate his body to medical science and I helped him to fill out the paperwork which would make this happen. He wanted to donate his corneas too, and I remember he and I having a three-way phone conversation with someone from the donor register team to sort this out. Phil told them quite clearly that he would be 'dead within weeks' and expressed no fear or sadness about that. He was a man with no family but a lot of friends and he was completely accepting of his situation. When he died less than two weeks later it was with no regrets, or remorse, or anger. He felt he'd lived a good life and was now ready to go.

Other people seem to accept the situation on the outside, but when you talk to them you notice a chink in their armour. I dealt with a lady in her eighties who'd been admitted with an abdominal pain that turned out to be terminal cancer. She lived at home with her husband and had been a real matriarch, still enjoying life to the full (including regular swimming) just a few weeks before she was diagnosed. She was taking a lot of painkillers but nonetheless seemed to accept her situation. I sat with her several times until, one afternoon, she just broke down and really cried. And then it all came spilling out – she wasn't worried about dying per se, but she wondered how her husband would manage, how he would feed himself, look after the house, keep the garden tidy, do the shopping. In short, all the things she'd done. She was trying her best to be stoic, but underneath that were a lot of worries that we could now help to alleviate during the time she had left.

The dynamics of families who, quite understandably, struggle with a terminal diagnosis is illustrated by the story of Ravi, a British man of Indian heritage in his fifties, with a wife, Sania, and two children aged fourteen and two. Ravi had been to his GP several times with changes in bowel habits, some bleeding and weight loss. Each time he'd been sent away with a 'nothing to worry about'. However, pressed by Sania, Ravi was eventually put on a two-week waiting list for a scan. When the results came back, he was diagnosed with colorectal cancer that had 'metastasised', or spread. It was incurable, and any treatment he would receive would be palliative only.

Had this been diagnosed in time, it's possible the cancer could've been treated successfully. That didn't happen, of course, but in any case, colorectal cancer can go undetected for a long time, during which time it spreads. When we met him, Ravi had been under an oncologist at a nearby cancer centre for about a year and was receiving palliative chemotherapy.

Ravi had been admitted to Northwick Park with severe abdominal swelling and pain. He was weak and fatigued but despite everything he'd still been trying to work remotely from home. When I first saw him he was lying on a bed in the hospital wearing a large jumper which, I later discovered, was disguising how malnourished he'd become. Cancer can really reduce the appetite, leading to rapid weight loss. Ravi was in a bad way but he, Sania and I managed to have a positive, helpful chat about how things were going, though it was clear there was a lot of anger and frustration at the fact he'd had a delayed diagnosis. He was now waiting for further results but in the meantime we agreed we'd try some different things to manage his pain. The scans made it clear that the pain was being caused by the cancer spreading through his bowel and abdomen. He had been started on a slow-release morphine tablet twice a day at home, with extra morphine as he needed. Ravi said the morphine helped his pain but he was worried about becoming constipated (a common side effect of opioids), so we added in a stronger laxative, which meant that he felt happier about asking for more morphine when he was in pain.

I saw him the following day. He was now in a hospital gown,

which made it clear how underweight he was. Sania had been trying to feed him as normal but he'd had no appetite. However, the sudden weight loss had led to criticism of Sania by Ravi's extended family for 'not feeding him properly'. This isn't an uncommon reaction – as I explained earlier, we all want people to eat when they're unwell because instinctively we feel it will make them better – but such blame can be hard for a partner already struggling with a terminal diagnosis.

After the three of us had spoken, Sania asked to talk to me in the corridor. She was an intelligent woman and she knew her husband was deteriorating quickly. Fear was written across her face.

'Kelly,' she said, 'things aren't good, are they?'

'Having seen him today, Sania, things really aren't good,' I replied. By this time we'd had the scan results. The disease had progressed significantly; his bloods were awful and he was going into liver failure.

'He isn't well enough for treatment, is he?'

I shook my head. She was brave enough to articulate this truth and seemed to accept the severity of the situation. Her main worry was how she would break the news to the rest of the family, including her two children. Instinctively she seemed to understand that Ravi's family would fight to keep him alive at all costs, and that this might not be the best course of action.

'I'll help you to talk to them,' I said, taking her by the arm. 'I know you've been let down in the past but this time you've got our full support.'

She told me she needed particular help telling her son. He knew his dad had cancer, but not that it was incurable. Ravi and the boy were close; he didn't want to upset him unnecessarily.

And the extended family considered that children shouldn't know about such difficulties. So there were a lot of pressures coming from different quarters to manage expectations and the flow of information. Not easy when in the midst of this, someone is dying.

Luckily, Sania had an ally in her sister, Sufia, who supported her and accepted what was happening. She was pivotal in helping to take the pressure off Sania at the various family meetings we had, during which we were bombarded with 'what if' questions about various treatments they'd heard about, special food they'd been told could reverse the cancer's spread, new antibiotics that were appearing on the market. In palliative care you often find yourself saying 'no' (in the nicest way possible) because while you understand a family's grief, you don't want to give them false hope.

The family, including parents in their eighties, were naturally desperate to find a cure. To which I'd say, 'Well, this is what we're hoping for as well, but actually at this moment this is how things are.' I couldn't sugar-coat this pill; instead, I had to unfold the bad news slowly, letting them talk to the consultants and gently leading them to the point where they could see for themselves just how bad things had become for Ravi.

Ravi's sister was particularly upset and angry. She sat upright, arms folded and found it hard to make eye contact. When I explained that her brother was very unlikely to get better she cut right across me.

'You cannot say that!' she said. 'You can't say that he's not going to get better!'

I stayed calm, not wanting to inflame the situation any further. She was devastated, and lashing out at anyone she might consider in some way responsible for this situation. I knew that at some point she would break – that her anger and resistance to the truth would fall away and that she would break down. Only after this would she be able to accept and come to terms with what was happening.

The family were adamant they didn't want me to talk to Ravi about the fact he was dying. I told them I wouldn't force any information on him but that I also knew Ravi was a smart guy who understood his illness.

'If Ravi asks me questions,' I said, 'I'll have to answer them honestly. I can't lie to him.'

His sister scowled at me. 'If you tell him he's not going to get better then he'll lose all hope. He'll just give up and die.'

'All we want to do is make what remains of his life as positive and comfortable as possible,' I said. 'And I need the help of everyone in this room to do that.'

The sister went quiet. 'Ravi needs to understand what's happening,' I added, 'because apart from anything else, he needs the opportunity to talk to his children.'

Sania nodded. 'I think you should talk to Ravi soon,' she said. Later that day, I went to visit him with Sania in tow.

I prompted him with some gentle questions about how he was feeling. He was still troubled by constant pain but was hoping that a procedure to drain the swelling in his stomach might help with that.

This gave me the opportunity to go in a little deeper. 'What we're worried about, Ravi, is that even when we drain the fluid away, it might make you feel a bit better but it's not going to change what's happening,' I said.

He nodded. 'Go on,' he said, 'tell me more.' Out of the

corner of my eye I could see Sania staring at me in expectation.

'We've got all the scans,' I said, 'and we can see from the way things are deteriorating that you're not getting better.'

Ravi was quiet for a moment. I didn't need to say anything else. Sania came to the other side of the bed and was tearful but really strong.

'You need to be able to say things that you want to say,' she said. 'None of us want this to happen. We're all hoping that things are going to change, but this is how things are.'

It was obvious the two of them needed to talk, so I left the room, taking 'the elephant' with me. Once that particular creature is gone, couples and families can talk more freely. After a while Sania came out. 'We need to get Sanjeev [their son] in to visit this afternoon. I need you to help me have *that* conversation.'

My stomach turned over. Such conversations are never easy, but when children are involved, well… let's just say that I skipped lunch that day as I psyched myself up to talk to this young boy about the illness affecting his dad. I talked to my colleagues who, as ever, gave me great advice and support. Then I went back up to the ward, where Sania, Sanjeev and Sufia were waiting.

For a twelve-year-old in a horrible situation, Sanjeev was calm. He was also well prepared, having written down various questions he wanted to ask me. He knew what his dad's cancer was and what treatments he'd had. He asked me whether there was any more chemotherapy available.

'The problem now,' I said, 'is that the disease has spread to the peritoneal cavity, which is like the balloon that surrounds everything that happens in your abdomen.'

'Can you remove the peritoneal cavity?' he asked. Clearly, he was an intelligent boy.

'I'm afraid not,' I said. 'It's not like the cancer is in the bowel and we can just take that out. It's now spread like a spider's web around everything.'

There was a pause. I could sense what was coming.

'Is he going to get better?'

I could feel a burning sensation creeping up my throat and pricking at my eyes. I struggled to keep my composure as Sanjeev fixed his gaze on me. I looked directly back at him.

'I'm sorry, Sanjeev,' I said, 'but I'm afraid he's not going to get better. I have to tell you that he's going to die.'

There was no other way. Sanjeev was a smart boy, and had I tried to couch it in any other terms he'd have known. But in that instant his world crumbled. He placed the sheet of paper containing his questions on his lap, his head slumped forward and his shoulders began to shake as he sobbed quietly.

By his side, Sania was crying too. She took his hand in hers and stroked it, telling her son that he still had time to be with his dad and that they had a lot of important things to talk about. I judged it was the right time to depart. Sufia also looked ready to leave.

'You both need time together now,' I said. 'We'll be right outside.'

I closed the door to the room and leaned against the wall. The overwhelming emotion I'd felt could be contained no longer. Sufia gave me a hug. She was crying too.

'My God, Kelly,' she said, 'I don't know how you do your job.'

'Sometimes it's just really hard,' I said. And it is, especially when it involves young people, and those who will grow up having lost an irreplaceable parent. You're aware that a slice of sunshine has been snatched from their lives, never to be returned.

It was decided that Sanjeev would stay over in hospital for the night so he, Mum and Dad could have plenty of time together. The following day we made contact with a hospice local to the family so that they could get as much support as they needed, now and in the future. A bed was available at the hospice, so I went to deliver the news to Ravi and his family, and immediately I entered the room I felt the atmosphere had changed considerably. I'd been seeing him for two weeks now and there'd always been anxiety and distress in the air. This had gone, to be replaced with a feeling of calm and peace. It was an amazing transformation. Ravi looked settled and more comfortable than I'd ever seen him. He'd had the opportunity to talk openly and honestly to his family, and he looked so much happier for it.

Four days later Ravi died, surrounded by his loved ones. It was almost as if he needed to have that deeply personal conversation with them all before he could finally let go.

Some months later, I met with Sania and Sufia. They'd asked to see me because they wanted help putting together a timeline of events so they could address some issues raised about Ravi's late diagnosis. They wanted to say thanks too: to all the palliative staff who'd helped them through those final few days. Sania smiled at me. She looked careworn and troubled, but events were very raw and recent.

'You're a wonderful family,' I said, 'so please take care of each other.'

She smiled again. 'I know,' she replied. 'We'll get there.'

Chapter 11

In the last chapter I mentioned how the proximity of young people to a situation where someone is terminally ill can be very distressing for everyone involved. Ravi's sister Sufia told me she didn't know how I could do my job, to which I replied that sometimes it was hard. In turn, I don't know how paediatric nurses do what they do, especially when they're looking after children with terminal illnesses. The fact that many of them are younger and don't yet have their own children may be a factor. In any case, it's a very tough but exceptionally rewarding job – just one I personally couldn't do.

Which brings me to India, the youngest person I've ever looked after at Northwick Park, and possibly one of the strongest and brightest. In this chapter I want to tell her story in full, a story that is full of bravery, positivity and determination. An insight into the reality of receiving a terminal diagnosis at a young age and how this affects the young person as well as those they love. And how the devoted love of a family, spouse and friends can profoundly influence the life of that young person when they are dying. Also, India's story demonstrates what some unlucky young people have to go through while those their own age are out having fun, studying, taking holidays, forming relationships and generally taking life for granted, just like India should've been doing, too.

When I first met India in the early days of January 2016 she had been through a huge amount of surgery for colorectal cancer. She was almost twenty-two, was a student in Norwich and had been married to Matt for just six months. She had also suffered from colitis for a number of years. India was very young to have a diagnosis of this type of cancer – it's not unknown, but it is very unusual. The major surgery was carried out with the intent to remove all of the cancer, which would later be followed up with chemotherapy and possibly more surgery to ensure all of the cancer had gone.

She knew that at that time she was too unwell for further major surgery or chemotherapy but was optimistic that she'd get stronger so she could go through these treatments at some stage. However, the surgeons treating her started to become concerned about India's worsening pain and poor recovery post-surgery and were sufficiently worried to call us in. Initially, this was for pain management. India was experiencing a lot of discomfort and was on a cocktail of drugs including morphine that made her drowsy but weren't doing much to alleviate her pain. So we were asked to get involved, which is normal when people with cancer are experiencing extreme discomfort. We would be reinforcing the idea that, at this stage, we were there to help with pain management because as far as India was concerned, this was still a journey full of hope. The very words 'palliative care' can have the effect of snuffing this out, and in someone so young that's the last thing you want to do.

Despite her weakness and frailty, India shone out like a beacon. She was a beautiful girl: friendly, open, relaxed in company and hopeful that her desperate situation would pass. She was a Christian, trusting that God would help her through these difficult times. At her bedside were her husband, Matt, and her mum, Melanie. Matt was Mr Sunshine – always smiling, happy and totally supportive of his young wife. He constantly asked us what he could do to help and he was a real ray of hope and optimism. Melanie was a kind, caring woman who shared a lot of her daughter's characteristics. The three of them had determination, optimism and a fighting spirit they hoped would carry them through to a brighter future. India's maiden name was Lockhart and she'd married a Lewis, so they quickly became 'Team Lockhart-Lewis'. I didn't see her dad Paul as much because he liked to come in when there were fewer people around so he could spend time with India on his own – just the two of them, dad and daughter savouring precious time together. I compared him in some ways to my own dad: quiet and happy to let the attention be on others, but always there if needed. He was a father in the unbearable position of seeing his little girl suffer. Samuel, her big brother, was calm and collected, there when she needed him most.

Each time I walked into India's room, I was greeted with big smiles, yet behind these there was worry. Real fear. You often see it in the eyes of even the toughest patients and families. As ever, the elephant had taken up residence in India's room, and although we were nowhere near ready for a conversation about it, its presence was apparent nonetheless. India's doctors were planning to go ahead with surgery on her bowel and were hoping that if she got through that, there would be further operations to make sure every scrap of cancer was cleared out of her.

At that time, India's situation was presented as serious but 'treatable'. 'Treatable' is an ambiguous word. It means that things can be done, but doesn't necessarily imply a cure. All it means is, 'There may be options of medications or interventions that MAY make a difference to the cancer'. At this stage, the implications of 'treatable' weren't being fully discussed with India and her family. She was still only twenty-one and hardly at the stage to be considering any alternatives to 'curable'.

Surgery took place towards the end of January. At first it seemed she was doing well but very quickly the surgeons established that the cancer had spread to her ovaries and the lining of her abdomen. This wasn't good news and very gently we discussed the possibilities for chemotherapy to tackle the spread while acknowledging that India was far from well enough to undergo such treatment yet. And she was still experiencing large amounts of pain, the control of which left her drowsy, and frustrated if she pressed her bell for more morphine and the nurses took their time arriving.

Most days India would keep cheerful. Small things, like managing to walk to the loo unaided and having a shower and her hair washed, made her smile. Yet there were other times when she became tearful. The wound from her surgery wasn't healing well and each day she was feeling weaker rather than stronger. She knew everyone was trying their best, but increasingly I could tell that she knew things were far from good, and that they might not get much better. I would chat to her while plaiting her hair, and she'd show me her wedding photos from just six months previously. It was hard to equate that happy, smiling young bride in those pictures with the poorly, frail girl who could barely sit up to have her hair done, but all the time we tried to keep everything light and bright.

Behind the scenes there were many intense conversations going on. The cancer had spread to many different places including the peritoneal cavity and, like Ravi from the previous chapter, the concern was that this was a spider's web impossible to remove. Further operations were futile; all that remained was the possibility of chemotherapy and even if she were strong enough, this would only be palliative, i.e. trying to buy her a bit more time. The palliative team had several conversations with India's surgeon, a lovely guy who completely understood and empathised with the difficulties we would have breaking such terrible news, especially to someone so young. We knew we had to tell them but, as ever, fear was present among all of us. We tried to anticipate how India and her family would react and how well they would deal with it. But while this to-ing and fro-ing was going on, we were all aware that we would have to tell them something, and soon.

One afternoon, at the beginning of February, I had a meeting with India, Melanie and Matt. Melanie started to ask a few questions about the healing process and it was clear India was becoming uncomfortable, so I suggested that she and I went outside for a chat.

Melanie and I went into a small meeting room which over the next few weeks would become a regular rendezvous point. We sat down, face to face. She looked at me for a moment, then said, 'I don't think India is well enough for chemo, is she?'

'No,' I replied, 'definitely not at the moment.'

'Look me in the eye, Kelly,' she said, 'and tell me she is going to get better.'

I knew where this was going and braced myself. I admitted that no, it was very unlikely she would get better. Again, Melanie paused before speaking.

'I need you to tell me everything, Kelly. I can't see she will ever be well enough for chemo, and I'm really worried that India will die without any of us knowing that she's dying. So I need you to be honest with me now.'

This was the moment – the one we palliative staff had all experienced many times in the past, and the one we still dreaded.

I told her everything. How she wouldn't be well enough for chemotherapy and that even if she were, it could only slow the progress of the disease. Melanie listened intently, then asked me about the prognosis. 'It's important for me to know this,' she said. 'We want to enjoy the time that's left with India.'

I replied that it was hard to know, given the rapid advance of the disease and the various complications. 'It could be months,' I said. 'Or it could be weeks…'

Melanie was sure that India wouldn't want to die in hospital and we talked a little about what would be needed to get her home or to a hospice. We discussed this, and agreed we'd have a talk with India when the time came.

'I've only got one more thing to ask, Kelly,' Melanie said, 'and that is that you're honest with me about everything from now on. India wants to take things one day at a time, and I respect that.'

'I have to admit that I'm worried about how much India understands about what is happening,' I said.

'She knows it isn't curable,' Melanie replied. 'All she wants is another couple of years to live, but even she knows that's unrealistic.'

It was almost too hard to concentrate, such was the atmosphere in the room. I was talking about the impending death of a twenty-one-year-old to her mother while just a few feet away, the poor girl and her lovely husband were trying to keep as positive as they could.

Melanie told me that India and Matt still had hope and were relying on their Christian faith to get them through. The congregation at the church they all attended were praying for India constantly. I said to Melanie that I should really talk to Matt and she agreed.

The following day I met Matt in the hospital cafeteria, as requested. I talked slowly and carefully, not wanting to burst his sunny bubble, while knowing that was exactly what I'd do.

'She's been through so much,' I said, 'and I know you're all hopeful and praying hard for her. But you know the scan results aren't good at all. When you look at her, what do you see?'

He paused for a moment. I could see he wanted to give me an upbeat reply totally within his nature. I also knew that he was an intelligent guy who was in touch with reality.

'When I look at her,' he replied slowly, 'I can just see the life draining out of her.'

I nodded. 'You're right, Matt. This is overwhelming for her, isn't it?'

Not once during this whole thing had I seen his smile fall away. Now I could see him struggling to process what had just been said.

'I hope you don't mind, Kelly,' he said, 'but I think I need to be on my own now.'

'Of course. But just one thing before I go. We need to think about how we talk to India about this. We'll support you all the way – you know that.'

In response, he nodded, his eyes full of tears. 'It's her birthday in a few days,' he said.

The following day Kerry and I went to see India and Melanie. As ever, we would be led by India, who by this time was aware that the atmosphere had changed from one of hope to one that seemed to involve a lot of tears and whispers in corridors. We arrived to find that the doctors had just left and had been talking about chemotherapy. India was tearful and confused, asking us to tell her exactly what was going on. I went through everything, eventually explaining that the aim of the chemotherapy was to slow down the cancer's growth.

India stopped me right in my tracks. 'So are you telling me that the cancer's terminal?' she said. 'Am I going to die, because if I am, I need to know. I need to know what's happening to me.'

I bit my lip, hoping she wouldn't see my own distress. Then I pulled my chair closer to the side of the bed.

'Why are you asking me that?' I said.

'Because things are getting worse, aren't they?' she said, tears falling down her hollow cheeks. 'I'm not getting better. I know it.'

'No, you're not getting better,' I said, 'and we're worried that your body won't ever be strong enough for the chemotherapy.'

There were no words. India was angry, distraught, scared, tearful. Who wouldn't be? Within the space of five minutes she went through a whole world of emotions that other people can take days or weeks to process. She had a whole life ahead that was now being snatched away. Melanie cried. Kerry cried. So did I. We talked for a long time about life and death, and what it all meant. There were more tears. Eventually India settled down and began to speak with reflection.

'I need to know everything that's going to happen to me from now on,' she declared. 'I'm not giving up. Matt and I have loads of plans. I'm going to keep fighting this. God will support me.' But she knew – and all of us in the room knew that she knew.

This was the moment to bring a positive note into the most awful discussion imaginable. India's birthday was only a few days away and Mel had already asked me about the possibility of getting her home for the day. 'How about we try to get you home for your birthday?' I said. 'We can arrange the transport and all the meds you need. You can spend the day with friends and family, away from these four walls. What do you think?'

For the first time in ages, India's face lit up into a smile.

'That would be fantastic,' she said.

We swung into action and by the end of the day had almost everything sorted for her visit home. That day, 9 February, I visited her before she was wheeled into a high dependency unit ambulance. She was thrilled to be making the journey home, even for the day, and was looking forward to her birthday celebrations. I'd got in contact with the Peace Hospice, which covered the area where India's parents lived, and they'd agreed to send out two Hospice At Home nurses who would visit to make sure everything was going well, and to give symptom management medications to India, if required.

India returned to hospital at 6pm on the day of her birthday.

I visited her the following day and she was very tearful. It was to be expected. She'd had an amazing day at home and hadn't wanted to return to hospital. She talked of going home permanently. I noticed that she appeared very pale and weak, and that her pain levels had increased. There was a possibility that she could be discharged home and into the care of the HAH, which would be ideal.

In the days that followed, India began to deteriorate rapidly. Her pain worsened and by now she was almost always distressed. She was frustrated that the pain relief being given to her never seemed effective enough and was anxious about the possibility of going home, wondering if it would work as well as she and her family thought. By now, it was recognised she was dying and time was against us. Again, the palliative team got to work, and on 17 February she was finally discharged from Northwick Park to her parents' home, and into the care of district nurses and the HAH team.

It was the last time I saw her. Ten days later, on Saturday, 27 February, India died surrounded by those she loved the most – Matt, Samuel, Mum and Dad: Team Lockhart-Lewis. In the job we do, we're more than used to receiving news that someone has died but this hit us particularly hard. I knew India had been well looked after at home but, even so, the fact that I'd got to know her and her family and that she was so young was personally devastating.

Because we're there at the end of someone's life we sometimes get invited to that person's funeral. Generally we don't go; for me, it feels like crossing the line from professional to personal and maybe it's part of my protective barrier. But with India, I didn't think twice. Kerry and I went along to St Andrew's

Church in Chorleywood – where India had been married the previous summer – and it was an amazing celebration of her life, full of young people singing, clapping and giving personal tributes to beautiful, brave India – already deeply missed and obviously dearly loved by everyone.

Chapter 12

If you've stayed with me so far, you'll know by now that looking after sick and dying people as part of a palliative care or hospice team can be pretty harrowing. As a palliative or hospice nurse you need excellent listening skills and empathy in spades. You need to deal with people's grief – patients and families – while keeping your own emotions in check as far as possible. Last, and definitely not least, you need a good sense of humour. Surprising, right? Not at all. If you don't enjoy a laugh this job is definitely not for you. We need humour to keep us balanced and sane, and at Northwick Park the palliative team office is definitely the loudest in the entire place.

We laugh and joke about the stuff everyone in workplaces across the country jokes about. Nothing unusual about that. But, as I've said, our humour is also tinged with the darkness we deal with on a daily basis. And quite often we're the butt of our own banter. For example, I dealt with a lady in her late eighties whose chronic obstructive pulmonary disease (COPD) had suddenly become worse. She went into respiratory arrest and was snatched from the jaws of death by a lot of oxygen and steroid boosts. So she stayed alive but was seriously unwell and by the time I saw her she was on a BiPAP machine, which pushes air in and out of the lungs to help with the exchange of oxygen when the lungs are in a bad way.

Really, though, she was dying and the BiPAP machine was pretty much all that was keeping her going. She'd been conscious the previous day but her son and daughter, who were now gathered at her bedside, told me she'd been asking for her husband, who had died thirty years previously. So it seemed she was slipping away and had entered the stage at which people start to 'see' or remember people and events from the past.

Her children told me that she would not want to live like this, fighting for breath and suffering. We talked about removing the BiPAP mask and allowing nature to take its course, but the siblings were worried that the other patients in the bay would hear what was going on and become distressed. Even with their mother so poorly, and with difficult decisions to make, the son and daughter's concern for others demonstrated just what lovely people they were. Which made what happened next so embarrassing…

I checked to see if there was a side room we could take the old lady to, where we could remove the mask and allow her children to say their goodbyes without all and sundry listening in. Unfortunately, there were no spaces available and whatever happened next would need to take place in the bay.

I relayed this to the brother and sister. 'Well, that's fine,' the brother said, 'and we've both agreed that the mask should come off so Mum can be free from her suffering. So we're happy to do this here.'

The three of us sat down and discussed what would happen next. I told them that we'd give their mum some medication first, just to settle her and make her peaceful. Then the machine would go off, followed by the removal of the mask and she would be allowed to die peacefully in the presence of her family. I explained this gently to the couple, who listened to every word and nodded in agreement with the procedures I was outlining. So far, so good.

After the sedative had been administered the brother and sister said their goodbyes. 'Are you ready for me to turn the machine off now?' I whispered. Yes, they were ready. I clicked the switch to the 'off' position and instead of the light disappearing, the whole machine started bleeping loudly. I tried again – same result. The siblings were looking at me expectantly as I could feel myself going redder and redder. I tried again and again, until I realised that I'd only flicked the standby button, not the main switch, hence the bleeping to warn me that something was wrong. Finally the machine went off, but as I turned round to tell the couple that it was done, I caught my elbow on a full jug of water on the bedside table and sent it flying – all over the table, the floor and into the next bay.

'Oh good grief, I'm so sorry!' I said. The couple looked at me sympathetically.

'Don't worry, dear,' said the woman, 'it's fine. We understand that this isn't easy.'

'No, it isn't,' I said, 'but I can assure you I'm never so clumsy. I don't know what's got into me today.'

There was one more machine to switch off – the one which monitored her blood pressure and heart rate. I went to move it so I could gain access to the back of it, but somehow I managed to get it stuck fast under the bottom of the bedside table. Again, I could feel the heat of shame burning across my face. I pulled and pulled, but it was stuck firm.

'Would you like me to help you?' the son asked kindly, noticing my plight.

'No, I'm fine,' I replied, through gritted teeth. 'I'll just give it one more try…'

And with that, I gave it such a tug that it suddenly broke free, toppling over and taking me with it. The poor son rushed round to the other side of the bed, dragged the machine off me and offered his hand to pull me up. By this time, despite the fact their mother was now in her last moments, they were both laughing heartily.

'It just isn't your day today, is it?' smiled the daughter.

'I am so, so, sorry,' I said. 'I can't believe all this is happening while… you know…'

'Don't worry,' said the son. 'It was a bit of a tense moment but this has helped to cheer us up no end.'

Needless to say, I was the object of ridicule in the office for days afterwards.

Then there was an elderly Indian lady who was dying on the hospital's Jenner ward. All the conversations with the family had been had and we dropped in every day just to check on her and manage her symptoms. She had a big family who were there most days and, as usual, we would assist by answering questions and keeping them up to date with developments.

The family made the atmosphere around the bedside light

and comfortable. They sang, chanted and said prayers for their relative and generally made this difficult process so much easier. One afternoon I went in as usual and, after chatting with various members of the family, leaned over the bed to do a few checks.

'Hello, Mrs Desai, how are you today?' I said. 'I've just come to do my daily checks as usual. Nothing to worry about.' We always talk to every patient we deal with, irrespective of whether they're conscious or not. We even do it after they've died, telling them that we're about to wash and change them, and just get them ready for the next stage of their journey. It sounds silly, I suppose, but it's actually very respectful. They may be dead, but they're still a person, still someone's loved one. You can't ignore that fact and we're always careful to keep up standards in this respect.

I took Mrs Desai's hand in mine, to check the strength of her pulse. The hand was cold. There was no pulse. I looked at her face. There were no signs of any breathing and her lips were beginning to take on a bluish tinge. *Oh no*, I thought. *She's already gone, but the family don't know it.*

One of the lady's sons smiled at me. 'Is she comfortable, do you think? Does she look OK?'

She's very comfortable, I thought, *but rather beyond OK.*

'Excuse me a moment,' I replied. 'I just need to pop out for a second…'

In the corridor I saw the nurse who'd been attending Mrs Desai. 'Do you know she's died?' I said.

'Oh God,' replied the nurse. 'Give me a sec, I'll just take a quick look.'

The nurse slipped into the room and was out within seconds.

'You're right,' she said. 'Shit! What do we do now? What do we say to them?'

'Don't worry,' I said, 'I'll deal with it.' And with that I went back into the room as calmly as possible and once again took hold of Mrs Desai's hand.

'I think you should all come around the bed now,' I said softly. 'I think Mum is taking her last breaths.'

The gathered relatives started to cry and pray, placing their hands on the old lady. I stood back and watched, wondering if they'd spotted anything wrong.

'Do you think she's gone now?' asked the son. 'Has she died?'

'Yes,' I said, nodding. 'I'm sure she's died…'

Another story to take back to the office – it's these moments of humour that keep us going, I think – it's not like we're mocking anyone, in fact we only ever mock each other, but we need laughter to get us through. Sometimes it's the most stressful situations that we can look back on and appreciate the funny side of. We had been caring for a patient in Central Middlesex Hospital (CMH) – one of the hospitals in the Trust. We are not based there so have less involvement with aspects including discharge planning. The patient had been referred to St Luke's hospice for end-of-life care and when a bed became available, we called the ward to let them know and ensure they booked transport. Hospices like patients to arrive early on in the day to give them plenty of time to properly assess and plan the care while the doctors are around. At about 2pm we received a call from St Luke's to say that the patient hadn't arrived yet. Usually CMH were very on the ball with booking transport, so we called them to find out what the delay was.

'He left at about 10am,' we were told by the nurse in charge. Strange.

While we were all scratching our heads, we received another call – this time from St Luke's hospice in Basingstoke. The patient had arrived at their doors at about midday – they certainly weren't expecting an admission from London. So the ambulance crew turned around and made their way back to the correct St Luke's. Clearly this was all very distressing for the patient who went on to develop breathing difficulties and ended up in Basingstoke A&E. Eventually, he made it to the correct St Luke's at about 6pm, and they kindly agreed to admit him late rather than insisting he went back to CMH, which they could have done. It turns out that the discharge coordinator had clicked on the wrong 'St Luke's' from the drop-down menu and when the transport team arrived, they had challenged this.

'Are you sure it's St Luke's in Basingstoke?' they had rightly questioned the discharge destination.

Only to be reassured by the nurse sitting at the front desk: 'Yes, if that's what has been booked, it must be right.'

What a day!

Having said that, it's not unusual for us to be involved in planning a non-local discharge. In the team, Kerry and I have a reputation for managing to get people to their preferred place, even when this is in a different country. So far, we have organised transfers to Wales, Ireland, Kent, Romania and even Nigeria. So much planning goes into these transfers. We have to liaise with the airline, transport teams and ensure the hospital/hospice or home at the discharge destination has all of the correct information to care for that person when they arrive.

All medications for the journey must be arranged and oxygen, if needed. If the patient is bedbound and needing a stretcher, the family have to pay for a whole row of unused seats as the seats will be removed to allow space for the stretcher. We have to complete paperwork with the patient, stating that they are taking the risk of dying during a flight and if they do die, the plane will not be diverted. Very blunt and honest conversations must take place in advance. It is so nerve-wracking waiting to find out if the patient made it to their destination – finding out whether all the planning paid off – but so far everyone has made it and the families are so very grateful for us going that extra mile – literally.

Sometimes it's the patients who go out of their way to make us laugh and it's incredible how some people just seem to keep up a level of humour and fun, even in the direst of circumstances. My thoughts go immediately to Peter, a guy diagnosed with oesophageal cancer, with the most incredible will to live I've ever experienced.

When I met him, Peter was in his sixties and had come to Britain as a young man. He was a larger-than-life character and whenever I met up with him his first words were always, 'Hey, baby!' Things weren't looking great for him, health-wise; cancer of the oesophagus is notoriously difficult to operate on because of its location and often the way it presents means that only palliative treatment is possible.

Peter was in this position, but he had a will to live that I've never seen in anyone else in all the years I've been nursing. This was largely down to his personality, which simply refused to submit to cancer's demands. Also, soon after he'd been diagnosed his daughter had become pregnant. This would be his first grandchild and Peter was determined he would live to see them born.

He was already very unwell when he heard the news about his daughter. His cancer was advanced, and he'd undergone palliative chemotherapy and radiotherapy. He was regularly admitted with problems swallowing, caused by the tumour pressing into his oesophagus. He underwent numerous procedures to resolve the blockage, which involved pushing a camera down his throat into his oesophagus to identify where the blockage was and inserting a stent, which pushed the tumour aside and allowed food to be passed down into the stomach. By the time I met him he'd had three separate sessions of this treatment and had lost a lot of weight. Eventually he had a peg inserted – a feeding tube that went directly into his stomach and took away the pressure of needing to eat and drink enough to maintain his weight. It isn't a particularly comfortable way to live but Peter was determined to keep going until his grandchild was born.

Whenever he arrived at Northwick Park we'd invariably get a call from downstairs in A&E to say, 'You need to come down and see this man. We think he's dying and he's known to your team.' When they said who it was I'd reply, 'Are you sure he's dying? He actually looks like that most of the time.' And he did. He was incredibly skinny, and I used to wonder how his stick-thin legs could possibly support the rest of his body. He was usually brought in because he'd been unwell for a few days at home but had battled on until his wife could no longer manage and called an ambulance.

So multiple times we'd go down to A&E and say, 'Yep, that's Peter.' He was often quite sleepy by the time he'd been brought in but I'd give him a little shake, he'd look up, smile, and say, 'Hey, baby!' before nodding off again. Whenever he said that, I knew that he was going to be OK.

One afternoon I was called to the ward to see him because the nursing staff were considering sending him home but weren't sure if he was well enough. He'd been in bed for a few days and seemingly hadn't been able to get up. When he saw me he cracked a broad smile and went into the whole 'Hey, baby' routine.

'Come on, Peter,' I said. 'Let's see if we can get you up.'

He was nothing less than skeletal by this stage, but the man had a will of iron and, inch by inch, he hauled himself out of bed. Using a walking frame, he made his way out of the bay and towards the loo. The occupational therapist and the nurse looking after him nearly fell over because they considered he was at death's door. Yet here he was, making his way virtually unaided to the bathroom.

He was discharged soon after, but was back about three months later. I could hardly believe he was still alive, but he was still cracking jokes and brandishing his phone, which contained photos and videos of him holding his newly born grandchild. He battled on for about five months afterwards and it wasn't easy to know when he'd reached the point where he was actually dying, having teetered on the edge for so long. His deterioration was slow and although he was terribly malnourished, somehow he managed reasonably well. His wife was amazing, supporting him through this entire time, and looking slightly more rundown each time we met. People like Peter never do this well without someone strong by their side – the role of the carer should never be underestimated.

There came a point, though, when events took a turn for the worse. He was admitted to hospital and as he was being wheeled up to the ward his wife whispered, 'Kelly, I think this will be the last time.' He was still smiling and saying, 'Hey, baby', but he was confused and having minor hallucinations. As for the weight – well, he absolutely couldn't have lost any more than he already had. He wanted to be home and his wife wanted it, too, but she was realistic about the fact he'd be hard to look after in his final days. We arranged for him to go into the hospice, expecting him to die very soon, but in typical Peter fashion he hung on for another three weeks.

He was a lovely guy, and incredibly stubborn. Many of the people we see who outlive their prognosis seem to have that strong-minded streak. Peter wanted to live long enough to see his first grandchild, but I suspect he'd always had a determined nature. He looked death in the face and stared it down, time and again. I've had conversations with relatives about a loved one and when I've asked them what they were like when they were well, the reply is that they were 'a stubborn old bugger'. Invariably, these are the people, like Peter, who simply refuse to fade away quietly.

Then in some people, the fight to survive comes from another place altogether. Rosa was from a large London-Italian family and, while she was pregnant with her second child, was diagnosed with colorectal cancer. This was obviously devastating news. After many discussions with multiple oncologists, surgeons and specialist nurses, the plan was set. Rosa would go through with the pregnancy, having a Caesarean section to reduce potential complications, and have all the oncology treatment afterwards, to include surgery and chemotherapy.

Almost as soon as the baby was born, treatment commenced. It was always a risk to go through with the pregnancy as any delay means the cancer can grow and spread. But this is what Rosa and her husband had decided. They'd waited a long time to conceive and wanted their older child to have a brother or sister.

Despite positive signs early on, Rosa started to deteriorate about a year after treatment had started. Scans revealed what they were all dreading – the cancer had spread and she now had widespread disease through her colon and her abdomen. Rosa and her family had picked up on some discussions between the doctors and oncology nurses and felt that more could have been done to treat her cancer. They were getting conflicting information about whether the correct treatment regime had been followed and whether the surgery was aggressive enough.

When I met her, the baby born by C-section was about two and Rosa also had an eight-year-old. By this stage, she and her family were looking into all possible avenues for treatments that might buy her more precious time. Needless to say, we were dealing with a woman who was very, very angry indeed. Her family trusted absolutely no one and as well as being angry she was also terrified, both at the prospect of what would happen to her as well as the thought of leaving her children without a mother. The only mitigating factor was that she had an incredibly supportive and loving family who, despite their own anger, were prepared to sit down with me and other members of the palliative care team to discuss the options in a constructive way.

Gradually and carefully we gained her trust. One of the consultants on our team, Gilli Erez, put in a lot of work on this front because Rosa and her family needed to have absolute faith that she was being well looked after. Rosa was desperate to get that little bit better so she could have further treatment and we were always careful never to shatter that hope.

When I went to see her one cold winter's afternoon she looked awful, and was agitated and restless. Her legs were swollen and she couldn't get comfortable. At that point I actually thought she might be dying. Before she began to deteriorate she'd been on a new drug that, for a short while at least, had kept her cancer under control, stopping it from getting worse. Rosa's family were desperate to get her back on this medication, but she had to be stronger in order to be able to take it.

I was concerned about her that day and asked her brother to come in. I told him what I thought and he agreed this looked serious and asked their parents to come to the hospital. They were absolutely crushed by the news, but they also knew their daughter was strong and determined. And at the back of my mind, something about Rosa's appearance nagged at me and I wondered whether she really was dying or whether there was something else going on.

'I'm worried she might be dying,' I told her brother, 'but I'm not sure whether the morphine is making her more poorly than she should be. Perhaps we could reduce the dose and see what happens.' The morphine had been started because Rosa had a blockage in her bowel caused by the tumour. It had been really effective at managing her pain. Rosa had not eaten solid food for a few days to rest her bowel as sometimes the obstruction can resolve spontaneously, which it thankfully did. As the obstruction resolved, the pain improved, but I hadn't then thought to reduce the morphine dose.

We halved the morphine that was in her pump and the next day I came to see her, anxious as ever about what had happened since the day before. I was delighted to see that she was much brighter. Rosa was awake, much more comfortable and less restless and it felt as if we had a little bit of a breather again. Far from losing trust in me, the family were delighted that I'd misread the signs of dying. For them, the fact she'd rallied meant she'd discovered the strength she needed to make something of a recovery. They were realistic enough to know that there was no cure for Rosa; they (and she) just hoped for as much time as possible, and as a team we shared that hope.

We'd already started the talk about the hospice because the family desperately did not want her to die in hospital, for obvious reasons, or to be there any longer than was absolutely necessary. At the beginning of the week, she appeared brighter, with the result that her oncologist agreed she could start chemotherapy again. It was just a tablet form of chemotherapy but still, a treatment that offered the hope they were hanging on to. We knew she would be more comfortable at the hospice and we hoped she would allow her children to visit. Up to this point she hadn't wanted them to visit her in hospital – such places just had too many bad associations for her.

Yet, day by day, I noticed she was becoming more withdrawn. Her usual chattiness had gone, replaced by a lack of engagement with us and her family. People actively dying tend to sleep more but Rosa was very much awake during this period. It's hard to know exactly how much she knew, and although she was still determined to go on, her demeanour seemed to suggest that the inevitable wasn't far away.

The nurses on the ward were struggling with this, and with

the fact that her children weren't by her side. But not everyone wants this. It can be incredibly distressing, especially for those people who desperately want to get better in order that they can spend more time with their children. Rosa just wanted to walk out of that hospital as a person completely free of cancer. The fact that she couldn't led her to make decisions about who could and could not visit that some staff didn't quite understand, and we worked with some of the nurses to help them see that it's a very individual choice.

On the day of transfer I went down to see her to make sure everything was ready to go, knowing it would be a complex operation. Unfortunately, she'd really deteriorated overnight and this time, it was clear she was dying. We needed to get her to the hospice without delay – the last thing anyone wanted was for her to die in hospital. It would've been the final blow to this kind, generous and hopeful family.

Again, I spoke to her brother. We had the 'dying conversation' once more, but this time I didn't have to explain: he could see it for himself. He was a real bear of a man, about 6ft 4in, strongly built with a big beard, but when he hugged me I could feel the weight of his pain and devastation, knowing that his beloved sister would soon die and the battle would be over. The family were gathered that day and after I'd told them what I thought, I left them to their grief. They were a close family who, even after their trust in the NHS had totally collapsed, had allowed me into their lives, but now I felt they needed to be alone to share their feelings.

Rosa left the ward later that afternoon and as she was wheeled to the ambulance even the staff were crying. They would miss Rosa and her family and all the charisma and soul they brought to the ward. She died in the hospice the following day with her family by her bedside.

Her family are still seeking redress for what happened (or didn't happen) during her cancer treatment, but being the good people they are, they showed their gratitude to the nursing staff who looked after Rosa during her final weeks by coming on to the ward to give them their personal thanks. For me, it was an honour to be associated with them and to have the opportunity to gain their trust.

Chapter 13

At Northwick Park Hospital the palliative care team rolled into the new decade with the usual daily highs and lows that accompany the work we do in a busy, demanding and often complex environment. When I say 'usual', I contradict myself: there are very few average days within our team because each day brings new and varied challenges.

In early February 2020 we seem to be short-staffed – the usual collection of winter coughs and colds, plus people taking mood-boosting short breaks to Spain or the Canary Islands. When staff levels are low, pressure is brought to bear on the more experienced people in our team because we are automatically allocated the more complex cases. On this particular day I arrived at work at 8am as usual and spent a couple of hours catching up with the previous day's work before printing out my list of patients to see, throwing back a strong coffee and heading out to the wards.

Walking towards my first port of call, I took a two-minute detour to a small kiosk located just off one of the main corridors. The kiosk provides numerous services: dry cleaning, phone repairs, multiple phone accessories and best of all, an opportunity to have a deep and meaningful chat about everything and nothing with its operator, Dilip. Dilip has worked at Northwick Park for nearly fifteen years, spending most of his day there in the kiosk, watching the fascinating scenes of the hospital go by. A complex family history has made him a thoughtful yet deep person and just a few minutes with Dilip allows me a short escape from the pressures of work, setting me up for the rest of my day. He doesn't mind that I have a moan about the state of the world, the way it is being ruined by fake and shallow people, the lack of kindness, and the frustrations caused by people being in jobs they can't or won't do properly!

After we chatted, I continued my walk towards my first patient. I scanned my list quickly just before I entered the ward. Now I was pleased Dilip and I had had that uplifting little conversation because this was going to be a very tough start to the morning. Jane was in her early sixties and suffering from pancreatic cancer. The notes said that she was neutropenic, i.e. that she basically had no immune system, making her highly vulnerable to infections, which could kill her. She was also in bowel obstruction, and discovering this, my heart sank.

There is no easy way of describing the effects of bowel obstruction, no terms in which they can be politely skirted around. So let me put it as plainly as possible: when someone is in bowel obstruction they are suffering from a blockage in the bowel that stops ingested food and drink from making its way through the digestive system and causes pain and persistent vomiting. This blockage eventually becomes so bad that the faeces, which cannot escape in the usual way, arrives in the stomach and is vomited out of the mouth. This starts as a liquid before quickly turning into solid matter. You can give the patient anti-sickness injections but these rarely do much good because the act of vomiting is a mechanical one.

In short, it is horrendous, both for the person in bowel obstruction and the nursing staff dealing with it. Nurses are used to cleaning people up and generally have cast-iron stomachs. But even the words 'bowel obstruction' can cause the toughest and most experienced nurses to blanch and wish they were somewhere else at that moment.

One way of treating the condition is to insert a tube into the stomach, releasing liquid and helping to get rid of gases that have built up. Again, it's horrific to be on the receiving end of this treatment, and this was the scene which greeted me as I entered the ward.

Jane's daughter was visiting that morning. She was in her mid-twenties and evidently finding the situation extremely hard to cope with. The smell that comes from the intubation procedure is noxious and embarrassing, and I could tell straight away that the young woman was really struggling to contain her emotions. I tried to reassure her, telling her that her mum would feel better after the procedure to insert the tube was finished.

'But what about the cancer?' she said. 'That's going nowhere, is it?'

'I'm afraid not,' I said. I couldn't reply otherwise. Pancreatic cancer is extremely aggressive and one of the problems is that it is often late in revealing itself, making it almost too late to treat.

Even if it's treatable by way of removing the pancreas, it can leave the patient with serious long-term ill health. Pancreatic cancer causes all sorts of side effects, including bowel obstruction and obstructive jaundice, where the bile duct becomes blocked and the patient turns a nasty shade of yellow, as well as experiencing nausea, vomiting and loss of appetite. Progression of the disease is often rapid. Given all of the above, this is often a blessing in disguise.

I spent about thirty minutes talking to Jane's daughter about her hopes for her mum's future versus the reality of the situation.

Next on the list was a woman in her fifties with cancer that had spread across her body, including her brain. She'd had a terrible night's sleep and was restless, agitated and tearful. I was able to bring her better news, in that a local hospice was able to offer her a bed subject to a care plan, which we (the patient, her family and nursing staff) now needed to implement. The idea of a place in a hospice being 'good news' might seem bizarre to many but believe me, for this woman and her family, who had suffered terribly, it was a relief to finally hear something positive.

After this I went straight into a meeting with the family of Edna, a ninety-one-year-old who had both cancer that had metastasised and again, bowel obstruction. The old lady had been a twin, and in the meeting was completely open and honest about feeling ready to join her brother who had died some years previously. She was adamant that she didn't want any resuscitation, should it come to that, or anything else that would prolong her life.

'I'm not very keen on suffering,' she said, looking me directly in the eye, 'and I don't want to be a burden to my children.'

Cue protests from Edna's children telling her that she had never been a burden, and never would be. She raised her hand to silence them.

'Now I don't want to hear any more of that,' she announced. 'I've had a very good life and you all need to get on with yours. And that's final.' Following that, we were able to work on a clear plan for Edna's end-of-life care. As I walked away, she gave me a big smile and a thumbs-up.

After lunch I went along to Fielding ward to see Fred, a man in his seventies diagnosed with malignant melanoma. He'd been admitted two days previously with pustules all over his body and appeared to be deteriorating significantly. He was agitated, and not only because his body was giving up on him. Fred was desperate to go home because he wanted to see his beloved dog for the last time.

'Is there any chance I can just go home to see Bella?' he asked me with tears in his eyes. 'I know what's happening to me, and I'll feel so much better if we can be together.'

My heart went out to him. It was a simple last request, but one fraught with complications. We would have to arrange transport immediately, along with all the machines and medications that needed to accompany him. Then we'd have to make sure the district nurse team could go in at a moment's notice if he needed medications to manage his symptoms. In other words, it would be a complex task. Nonetheless, in a situation like this we will try to move heaven and earth to make something happen, so I went to the nurse in charge of the ward to discuss the situation.

She agreed to do anything she could to help this happen and started on the task of booking transport and sorting the district nursing referral while I continued conversations with Fred and his daughter about the practicalities of this complex discharge home. I hadn't long left the ward when I got a call from the ward sister, who told me that Fred had suddenly started to deteriorate. She thought he might be dying.

'I'd love to get him home,' she said, 'but I think he's too unwell to move. I'm not sure he'd actually make it home. What do you think?' I took one look at him.

'I agree,' I said. 'He's just too unwell.' My brain was buzzing – there had to be something we could do… 'So what do you think about bringing the dog to him, here on the ward?'

I knew it would be a tough call. Our team tries its best to fulfil patients' requests, especially when they're dying, but we're up against other forces in the hospital who, for generally good reasons, can't help us. They will try, but rules are rules and that's understandable. It's much easier to accede to such requests in the hospice environment. When I worked at The Peace in Watford we had dogs, cats, rabbits and caged birds in to visit. I even remember someone bringing a horse into the garden so its owner could say goodbye. So it can be done, but it's not always practical in a hospital setting where there are many other things going on.

The nurse in charge bit her lip. 'Oh, Kelly, I'm not sure about a dog coming in,' she said. 'Personally, I don't have a problem with it, but there's been an outbreak of diarrhoea on the ward and you'd really have to speak to Infection Control first. Sorry, Kelly, you know how it is.'

I do know how it is. If there is infection on a ward hospitals must take every measure to stop it spreading and, entirely predictably and necessarily, that was what the staff member from Infection Control said to me when I went to request permission.

'I'm really sorry, Kelly. There's no way we can have a dog on the ward while this is going on. It's not fair on the other patients. It would be irresponsible.'

'Is there any way around it?' I said hopefully.

'The only way is to find a day room on the ward. If you can do that, the patient can be wheeled in there and the dog can come up to see him. Afterwards we'll have the room deep-cleaned. That's the only option if you can get it sorted.'

I didn't hesitate. I went back down to the ward and requested a day room from the nurse in charge. There was one free – amazing! By this time Fred's daughter had arrived so I quickly explained the situation to her.

'But how are we going to get Bella in?' she asked. 'Mum's at home but she can't drive. There might not be time for me to go home and pick her and Bella up.'

We both looked at Fred. There was no doubt he had a very, very short amount of time left. Hours, if he was lucky.

'Let's ring a taxi,' I said.

I went downstairs to our team's office and did just that. The taxi firm understood the urgency and promised to dispatch someone straight away. Then I caught up on a couple of bits of admin before heading back up to the ward where Fred was, so that we could transfer him to the day room to await the arrival of Bella.

When I arrived I could see Fred's daughter sitting by the bed, holding her dad's hand. As she turned to me, tears were streaming down her face.

'He's gone,' she said. 'It's over.'

She kissed his hand, now cold. I leaned over and took his wrist gently between my fingers. No pulse.

'I'm so sorry,' I said. 'We did try. I'm so sorry that we didn't get Bella here in time.'

I knew that Fred's wife would be here with Bella soon.

'Maybe we should let her see him for the last time anyway?' Fred's daughter said.

I looked around. There weren't many patients in the bay. If I asked those who were there nicely, and if we pulled the curtains around Fred's bed, and if we made it a very quick in-and-out visit, perhaps it would be all right. Quickly I went around the other patients, asking if they were fine with dogs. I'm not sure I phrased it in so much as a question than a statement (reducing the risk of someone saying no) and I'm not sure they all understood me. After all, this was a care of the elderly ward, and usually many of the patients have some element of cognitive impairment. But in the absence of a refusal, we got everything ready. Five minutes later I was called to the front entrance – a taxi driver was just unloading an old lady and a dog from his car. Could I come to meet them?

Bella was a beautiful golden retriever who drew admiring, if surprised, glances from staff, visitors and patients as she trotted along the corridor to the lift. Fred's wife, Dorothy, looked exasperated, having been waiting at home that morning for her dying husband to arrive before being rushed into a taxi with their dog to come and say their goodbyes. Dorothy asked me straight away how Fred was and I told her. Shortly she would be seeing him for herself and it was best to let her know now. Shaken by the news, she continued walking with me down the corridor, being pulled along by Bella. I knew I was breaking Infection Control's rules but once on the ward we took Bella straight to Fred's bedside.

It was incredible to witness what happened next. Straight away, the dog picked up on the fact that something wasn't right. She put her paws on the bed and looked at Fred quizzically before gently licking his face. She sniffed the air around the rest of his body before lying under the bed, her whole body pressed to the floor. She understood, all right. Poor Fred hadn't had the chance to say goodbye to his beloved Bella, but she'd certainly said her farewells to him.

I was pleased that we'd had the dog in, but also despondent that it didn't happen in time. While it couldn't be helped, you never like to feel you've failed someone. I left the ward feeling a bit low, trying to reflect on what a crazy morning it had been. And then I went to see Edward…

Like Peter in the last chapter, some patients somehow have the ability to transform your difficult day into a good one. Edward was one of these. Ninety years old, with advanced prostate cancer and in considerable pain, he was nonetheless smiling and full of life when I went to visit him later that afternoon. His bed was damp, the result of having spilled cornflakes and milk down himself earlier on in the day, so I decided to give him a nice wash.

I chatted to him as I lay the bed down flat. 'Nothing to worry about,' I said, 'I'm just going to put the back of the bed down.'

'I'm not afraid,' he replied in a deep tone, and with that he placed his hands in the prayer position, as though he'd already gone to meet his Maker. I had to laugh, especially after the day I'd had.

'If my time is now, then take me Oh Lord,' he said, 'for I am ready!'

He kept up a string of jokes and comic asides as I dried him and got ready to change the sheets. When he saw the new bed linen, he smiled.

'Aha! Is that my shroud? It looks very clean and white. Do pop me in now, then place me carefully into my coffin!'

I laughed again.

'I'm only half joking,' he said. 'I think I've put off this dying business for as long as possible, but when the moment comes I'll be ready.'

I walked away smiling. Despite his pain, Edward was good for the soul and in a job like this, we all need a bit of sunshine now and again. Before I left for the day I related the dog story, plus the encounter with Edward, in our monthly supervision session. This is run by Frances, a psychologist, and it's a chance for us to offload everything we've seen, heard and experienced over the previous few weeks. Frances is a lovely person and excellent at her job, having worked with palliative care teams for a long time. She always begins each session by asking, 'Has anybody got anything that they'd like to talk about?' Inevitably, we all say, 'No,' then spend the first couple of minutes thinking about how we're going to get through the hour before someone pipes up with something and we're off. Then things really start moving and more often than not we run out of time.

My colleague and friend Kerry was in on the meeting, as usual. She'd been looking after a young woman called Sisira. She was twenty-six years old and had a metastatic colorectal cancer. She'd initially been to her GP with difficulty in breathing, which was later identified as lung disease on the back of a colorectal disease that hadn't been previously diagnosed.

The cancer had spread from her colon into her lungs. Kerry had spent quite a long time supporting Sisira and her family.

They were Sri Lankan, and although they were poor, Sisira's father had given up work to look after her. She was desperate to stay at home as much as possible and live a normal life, even to the extent of being able to go up and down the stairs without too much difficulty. On their behalf, Kerry had contacted a stairlift company, who'd put a stairlift in for free.

Kerry had become close to Sisira and her family, and we knew this day's supervision would be difficult because Sisira had died just that morning. Not surprisingly, Kerry was very emotional and at first didn't want to talk about it. So I told everyone about my experience with the dog, then Edward, and it seemed to break the ice. Kerry started to open up and told us she'd been to visit the family that morning, to find about thirty of them gathered around Sisira's bed, praying, chanting and sharing memories of this vibrant, lively young woman. Like me, Kerry isn't a crier, but she filled up with tears as she told us how welcome she was made to feel in this intimate setting.

As always, the experience of sharing difficult moments helped us all to put that difficulty into context and express the feelings we have as human beings, not just nurses. And it's not only emotionally draining encounters with patients; during this session we get the opportunity to reflect on our own behaviours. I know that sometimes I am difficult to be around in the office and I am not proud to say that my stress is sometimes released at the expense of my colleagues. Supervision gives us the opportunity to apologise and discuss better ways of working together.

I arrived home at about 5pm feeling that I'd had quite a day of it, on the whole. Ups and downs, laughs, tears, frustrations and kindnesses. As I said, just an average day in a job where average days are challenging, to say the least. I made dinner, then Mark and I chatted for a while about this and that. Thankfully he's a good listener and over the years we've been together has heard just about everything there is to hear about my strange but wonderful job.

Later that evening, I took a stroll up the hill with Ronnie to visit one of my good friends, Sinead. There's no better distraction than being in her house, with her two children running riot and her husband, Ben, ranting and raving about some recent issue or another. Today was no different; Ben was on one. He was talking all about some virus that was currently spreading like wildfire in a Chinese city I had never heard of, a place called Wuhan. He loves a conspiracy theory and I was convinced this was another one of his crazy, mind-blowing stories that would amount to nothing but scaremongering. Never one to keep my opinions to myself, we ended up in a full-blown debate. I even felt Ronnie digging me in the ribs, meaning 'time to shut up, Mum', but I carried on.

'You're out of your mind,' I told him, as he explained how within a few weeks the whole country would be shut down, schools would close, and life as we know it would change forever because of this deadly disease. Honestly, I laughed out loud. I had never heard anything so ridiculous. Even when he showed me footage on his phone of emergency hospitals being built in China, I couldn't be convinced. Eventually I walked away with Sinead, who looked back at me and rolled her eyes.

'Try living with him!' she said.

Soon after that, Ronnie and I headed home. I'd had one of those days. I didn't need any more doom and gloom, thanks.

Part Two

AFTER

Chapter 14

Like so many others in all sections of society and all parts of the world, I was wrong about Covid-19. It took me and billions of others completely by surprise. I'm a nurse, I work in a hospital, and I know exactly how viruses spread, and just how contagious they can be. Unlike Ben, I just didn't see this coming and perhaps didn't take it seriously enough. I certainly wasn't the only one.

Few of us were truly prepared for what happened next. There was a well-justified fear that the NHS would be overwhelmed if what was now being described as a 'pandemic' would hit Britain as hard as it seemed to be doing in places like Italy. Yet we all continued to act as if nothing much was happening. We socialised as usual, sometimes at mass gatherings like football matches and race meetings. We didn't move as quickly to 'lockdown' as other countries, with devastating results that became apparent just a few weeks later. Some of the thousands of Covid-related deaths in Britain were unavoidable; others weren't. We've all talked about the 'should've', 'could've' moments that might have made a huge difference, but hindsight is a wonderful thing, of course, and we have to remember that very few of us in the NHS or at senior government level had any experience of dealing with a pandemic like this. We all had to make it up as we went along; sometimes that 'on the hoof' thinking really stood out, other times it didn't.

However, this section of the book, written with hindsight and hard-won experience in the aftermath of Covid-19 taking a grip on the UK, isn't meant to be critical or political. Politics and opinion will no doubt creep into it – that's unavoidable, even if I have no personal axe to grind about anyone involved in the response to the virus. We did what we did, and for a moment at least, the country was overwhelmingly united in a tough battle against a silent, sinister and often terrifying enemy.

As we know, the NHS has been at the forefront of this fight. Time has given all of us – doctors, nurses and non-medical staff – a perspective on the grim situation we have faced and how we responded to it. For many, it's been the chance to step up to the plate and put all of our skills and knowledge into the situation. For others, the worst days of Covid-19 brought trauma, fear, guilt and regret. We are all different, and we all respond in different ways to that which challenges us. What we're all agreed on is that the level of support for NHS staff right across the country has been unprecedented and humbling. For years we've battled against underfunding, working in old, decrepit hospitals with constant bed and equipment shortages. We have faced complaints from patients, families, managers, politicians, the press and the public on a daily basis. Yet, we still pull ourselves out of bed each day and go to work, knowing that at least some of what we are doing was helping to save lives. Then, in those first few weeks that seemed like an eternity, we were national heroes, every one of us. We saw the banners and the homemade signs in the windows, we heard the cheers and the clapping. And even if a cynical few of us wondered where such support had been during all the 'bash the NHS' years, we appreciated every single word, every gesture of support.

The following chapters are my memories of the fight against Covid-19 during the incredible, fast-moving weeks of spring 2020 when the world was turned upside down. I kept a diary during this period and I've shared extracts from this, where appropriate. These pages also include the memories and reflections of a number of my colleagues at Northwick Park. These are people I work with every day, highly experienced professionals, who have all played their part in our hospital's struggle with Covid. Not just that, but they are people too, ordinary men and women who came into work at personal risk to look after scores of sick and dying people, before going home to loved ones who worried about them constantly. I feel it is important to include these voices alongside mine because they help to reflect the wide variety of experiences and emotions felt during this period.

The London Borough of Brent, where Northwick Park is located, has some of the poorest and most diverse communities in the UK. Even as Covid-infected patients were arriving in small numbers we knew we'd be hit particularly badly, and we were. In fact, at some points, Brent had the worst death rate of any local authority in England and Wales per 100,000 population. A high proportion of these were among Black and

Minority Ethnic Communities (BAME), who number among the poorest of Brent's 330,000 population. These people are among Northwick Park's regular customers, and it was the same group that we witnessed dying daily on our wards. We also dealt with their grieving families, most of whom were unable to be anywhere near their loved ones as they died. For us in palliative care this was particularly hard to take, as our whole reason to exist is about helping sick and dying people to spend what remains of their lives in comfort, and with families fully involved in the process of 'dying well'. During Covid, many people didn't die well at all, but despite this, their families showed extraordinary degrees of acceptance and resilience.

So here is an account of what happened at one UK hospital during the spring and early summer of 2020…

When the first handful of patients started to arrive at the Trust's hospitals with Covid-19, the whole atmosphere changed almost overnight. Thanks to the news from abroad, the warnings about this virus had become louder and louder – the city of Wuhan in full lockdown; the emergence of cases in other countries, especially Italy; the TV pictures showing patients on ventilators being treated by staff in full protective gear; the ambulances full of bodies arriving at the mortuary and being handled as if they were toxic waste. The drums were beating louder and louder, and when there were reports of the first deaths in Britain from this new and obviously highly infectious disease, our Trust began to plan for an emergency situation.

In those first few weeks I was working at Ealing Hospital, covering for a member of staff. All hospitals are similar but no two hospitals are the same, and given I was working with staff and patients I didn't know in a place that was unfamiliar to me, I was out of my comfort zone for that short period. Added to the feeling of disorientation was the change in temperature, not just at Ealing Hospital but right across the NHS, and not long after, throughout the whole country. What had been written off a few weeks previously (by a large majority of people, including me) as something happening 'over there' was now on our doorsteps. In the case of our Trust, quite literally. A trickle of people arriving at A&E with the classic symptoms of first-wave Covid-19 (high temperature, persistent cough, difficulty in breathing) turned into a flood, and before too long, the wards across all the Trust's hospitals were full of Covid patients. Sinead's husband Ben was right – this was going to be massive. Luckily, senior medical staff had sensed this some weeks before the whole country woke up to the fact that the world was about to change for the worst.

Mike Dean, Consultant, Anaesthetics and ICU, Northwick Park: *Our department was aware something was brewing in mid- to late January, and from early February onwards, active preparations were being made. The virus was mushrooming in China and starting to spread throughout Asia. Initially it was felt it would probably just settle down but as time passed, it became more real. For us as a Trust, it became real pretty quickly. We have a large number of patients with international connections and in mid-February, we had a patient who came from Singapore with a respiratory illness. He didn't have Covid, but it was a shot across the bows for us. It was a really useful wake-up*

*call to demonstrate how unready we were for the onset of a
severely infective and highly contagious respiratory illness.
I was involved in the initial planning stages, and it was
obvious we needed to be making much swifter preparations
than we were able to. By the time the daily Trust meetings
were happening, the virus had reached Italy and it was
terrifying to watch that country crash and burn when we
knew full well that they have twice as many ICU beds as
us. If they couldn't cope, there was no way we could.*

As the crisis unfolded, it was clear that we were going to be
overwhelmed by demand for beds. The numbers of Covid
patients that were expected every five days actually doubled
every two days. Very quickly, almost every bed was allocated
to a Covid patient – an extraordinary, incredible situation
that produced widespread anxiety and panic. Every couple
of days another ward went Covid and already patients were
needing ventilators and CPAP machines. CPAP (continuous
positive airway pressure) is a machine that helps force air into
the lungs, keeping the airways open. Patients will be awake,
wearing a tight-fitting mask, and it's the final measure before
needing ventilation.

As a department, the priority for us was to get non-Covid
patients out of the wards and home as soon as possible. The
skills we already had for discharging palliative patients –
arranging transport and equipment, scheduling district nurse
visits and sorting out care packages – were brought to bear on
patients we wouldn't usually have dealings with. When this first
began, I was still at Ealing Hospital and I was approached by
a consultant who asked me to see a patient with heart failure.

The man was unwell, and was being supported by his daughter. Although her dad hadn't yet had the full amount of treatment he should be having, we needed to talk about his immediate removal from the hospital.

She was the type of person you could have an honest conversation with and she could see for herself the drama that was unfolding all around her. So I decided not to beat around the bush.

'Things have become so bad that if we don't get your dad home as soon as possible, he will most likely catch coronavirus and die,' I said. 'That's the reality.'

She nodded.

'I know he's not had all the treatment he needs but we'll do our absolute best to keep him going while this thing is on. Honestly, he'll be safer at home than he will be on the ward.'

She didn't need much persuading and by the end of the following day he went home to an uncertain future, but at least one in which his chances of being killed by Covid-19 were lessened.

Meanwhile, the fear and tension among the staff was creeping up steadily. There seemed to be conflicting advice about who needed personal protective equipment (PPE) and who didn't, how long you needed to wash your hands for, whether patients being discharged from hospitals into care homes needed testing for Covid. At the beginning this wasn't a requirement – the advice was that they just needed to get out of hospital straight away, before it was too late. Unfortunately, for some it was already too late – they already had the virus and took it with them to care homes, with devastating results.

There are a lot of care homes in the Trust's geographical

area and at the beginning of the pandemic they wanted any residents in hospitals to return immediately, knowing these elderly people would be among the most susceptible to the virus. At the outset, people were sent home unswabbed and some of these became super-spreaders. Later, when it became clear this was happening, care homes insisted on potential returnees being swabbed and wouldn't take them if they tested positive. Sometimes, this group included those who had mild symptoms, or no symptoms at all. They stayed with us for a week before testing negative and went back to the care home. Others became unwell and died.

Randall Jones, Team Leader, Palliative Care, Northwick Park: *At the time, care homes were quite rightly concerned about patients being discharged from hospital back to them, saying, 'Has this person been tested?' The priority at that time was to create bed capacity within the acute hospital. Personally, I think the entire handling of this has been difficult from day one due to the constantly changing messages that were coming out. We probably wouldn't have seen the numbers we were seeing had we shut down a week earlier, as everyone at the time thought we should be doing except the Government. I feel an earlier shutdown could have saved lives.*

At the time of writing this book, Varuna Doorga had just joined the palliative care team as an assistant practitioner (healthcare assistant). Prior to this, she worked in a nursing home and was there at the height of the pandemic.

Varuna Doorga, Assistant Practitioner (Healthcare Assistant), Palliative Care Team, Northwick Park: *The panic period started when the first chest infection started spreading from one room to another, another and another, and then we had to isolate everyone. But this is where the challenge came. People with dementia are often quite mobile but weren't aware of what was going on. So we would say, 'You have to stay in your room,' and people didn't have a clue what we were talking about. So that was a challenge, to keep them in the room, because they would go in and out.*

Everywhere was a panic. There were lots of changes because it was a big care home. The hairdresser was shut, coffee shop shut, all activities stopped. And then we had to shut down.

One man started to feel unwell and seemed to have symptoms. At that time, we didn't think it was Covid because we knew that he hadn't gone out. We knew that, but it didn't click that his wife had previously visited. He wasn't reacting to oral antibiotics so it was agreed to send him to hospital. When the ambulance people came, they were shocked to see us working without masks. They said, 'Guys, you are not protecting yourself and others as well. Please go and wear your mask.' So then management started reviewing the policy and then from that they said everyone should wear a mask.

The man went to hospital on Monday. He stayed there for two hours and after two hours, he was sent back to die because they couldn't do anything. When he was admitted, they had to take a swab because he was coming in for a chest infection. The swab came back and the bombshell dropped that he was Covid positive. All the staff who had been in contact with him were very scared – many had children – and they were thinking, Oh my God, what are we going to do?

We were all having to learn very quickly about this disease and although everyone wanted to do the right thing, it was inevitable that mistakes were made. It was always going to be an impossible situation until we'd adjusted to this frightening new reality. And yet, there was also a strong sense of teams, hospitals, Trusts and the entire NHS banding together to fight something none of us had ever experienced in our entire careers.

Kerry Wloskowicz, Clinical Nurse Specialist, Palliative Care: *What I saw was a hospital pulling together. Yes, all of a sudden things got very hectic and very busy, but then I saw so much kindness. I saw people being nice to each other. I wasn't worried about Covid myself. I wasn't scared of it. Even when I got it and was off work it didn't worry me and I don't know if that was normal. I've come into this job as a nurse. This is something that you are trained for. We're health professionals. There was a feeling of 'What can we do to help this situation? Where are we best suited to work?'*

Kerry and I felt the same about the situation. We were staring at an approaching tsunami, yet despite the tension, anxiety and chaos of everything that was happening – not just within the NHS but across the entire country – we didn't feel much fear. In fact, quite the opposite. For me, there was a kind of excitement that we would be on the front line of this, and needed like we'd never been needed before. We had no idea how we'd cope, or who among us would fall sick and possibly even die. At senior NHS level there was deep concern that the service would simply run out of beds. This was becoming a very serious issue in our Trust once the numbers admitted with Covid began to rise. Our new medical director, Dr Martin Kuper, didn't mince his words. Staff were warned of a 'tidal wave' of cases coming our way, and that it was likely many people would die. We could be redeployed to different areas, we were told, and volunteers would be sought to help out in the worst-affected wards, including ITU.

We gathered to hear this news in our various departments, standing shoulder-to-shoulder as we normally would during staff meetings. Even then, as the virus was stalking the wards and the first patients were being ventilated, there was little thought about our own safety. We weren't wearing masks or gowns, and I'm not even sure if the term 'social-distancing' had even come into circulation at this point. Nor did we question any of this. We simply stood and listened, with the result that large numbers of staff quickly went down with the virus, leaving us seriously under-manned as the pandemic spread through the hospital. There were so many other things to think about that we didn't really consider how this might affect us as people. As ever, the priority and focus was on the patients, and how best we could treat them with the resources we'd got.

Mike Dean, Consultant, Anaesthetics and ICU, Northwick Park: *Suddenly you were exposed to considerations you wouldn't have thought of previously. We know what's needed to run an intensive care unit but* *when you're suddenly having to put ICU patients in a place not designed for critical care you think, Oh Christ! For example, I had a discussion about electrics, knowing that if they should fail in ICU, people will die very quickly. That's why ICU has the highest levels of electrical back-up, but only a few places in the hospital also have this. So by putting patients on a different ward, you're mitigating risks which are incomprehensible – as the guys from the Estates department said, such a risk is an inch wide but a mile deep. The chances of it happening are tiny but the consequences are massive.*

It was also a time when there was a huge amount of brilliant stuff going on. Some people just came to the fore and demonstrated abilities to think through problems and lead their colleagues, which was astounding to watch.

After my stint at Ealing Hospital I returned to my team at Northwick Park, glad to be back among colleagues I knew well and trusted implicitly. By the time I was back in my usual role there were no less than six wards full of Covid patients and the first deaths among those worst affected by the virus had started to happen.

For us, this was particularly shocking. Our core role, as I've mentioned, is to keep people living well until they die. There was simply no opportunity for this here because people were dying so quickly. A patient could arrive at Northwick Park in the morning with suspected Covid symptoms – shortness of breath, for example – then be settled into bed and given breakfast. As the day progressed, the shortness of breath would worsen to the point they needed to be on high-flow oxygen via a CPAP machine. By the time evening came, they were dead. The progression could be as quick as that. There was no time for last wishes or to say goodbye to relatives and friends. This was hard for us as palliative staff to take in, but doubly difficult for ward nurses who might only encounter a death every few weeks or so. It became clear that once those non-Covid patients who could leave Northwick Park had been discharged, our role would be about supporting both families and staff. By now, all visiting had stopped, making our usual face-to-face liaisons with family members just about impossible.

Randall Jones, Team Leader, Palliative Care, Northwick Park: *There was a lot of distress around patients dying, sometimes by themselves. So the team were upset about that. They were exhausted. They were tired. The most distressing things to them were that patients were sometimes dying alone and the nurses and doctors didn't have time to speak to the relatives to update them.*

So what we took from that was, 'What can we set up to support these areas to let relatives at least have one phone call a day to let them know whether their relative was dying, not dying, or getting better?' There was so much uncertainty that sometimes we had to admit that we weren't quite sure. Very quickly, we got that support up and running on the HDU, high dependency unit, here. Normally, HDU has about seven beds. Now it had twenty beds, everyone was on CPAP masks, having oxygen pushed into their lungs, and they're just one step away from intensive care. There was a need for someone just to ring relatives so we said, 'We'll trial it.'

A lot of the doctors had done some of the phone calls already for those who were dying. So we went down there, rang the relatives and said, 'This is your daily phone call. You will receive a phone call every day now at about the same time. We will give you an update from a medical point of view, nursing point of view, and you can still ring your relatives. Many of the patients have a mobile phone in the room but this is what we will do,' and it sort of snowballed. It took pressure off the nurses and the relatives thought it was great that someone was actually talking to them. The doctors loved it because a lot of those difficult conversations they didn't feel prepared to have or they were exhausted from having had so many of them, whereas that's our bread and butter.

Chapter 15

By mid-March, the Government had announced £300 billion in support for businesses affected by the pandemic. The death rate was creeping up steadily and it looked likely that sooner or later, we would be placed in the same 'lockdown' conditions that other countries were already experiencing. We were starting to notice panic-buying, especially of loo rolls and pasta, in the shops.

My hands were red raw from all the precautionary washing of them. This was pretty much the only safety advice non-critical staff were being given at the time. We just had to use our common sense. There was quite a bit of anxiety in our office about this, which occasionally spilled over into minor conflict. Some people were washing hands, cleaning desks, phones, mobiles, donning gloves and doing the whole thing again when they'd been on a ward. Others weren't as cautious. They would do the basics, like regular hand-washing, but didn't go to the next level, which would upset others. I remember my colleague

Liam making a cup of coffee for someone else, and when it was brought over, she said his fingers were too near the top of the cup, and could he make another one? He looked surprised and a bit hurt, but he did as he was asked, this time holding it by the handle.

On 17 March, I wrote this entry in my diary: *'I'm making my whole family eat an orange every day in the hope that more vitamin C will build up our immune systems...'*

With hindsight, it looks similar to attempting to use a pea-shooter to kill an elephant. I guess it reflects those early feelings of panic and uncertainty swirling everywhere. There was no cure for this, no mitigating its effects if you got a bad dose. The news at home and abroad was becoming steadily worse and, of course, those of us working at Northwick Park were seeing the escalating situation with our own eyes.

Like all my colleagues, I was worried about bringing Covid home with me from work, so I established a daily routine which I stuck to like glue. I changed out of my uniform at work and into my ordinary clothes, putting the uniform into a sealed bag. When I arrived home, I came into the house through the garage and removed my ordinary clothes, putting both sets into the washing machine before going up to have a shower. Once I'd changed into another set of clothes, I was finally ready to greet my family. It was a bit of a performance but it had to be done – the alternative was unthinkable.

We were told not to talk too much outside of work about what we were seeing and hearing at Northwick Park. Not because there was anything to hide; the fact was that we didn't want to panic anyone unduly. There was enough of that going on as it was. Externally, I tried to keep bright and cheerful, especially in front of Ronnie. He was only eleven, and about to face his school closing for the foreseeable future. Inside, though, I was scared. Every time I hugged him I could feel a wave of paranoia rising up from my gut. 'Supposing I already have it? Supposing I've given it to him?' 'What if he reacts badly to it?' 'What if I pass it to Mark or Livvie?' And so on, until my head was spinning with it. Even if I coughed once I'd wonder whether I should be in a different room.

Ironically, Mark, Livvie and Ronnie never worried about themselves. They were far more concerned about me, going into a Covid-laden atmosphere day after day, and although they always told me to be careful, they never once said, 'You shouldn't go in.' They know me well enough to understand that unless I'd been diagnosed with the thing, there was no way I'd shirk my responsibilities. Even so, Mark often said, 'You don't need to be everyone's hero', and at the time I struggled with that. I knew there were members of staff at the hospital who were worried about Covid to the point that they refused to go on the wards. Of course, you couldn't force anyone to do anything in such a situation, but at the time I found such an attitude hard to understand. Why wouldn't you want to be a part of what's happening? Why wouldn't you want to do the very thing you were trained for – nurse sick and dying people? As time went on, I softened a little, telling myself that people are people and we all had differing reactions to what was happening. Personally, I'd never felt prouder to put on that freshly laundered uniform each day and get out there for another stint on the front line.

On 20 March Boris Johnson announced all pubs and restaurants would close for the foreseeable future. There would be no school for Ronnie and millions of other kids from the following Monday. Offices were closed and employees told they would be 'furloughed' – a word few had ever heard of but which we would all quickly become familiar with as the days and weeks passed. Only shops selling essential goods would stay open. Most of us would be staying at home, only allowed out for a limited period of exercise once a day. We couldn't meet others, even close relatives, and even if we passed people in the street we had to step away from them. This was 'the new normal' and among the public there was a sense of bewilderment that it had arrived so quickly. Many people wondered if it was all really necessary. There were still 'only' 200 deaths nationally. Surely there was no need for such panic?

But they weren't seeing what we were seeing: the terror in patients' faces when they were lying in bed, struggling to breathe even as high-flow oxygen was being forced into their lungs. Patients scared and alone, seeing people all around them being treated for the same condition and with almost identical symptoms. Some of them were dying, some were being transferred to ITU in the hope they might survive. Others were being sedated and ventilated right there and then, in full view of other patients on the ward, because there was no time to lose, no time to stop and wait – the medical teams knew their bleepers would soon be sounding for the next emergency. Curtains around beds were rarely drawn because patients were deteriorating so rapidly that they needed to be in full view of the nurses and doctors at all times.

'This is all so new,' I wrote in my diary, *'that we don't know if the sickest patients will get better – what a horrible waiting game.'*

This deep uncertainty was intensified when, on 20 March,

the hospital declared a 'critical incident'. We'd simply run out of bed space for the tidal wave of patients being brought in with Covid and we were about to be overwhelmed. We were the first hospital to publicly declare that we might not be able to cope, which proves that in those first few weeks Northwick Park was at the epicentre of the pandemic in the UK. What a position to be in… Thankfully, other hospitals in the Trust, and further afield, responded rapidly and we were able to move some Covid patients to other places and make way for new admissions. Additionally, staff from other hospitals responded to the call for help.

Mike Dean, Consultant, Anaesthetics and ICU, Northwick Park: *It (the declaration of the critical incident) was a mix of exhaustion and relief. Up until that point there had been frustration, now suddenly people were coming to help. It felt as though the cavalry were coming. I lost count of the number of trainees who were in different parts of London, and across the UK, who were getting in touch after the critical incident saying, 'You're clearly in the shit, how can we help?' Every time someone offered a bit more help I thought, Thank God, finally people get it.*

The weekend before what would come to be described as 'lockdown' was the nearest to national meltdown I've ever experienced. Despite the obvious seriousness of events, people were still out socialising, meeting friends, going to whatever mass gatherings were taking place and making multiple trips out of their homes. I didn't know what to think or feel. There were so many mixed messages, people clearly did not understand how serious this was, but why? We were all seeing the footage from Italy and Spain, the total chaos, devastation and loss of life. Maybe people didn't believe what they saw or had the attitude that 'it won't happen to me'. The media are definitely guilty of sensationalising everything, so I think a great number of people thought it was being made out to be worse than it was.

By now, as I've mentioned, panic buying was in full swing but luckily NHS staff were given priority where there were queues. That weekend, I went to Tesco in the 'priority hour' and an old man, well into his eighties, walked into the line right in front of me. As he got to the head of the queue, the Tesco staff member on duty asked for his NHS ID. I wasn't at all surprised when he told her he thought it was the priority hour for the elderly. The Tesco worker stood firm – he wouldn't be allowed in until all NHS staff had had their turn. I felt for him – there was obviously no malice there – and I asked him if there was anything he needed urgently.

'Toilet roll,' came the reply. My heart sank. Everyone wanted toilet roll, including me, but due to panic-buying, it was in notoriously short supply. By the time I reached the toiletries aisle there were literally two packs of the stuff left. I didn't want to be the person to selfishly take both of them, so I put one into my trolley and left the other. Outside, the old man was waiting patiently. I handed him the pack of loo rolls, he smiled and I went on my way, telling myself that my box of tissues would have to last just a bit longer.

Back at work, the wards were becoming fuller by the day and yet, incredibly, there still hadn't been an order for staff to wear PPE outside of intensive care. The wards were full of Covid patients and staff were going down with it like flies. We were wearing masks by this stage, or to be more accurate, we were advised to wear masks when entering the wards, but otherwise we were in our regular uniforms. There was fear over the fact that full PPE supplies were running out all over the country and confusion about who exactly should be wearing it. It was obvious that ITU staff should have first shout, but delays in equipment fit for purpose for everyone else meant an increased chance of infection for patients and NHS staff right across the country. Some staff complained constantly about this and I could understand their fears; the thing is, we just had a job to do and we couldn't wait until a truck full of supplies turned up. There simply wasn't time.

Our role as a team also included the triaging of new referrals – making sure that links to families were in place, allocating the work of the team, preparing care plans, etc., as well as arranging discharges from hospital, often in complex circumstances. This can be a demanding administrative job and in normal circumstances we take it in turns, usually for a week at a time. Given that we now had various team members either off sick or self-isolating, we felt we should be working to our strengths and we all knew that one person among us was particularly good in this role – senior nurse Claire Windsor. As I mentioned earlier, Claire has been a palliative nurse for around twenty years. She is very calm, her decision-making is fantastic and her palliative care knowledge second to none. We often refer to her as our 'wise owl'. She agreed to take on the role, not realising at the time that she would be in the hot seat for eight weeks.

Claire Windsor, Clinical Nurse Specialist, Palliative Care Team, Northwick Park: *Mainly I was office-based, managing the referrals, telephone calls, trying to get the team to see people in the most appropriate way. At that time we weren't seeing patients who were proving Covid-positive because we were trying to reduce footfall of people involved and also there was concerns that there may have been a shortage of PPE. Then we started getting referrals for discharge support.*

We had our patients who were non-Covid or regular type of patients who were wanting to get out of here, understandably. There were people who were being diagnosed with Covid, who were dying very quickly, and so we weren't really able to see them. We were just able to give telephone advice, and we developed some symptom control guidelines. The ward staff would then have some guidance about what to do without calling us because things were just changing so quickly that they weren't always able to call. I remember very distressed calls from doctors on the wards. So many people were deteriorating and dying. They were just desperately asking for help and advice.

There were people who were dying of Covid very, very quickly, and others who had other co-morbidities, or were elderly and frail, and they happened to have a diagnosis of Covid but they weren't deteriorating and dying in that rapid way like some of our other patients. So with some of these patients, family members started saying, 'Can we get them home?' Now, ordinarily, that's our bread and butter and we do that without thinking, and we've got very good relationships with the community teams and we know how to organise delivery of equipment and anticipatory medications – all these things that we do without thinking. But of course when Covid came along, our rulebook was completely ripped up, and we were starting from scratch.

I can remember being on the phone to the doctor saying, 'This family is desperate to take this gentleman home. Can you help?' And I spoke to his daughter, who I think was a pharmacist. And she was just pleading with me down the phone to get her dad home. Of course at that time nobody was allowed to visit.

So there were people in hospitals, coming up to the end of their lives, and families couldn't see them, which was devastating. We really struggled with that because we're very much a 'can-do' team. I remember thinking to myself, I don't want to be obstructive. I really want to help these people. Can we get him home? Will the equipment company deliver equipment in this time? Will district nurses go in? What are the risks to family members? I didn't know.

I tried to think it through, just working on the hoof and I said to the daughter, 'Please just leave this with me. I'm going to do my best to work this through.' And I did. None of us had met this man. None of us met the family. It was all done over the phone with the family and the doctors.

And I was able to get this man home the next morning with a package of care, with support from district nurses. The whole route rulebook we'd normally follow was ripped up, which in a way was good because the red tape was also ripped up with it. His family were just so thankful. I found out that he died two days later at home with his family.

It was just a horrific time, but after that we were able to work out as we went along what we could do and what we couldn't do. We were able to get a lot of people home or to our local hospice, who were really great at taking patients.

It was exhausting. I can remember going home that night just absolutely drained, because ordinarily, what we would do perhaps without thinking about it, it was just taking so much energy and brainpower. It did feel like it was a war zone at times with so much going on, and people were just dying so quickly and in so many numbers, but at least were able to help in some way.

As Claire says, we broke rules. In the circumstances we felt there was no other choice. One of the big lessons we learned was that people didn't necessarily need to be in hospital to have treatment, and that community teams could manage patients at home with illnesses that in normal circumstances would only be treated in hospital. Relatives were being taught via the web to give loved ones injections. The local hospice, St Luke's, put together instructional videos on how to give these injections, something only ever done by healthcare professionals previously, as well as how to handle people needing personal care and move them carefully. There was little alternative but for us all to make it up as we went along, because people were terrified of coming into hospital, even with serious conditions.

For those who were here, and couldn't be taken home, there was so much pain and heartbreak, especially for relatives who couldn't visit.

For example, Mrs Wilma Roberts, in her eighties with previous breast cancer, had been deteriorating at home for the past few months with her husband doing everything he could to manage her poor health. He knew that if she came into hospital, he would not be able to visit her. He was just as elderly and very frail himself. But as she became less and less well, he was not able to manage. Wilma started to get confused and was not able to get out of the bed. Eventually, Mr Roberts called an ambulance.

Having been admitted acutely via A&E, Wilma was transferred to one of the care of the elderly wards and was being quite actively managed via blood tests, Intravenous (IV) fluids and IV antibiotics. She was having her vital observations such as blood pressure, oxygen levels and temperature monitored four-hourly. The doctors had discussed her situation with the family and put in place a DNACPR order (Do Not Attempt Cardiopulmonary Resuscitation). Some people get very distressed when we discuss resuscitation – mostly family members – but this is only one part of a person's treatment plan. It doesn't mean that other treatments will be withdrawn; it just means that this particular intervention or treatment has been deemed not appropriate.

Her bloods on admission had shown very high calcium levels. High calcium can be caused by a number of conditions but for Wilma, it was likely due to her breast cancer and made worse by dehydration due to reduced oral intake at home for the past few months. It can cause many symptoms, including increased pain, confusion, fatigue, lethargy and excessive thirst. Wilma was clearly suffering with many of these symptoms, so treating her high calcium level was done as a priority. Unfortunately, the treatment for hypercalcaemia takes several days to take effect and my worry about seeing Wilma so very unwell was that we did not have a few days. She looked very unsettled, restless, agitated, and was making lots of groaning noises. Wilma was extremely frail and it was clear that she had lost a lot of weight recently. Seeing someone like this is very distressing. Leaving them this way is unthinkable.

I had a decision to make: I needed to choose how much to negotiate with the team treating her. I knew the consultant overseeing Wilma's care and we often see things very differently. He is in the school of thought that palliative care is not needed until someone is dying imminently. So I went in gently...

'Do you think Wilma has a chance of surviving the next few days?' I asked tentatively.

'We can treat her calcium and see how she gets on,' he replied.

'OK, great,' I said, trying to be positive, 'but equally, she is very agitated, unsettled and I'm worried about leaving her like this. Can we please prescribe the symptom management medications so that the nurses can get her more settled?' By now, I was negotiating.

'We can do that.'

He pointed to the drug chart, picked up by one of his juniors, who prescribed the much-needed medications. I took the chart straight to the nurse caring for Wilma, asking her to give some pain relief and something for her agitation.

I felt happy now, knowing that we were trying to treat a potentially reversible condition but that Wilma's comfort was being prioritised. I called her family. They'd already spoken to the ward consultant who, despite not always seeing eye to eye with me, is very good at ensuring families and carers are up to date with the medical plan, and will often phone patients himself. I spoke to Wilma's son, Steve, down as the first point of contact on the records. Steve understood that his mum was really unwell. I took this a bit further.

'She is unwell enough not to survive,' I said, waiting to see how he processed this.

'I know,' Steve replied. 'Dad wanted to keep her at home but she got so confused and distressed, he couldn't manage. We knew that she probably wouldn't make it out of hospital.'

From this I knew he got it. Now I could ask my usual questions plus the new ones developed during Covid… 'Has Mum ever talked about dying and what would be important to her?' and 'If we can't make her better, what should we prioritise?' Then the new questions: 'You are allowed to allocate one family member to come and visit your mum for fifteen minutes. Would you like to discuss this with the rest of the family?'

Fifteen minutes – I hated even saying it. How awful. Fifteen minutes to say goodbye to your mum or your wife of sixty years. Steve told me that his dad really wanted to come in but he and his sister were both so worried because their father was such high risk. We talked about referring his mum to the local hospice where there were still risks but much lower as there are only twelve beds. The hospice was much more homely, and Steve's mum could have a room that looked out on to the garden. The best news was that her husband would be able to stay with her all day rather than the allocated fifteen minutes in the hospital.

Steve agreed this was a good plan; however, we also needed to think about the reality that she might not survive long enough to make it to the hospice. He asked a very direct question: 'What about the possibility of seeing Mum's body at the funeral directors?' No problem – I promised to make a few calls.

I called three different local funeral directors, who all told me the same thing – that they were not able to facilitate any viewings, even for patients who were Covid-negative. This was devastating to hear, not only for this family but for many families at the time who would lose loved ones and not even have the opportunity to say their final goodbyes. They were not allowed to view the deceased in the hospital either, so unless they came and said goodbye for their allocated fifteen minutes, they would never be able to see that person again. This is compounded for those whose relatives die in ITU, where there were no visiting rights for anyone, even after death. This explains why so many people were fearful of being ventilated at that time.

I called Steve back and told him the bad news. He said he would go away and discuss things with his sister and dad to make a decision. Later, he called back and said they had agreed to the hospice referral in the hope that we could get her there in the next couple of days and they would all get the chance to say their goodbyes. So the referral was sent.

The next morning I went to the ward at 9.30am with good news – the hospice, St Luke's, had a bed. I went to the bay where Wilma was and saw the curtains were drawn around her bed. I thought she might be having a wash, but I couldn't see the telltale sign of nurses' and carers' feet behind the curtain. This was not good news. I confirmed with the nurse that Wilma had just died.

At that moment I felt terrible. Then I saw the nurse in charge, a lovely old-school ward sister who puts compassion and common sense first. She had already called the family and invited them in to see Wilma. I was so touched. The restrictions in place made things extremely difficult for the ward nurses who had to tell distraught families that they were not allowed to visit. It just goes against the grain of everything we know, everything we have ever done. I called Steve and arranged to meet them at the main entrance so I could give them all PPE.

At 11.30am I met Wilma's family – her husband, daughter and son – at the main entrance. Here was a family in turmoil. Mr Roberts was a broken man, trembling so much with grief that he had to get his daughter to tie his mask on properly. We walked the length of the corridor – the longest walk I have ever had in all my years of working here – past the boarded-up Costa, and the WHSmith with its shutters down. We reached the ward and walked towards the curtained bed. Wilma looked like a sleeping angel. All of the agitation that was in her face the previous day was gone. Now she was at peace. I left the family with her, the raw grief tangible, with tears flowing. These were heartbreaking goodbyes for heartbreaking times.

Like all of us in palliative care I found the 'no visiting' rule extremely hard. I understood why it existed but it seemed to go against all of our natural compassion. I couldn't see why, given the correct PPE, someone with a dying relative couldn't come in to say their goodbyes. People were dying alone and to us, that was an abomination. After a while, the rules were relaxed somewhat, and some wards made their own autonomous decisions about visiting, but it was still strictly a no-no in HDU and ITU.

The upside – if there is an upside – were the levels of support we were seeing for what we were doing. And when I say 'we', I mean the entire NHS, not just Northwick Park patients and their families. As the crisis unfolded, our daily commute to work was marked by homemade signs of support in windows, banners on roundabouts and messages on advertising billboards. It seemed that after years of criticism, the whole country was now behind us. The first 'Clap For Carers' event on 26 March was the most incredibly lovely gesture: people coming out from behind locked doors and into the street to show their solidarity. For my colleagues, there were mixed feelings.

Mike Dean, Consultant, Anaesthetics and ICU, Northwick Park: *Suddenly, people knew what you did and commented on it. Yet personally I've never felt less heroic. You have the nation clapping, and you think, It must be for someone else because I'm doing a shit job. I don't know what I'm doing. People are falling apart and I don't know how to deal with it all. It's really weird, because in one sense you are the last line, this is it, and everyone thinks you're doing a great job, but that's not the impression you've got, because you're surrounded by it and you're simply dealing with one problem after the next. And you're always thinking, If we'd done this with the clinical stuff at the beginning, could we have done better? But of course we couldn't, it's hindsight. Now we know a load more about it that we didn't know in the past. But it's difficult not to look back and think, Should've done that... You tell yourself not to do it, but it doesn't help.*

For me, the first 'Clap For Carers' was an emotional moment, but right from the start of the weekly event, I felt I was clapping not just for my colleagues but for the entire nation. We were all affected by this in some way: everyone's freedom to work, play, socialise, worship and generally go about our daily lives had for the moment ended. Sometimes I felt almost lucky to be getting in my car and heading for Northwick Park each morning – millions more were trapped indoors, yet they were handling it with good humour and resilience. Nevertheless, at that moment I felt proud to be part of the NHS, and hugely supported by the British people.

Chapter 16

Diary entry, 27 March 2020: *Administered morphine today to a man who was dying and severely breathless. He has deteriorated so quickly, but still being nursed in a main bay as side rooms are so precious. He speaks Bengali and was calling something out. My colleague speaks Bengali and she translated: 'Help me!', he said. 'Help me…'*

Covid is a plague – it is spreading like the Australian bush fires, but it's invisible. And this is only the beginning…

Like those bush fires 10,000 miles away, it seemed that every time we dealt with one incident another would immediately pop up somewhere else. The man I've described above was initially Covid-negative but once he contracted the virus its strength completely overwhelmed him. I knew from his symptoms that he had it, but the doctors had been reluctant to re-swab him. We were already running out of swabs for new patients being admitted; it was seen as a luxury to swab someone twice. I went with a different tack: that he was dying and very symptomatic, so we could refer him to the hospice, but they needed a recent negative test. It worked, and they re-swabbed him, but we would probably have to wait at least twenty-four hours for the result. He tested positive and was moved from the main bay into a side room, but by then most other patients in the bay were infected.

This level of breathlessness being experienced was something I had never seen before. He told my Bengali-speaking colleague he felt as though he was drowning and by giving him morphine, initially as regular injections as needed and then via a syringe pump, we improved those symptoms, took away the breathlessness and made him feel less like he was suffocating.

His family were desperate to get him home, but this was impossible given his condition. I spent time talking to his sister, who came to meet me outside the ward, hoping and praying that by being there, the ward staff would permit her to at least spend a few moments with her brother. She told me a little of his story. He had been living in the UK for the past eighteen years, sending money home to his wife and children in Bangladesh. He was the sole provider for the family. Now, she was faced with the horrible task of having to call his wife and tell her that he was dying. Too unwell even to make it to his sister's home nearby, he would die in hospital, and alone. I could see the pain in her face even at the thought of making this call. How could this make sense? He was previously fit and well, with only mild underlying health conditions, including high blood pressure and type 2 diabetes. Now he was dying. She was allowed in to see him, just for a few minutes. This would be the last time she would ever see him – he died the following day, alone as expected.

By now, like almost every other department, the hospital mortuary was having to deal with the possibility of being overwhelmed. In normal circumstances they would be looking at dealing with a handful of deceased per day; very quickly, this turned into thirty or forty, so huge refrigerated tankers had to be brought in. It wasn't just capacity either: usually there aren't more than a couple of staff in the mortuary but many more were needed and soon, staff from other areas were redeployed there on a voluntary basis. Regardless of the actual circumstances, every dead body had to be treated as though they'd had Covid, so the PPE protocols had to be stuck to rigidly there too.

Whenever a person died they were given a respectful wash before being placed in a body bag for the porters to collect. The bag was labelled with a special sticker, which identified the body as 'highly infectious', and would be treated as being actively Covid. The porters would then wheel the body into a special lift to the mortuary, which is located underneath the hospital. Then the business of arranging for a funeral director would start. Space in the mortuary and the refrigerated vehicles was at a premium, so everything needed to move with speed and precision while trying to retain the values in this area for keeping this as respectful a process as possible. Luckily, funeral directors in this part of London are used to dealing with people whose religious beliefs require burial within twenty-four hours, so the process was relatively smooth. But as we know, attendance at funerals was by then strictly limited, causing even more heartache for bereaved families who might otherwise attend funerals in their hundreds.

Again, rules were bent to fit the new circumstances. Usually, families need to come in to collect a death certificate and register the death before a funeral can take place. At this point, however, the registrar simply received an email from the hospital, processed the death and sent all the paperwork to the family via email as soon as possible, sending the original certificate in the post. This way, the body could be released for burial much quicker than previously. Coronavirus made the process of attendance and collection that had gone on for years suddenly seem archaic.

The rapidity of changing circumstances and the mounting numbers of dead and dying were really beginning to show by late March and early April. *'Things are getting worse by the day and for the first time I actually feel scared,'* I wrote in my diary.

It was hardly surprising, given that so much was going on in all departments. Our team had so many difficult conversations with families, in which we had to explain that yes, their relatives were going to die, no, they couldn't come in to see them but, yes, we might be able to sort out a video call via a phone or a tablet. I called one woman whose mother had heart failure and looked likely to die, but not from Covid. There may have been a chance, in some shape or form, for her daughter to say goodbye but she had a young son who also had a dangerous heart condition and she couldn't put him at risk.

'It's the worst choice you can ever make,' she told me. 'Do I say goodbye to my mum, who I've always been close to, or do I keep my son safe? There is no choice, really, is there?'

I felt so sorry for her, having to come to terms with a decision like that, but she was just one of many individuals and families faced with the prospect of not being able to see their loved ones again without even a word of goodbye. I also dealt with a patient called Janet, who was only fifty years old but was living in a care home with a diagnosis of advanced multiple sclerosis (MS). She had been bedbound for the past two years and when admitted to hospital she was presenting with high fever, low levels of oxygen and extreme shortness of breath. In short, all the classic signs of Covid, for which she tested positive.

I spoke to the ward nurse looking after her and asked if anyone had called the family – so far, no one had at that stage. I explained that I was really worried about Janet, who seemed to be at high risk of sudden deterioration leading to a quick death. She had a respiratory rate of about 35 and she looked extremely weak and frail. The nurse reported that she was opening her eyes and engaging with them the previous day, but that day was barely responding at all. The nurse was junior, so I offered to make the call to the family for her and she gratefully accepted. Reading the notes, I noticed her father was her nearest next of kin and had regularly visited her in the care home before he himself had to shield. I decided to return to my office to make the phone call. I knew it would be a challenging one, as this type of call usually is, but slightly less so in a quiet office than a busy ward.

He knew as soon as I introduced myself that things were not good. I asked when he had last seen his daughter.

'Two weeks ago,' he said, 'and she wasn't looking too good then. After my last visit the nurses at the home rang me to say she'd taken a turn for the worse and they were calling an ambulance.'

I could sense the fear in his voice.

'They told me she was struggling to breathe,' he added.

'To be honest, I haven't stopped worrying about her since this whole bloody coronavirus thing started.'

Janet's dad knew she was at high risk of catching the virus, but felt helpless. He was devastated when he got the call from the care home – his worst fear had happened.

I explained that it was an unpredictable disease, but what we did know was that when people start to struggle with their breathing despite high levels of oxygen, they may not recover. Janet's dad had already spoken to the doctors over the phone when she was brought in and he knew that she would not be admitted to ITU or HDU, as her underlying conditions meant that she was unlikely to ever recover from such invasive interventions. He knew that the decision had been made that in the event of CPR, she would not be resuscitated.

Janet's dad sounded weary, but also the kind of person who would appreciate honesty without any beating around the bush. He'd obviously spent some years worrying about his sick child. So I told him the reason for my call, explaining that I thought his daughter was dying. Then I paused. It is sometimes useful to allow such pauses in these types of phone calls as, somehow, silence speaks louder than words. I waited for him to respond, not trying to fill the gaps with words that would make no difference to the awful truth.

'Right,' he said, breaking the silence, 'so how long has she got?'

'People who are as unwell as Janet seem to die very quickly with this disease,' I replied, 'and although that might be a few days I've got a feeling that Janet's time left might be much shorter. Maybe a day. Maybe just hours.'

At that time, there was a slight possibility that he might be able to come in for a very short visit and I told him this.

'I can't,' he said. 'I'm shielding at home with my own health problems… I'm not going to get the chance to say goodbye to my daughter, am I? She will think I have abandoned her. After all the years of her being in the care home, we knew she was starting to suffer and we knew something would cause her death – but none of us could have imagined how awful this would be.'

I think if pure emotion could have reached down the phone and grabbed me, it would have done. I turned to Claire, sitting quietly next to me in the office. She could hear and feel the gravity of the call I was making, and we held each other's glance for a few moments, inwardly reflecting on the damage being inflicted by this horrible disease.

The conversation continued but I could feel my head spinning. I wanted to cry. I wanted to scream at the unfairness of it all, knowing that so many other families were having to go through this, too.

I returned to the ward the next day. Janet had died in the early hours of the morning. Her sister had visited the evening before (for the allocated fifteen minutes) and had managed to make a FaceTime call with her dad – he at least got to see Janet in one way before she died but they will live on with so many uncertainties. Was she alone when she died? Was she in pain or suffering? Did she feel scared? Did she think we had abandoned her?

Diary entry, late March 2020: *Extent of the emotional toll starting to become clear as staff everywhere are looking tearful and distressed.*

Mike Dean, Consultant, Anaesthetics and ICU, Northwick Park: *Every shift, you would come in to see the staff who'd been there for the day or the night shift, people you knew well and who'd been through plenty of crap with you in the past. These had been the really resilient people and suddenly they're sobbing in corners. And it's horrible, utterly horrible. Staff are throwing themselves against this situation like it's the front line of a war, and they're saying, 'What the hell is the point? Everyone is dying, why are we bothering? We're putting ourselves at risk, this is the worst thing we've ever done and it's pointless. These people are simply dying. Why are we here?' And it's a very difficult question to answer because it's fine to throw numbers at it, to say what the national picture is, but it doesn't make a difference. If you have looked after five patients and they've all died you think, What is the point? And that's really hard.*

We didn't have much thought around keeping up morale because the bandwidth was taken up with the basics. So it was entirely down to pre-existing relationships. If you're having a good day, you help the person not having a good day. The senior nursing staff were fantastic, trying to keep people going, but it's really difficult when you're in personal jeopardy, the working conditions are extremely challenging and you have massive fatigue. You get into that position where you're doing day shift, night shift, day shift, day off, and you don't know when it's going to end. You know you're not operating at full strength and not responding to things as you normally would. You get in a tailspin because you're knackered and didn't sleep. When everyone is knackered and not sleeping and in the same position, there are days when you're just thinking, I don't know how we get through this. People come out of their PPE, they drink as much water as they can, they chew a bit of food and life has become functional. No one is chatting because they're too exhausted and they're too tired to cry. Then you go home and you can't switch off. You can't just stop thinking about what you're doing. There is this constant guilt that you're not there, which is illogical, but it wasn't just me feeling that, it was widespread.

Eventually, Mike broke. A moment came when he started crying and couldn't stop. He was told to go home and rest.

Mike Dean, Consultant, Anaesthetics and ICU, Northwick Park: *I couldn't stop crying for days. I was in a heap. It's the closest I've ever come to mental breakdown and it's horrible. On the one hand you think, I can't spend time constantly thinking about Covid, I need to get on to something else. But every time you look at your phone there are a million messages about it and it's all over the TV. I was so grateful to my colleagues for enabling me to have a few days away from the place, but God, the guilt of not being there. You'd have hundreds of WhatsApp messages about things going on at work and you'd think, Christ…*

Staff were suffering in all different ways. One nurse developed symptoms and stayed at home to self-isolate. Her husband also developed symptoms but became very unwell. He was taken into hospital and sadly died of Covid. She recovered, but was left with a huge amount of residual guilt, feeling that his death was her fault because she brought the virus home from work, even though she'd done the right thing by self-isolating. Another member of staff working in admin was evicted from her rented accommodation by her landlady, who was scared she would bring the virus to the property. The Trust was excellent, putting her up in a hotel before finding her a room to occupy on site.

Increasingly, we found ourselves supporting staff as well as patients. We would visit various wards to see what was happening and invariably find staff distressed and overwhelmed. One afternoon, I encountered a nursing sister on Crick ward who was beside herself with exhaustion. I wondered if she wanted a short break to sit and talk, and she agreed. She told me that because of staff shortages, mainly down to sickness, she'd had only two nurses to cover the previous night's shift, which involved the care of no less than twenty-four patients sick with Covid.

'I'm at breaking point,' she said. 'We all are. I've been doing extra shifts to try to help out but I'm so scared my immune system will be compromised and I'll get Covid, too.'

This was a strong woman, more than used to taking difficult days in her stride. But when those difficult days are relentless and you've lost so many good staff to sickness, sliding into despair is almost inevitable.

'We've asked for help,' she said, 'but everyone wants to keep their staff to themselves and agency nurses are too worried to come in. I'm not surprised, really, but it's not helping us much.'

There was little I could say or do to make things better. So many staff were in the same boat – struggling to go on while trying to remain true to the caring, dedicated nature of their professions. As we talked, one of the portering team approached, telling her he'd arrived for a patient transfer to another ward.

'Oh my God,' she said, her head in her hands. 'What next? I just don't have the time to get this together.'

The nursing sister knew she'd have to accompany the patient up to the ward to complete the transfer properly. 'Look,' I said, 'I've done this a million times, so let me do it. You carry on in here. It'll be fine.'

She looked at me with an expression of gratitude mixed with relief.

'Honestly, it's nothing,' I said. 'I'll pop in again this afternoon, see how you're doing.'

Later, I dropped by to find the nursing sister revitalised. She thanked me for what I'd done.

'It might seem a small thing to you,' she said, 'but it really took the pressure off at that moment. I'm so grateful.'

It was a small thing, and even though she was grateful, I felt useless. I couldn't for a moment give myself any praise. I wasn't on the front line having to see and experience what these nurses were going through. In a similar way to Mike, I felt as if I was doing all I could to help, but that it would never be enough.

Claire Windsor, Clinical Nurse Specialist, Palliative Care, Northwick Park: *At its worst, those of us who were at work – because at times we were a skeleton staff – felt anxiety just under the surface. If someone coughed, we used to say, 'Is that you, Rona?', after a meme that was going around at the time. We'd tried to joke but we all wondered if we'd be the next to get it. I used to get up in the morning and think,*

I've survived the night, let's go again. And in a strange way I was buzzing to come to work. It was adrenaline, of course, but I remember thinking, Please don't let me get this because I'm on a roll here. And then after a while, the adrenaline wore off and for me, it was like hitting a brick wall. I was exhausted and burnt out. With hindsight, being on triage all those weeks probably did that. Emotionally, I was just spent. I couldn't give any more. You know that saying, 'You can't pour from an empty cup'? That was me. When you want to keep going and keep giving, to put your hands up and say, 'I can't give any more' is really hard. So I had some time out and my workmates were very, very supportive. I was able to recharge my batteries at home, sitting in the garden, watching the birds with my beautiful Staffie, Susie, beside me. Just something as simple as being in nature.

Meanwhile, patients with suspected Covid were continuing to flow in the direction of Northwick Park. It was noticeable that the average age of those admitted seemed to be dropping by the day. At first it was older people, the seventy-pluses, with serious underlying health issues. Just a few weeks later, there were many more patients in their mid- to late forties and fifties, and while some had health issues others didn't, yet were still dying very quickly of Covid. When somewhere dies in a hospital bay where there are other patients, nurses can usually explain to those who have witnessed or were present in the room that the person who died was 'frail' or 'elderly' or had 'heart failure' or 'terminal cancer'. But now, patients knew they were fighting the very same disease as the person who died in the bed next to them. And the only question on their lips was, 'Is it me next?'

Chapter 17

April 2020

As March turned into April the effects of the virus at Northwick Park showed no signs of abating. If anything, it seemed to be getting worse, or at least building towards a peak. Nationally, things were looking no better. Like many other people, I listened to the Queen's 'We will meet again' broadcast on TV and although I felt boosted by it, there was also the feeling that this was now very serious indeed. That feeling didn't get much better when it was announced that Prime Minister Boris Johnson had tested positive for Covid and had been taken to hospital. Although we nursing staff had had weeks of seeing death and serious illness stalking the wards, somehow these two events brought home the fact the whole country was now in the grip of coronavirus. Where would it all end?

I remember starting to become more paranoid about 'symptoms' I thought I was experiencing – itchy eyes, dry cough, generally feeling rundown. I'd tell myself that I'd definitely got it, only to wake up the following morning feeling fine again. I'm not usually an anxious person but I was beginning to feel that at some point, my time would come and I'd go down with a dose.

My fears were compounded by the concern Mark had for my safety. Everywhere you looked it was Covid, Covid, Covid. People weren't talking about anything else and, as Mike Dean pointed out in the last chapter, the internet, TV, radio and newspapers meant you just couldn't escape the horror. Then, on 2 April, I got a call while I was on the ward. It was Kerry. She'd got Covid symptoms and was feeling very unwell. She was in tears, not just because she now had the thing that was killing people in the very place she worked, but also because she would necessarily need to stay off, just at the time medical staff were needed the most. The guilt factor again…

Kerry Wloskowicz, Clinical Nurse Specialist, Palliative Care: *I got it. I warned my family and I tried to keep everyone upbeat about it. People were dying, yes, but a lot of others were getting better. I didn't like the way the media portrayed what was happening, so I tended not to watch the news. I told my daughter, 'It's OK, we're going to get through this.' I missed the week my colleagues had a lot of discharges, comings and goings, and staff were missing. I didn't like not being there. I felt guilty. I still do bank shifts at the Royal Marsden Hospital and of course I couldn't do that. I knew my colleagues at Northwick Park were struggling. Kelly would call me and she'd be overwhelmed and I couldn't help. So that was the hardest thing – not being able to help.*

There was still panic among non-Covid patients desperate to get away from the hospital, so the discharges continued apace. I worked with one man in his sixties on a medical ward who, ten days previously, had been fit and well until he was admitted with stroke-like symptoms. Scans showed new brain metastases as the cause of his symptoms, as well as kidney and liver metastases. So there was an unknown source of primary cancer and he was too unwell for this to be investigated in-depth. I phoned his wife. She was distraught that she'd sent him into a hospital full of Covid when he had practically begged her not to. As his symptoms got worse, she'd felt there was no other choice than to call 999. Now he was basically being palliated and she felt awful. You can't take away those feeling of guilt, however much you reassure someone that they made a good decision and for the right reasons. Now we knew he had a cancer that he was going to die from, we could make a good plan for his end-of-life care. Of course, she wanted him home and I worked with her and the community teams to get him there with the right equipment and care in place – all via phone, of course.

We were now told to wear masks while on the wards. Incredibly, most staff weren't wearing them outside of HDU and ITU, which demonstrates how chaotic everything was at this time. We really should have been wearing them from the beginning, but like many others I found them uncomfortable and impersonal. Whereas a smile or an empathic look can really help a patient to relax, listen to what you're telling them and respond to what you advise, trying to speak to someone from behind a close-fitting mask just seemed to provoke fear and anxiety. From the moment I put one on I had to fight the compulsion to take it off and show the patient a human face. There wasn't a time when I didn't say, 'Hi, my name's Kelly, I'm really sorry that I have to talk to you from behind a mask.' Hopefully that went some way to calming things down, but goodness only knows what patients in HDU and ITU thought when they saw staff in full PPE – masks, visors, full body coverings, wellington boots. Even seeing the ITU team coming down the corridor was scary enough.

Deaths were coming thick and fast by now. I had a conversation with a lovely nurse seconded from the day surgery unit about an elderly lady patient she was looking after. I took one look at her and told the nurse I thought we should call her family immediately.

'Why?' she said. 'She looks stable enough.'

The nurse could see an elderly person who had eaten breakfast, got up to use the toilet and was currently lying in bed awake and alert. I saw an elderly lady on maximum oxygen therapy, whose oxygen saturations were dropping. I knew that because her treatment escalation plan (which details the level of care a patient will receive if their condition deteriorates – a very important document during the pandemic) was for ward-based care, she would not be offered CPAP or ITU. She would most likely die from this, and within hours. Such was the random cruelty of this disease as it struck down the most vulnerable – even those who, on the surface, looked reasonably well.

It was Easter, and members of the public were donating all sorts of Easter goodies to NHS staff right across the UK. We were getting our fair share at Northwick Park. Janet, a healthcare assistant in the respiratory ward, kindly offered to go down to reception and grab an Easter egg for me one day as I was working on that department. She told me she was back at work having taken a couple of days' compassionate leave because her fifty-one-year-old sister had died of Covid.

'I've just sat at home crying all the time,' she said, 'so being back at work is a good distraction.' And off she went before I had a chance to argue, to get me an Easter egg. Those little acts of kindness will stay with me forever.

Like many of my colleagues, I found the gestures of kindness by staff and members of the public truly humbling. But this wasn't a sudden and complete U-turn in attitudes, and alongside the kindness was increasing unrest. Relatives were now banned from visiting family and while this was accepted at first, as time went on there were more than a few mutterings from people loitering at the hospital entrance. One family who had already been escorted from the premises by security, having tried to push their way in, had somehow got hold of a junior doctor's mobile number and were harassing him constantly with abusive messages.

They claimed their relative had dementia, and there was a loophole in the guidelines which said that if a loved one with this condition was very distressed there might be some leeway about seeing them, if only to calm down the situation. However, she was being nursed on HDU so there was absolutely no visiting allowed. The treating team were deciding on her treatment escalation plan and whether she would be deemed as fit for potentially life-saving surgery for a bowel obstruction. Due to her level of frailty and co-morbidities, including the dementia diagnosis, it was decided that surgery would not be appropriate, meaning a more conservative approach to care would be taken. At which point, the family confessed to having made up the dementia diagnosis so that they could visit her – a lie that could have caused serious repercussions.

In all honesty, there were very few cases like that. If people did turn up and were told they weren't allowed on the ward, by and large they accepted it. For some, just being in the vicinity of the hospital was enough to feel close to their loved one. Sometimes people waited in the corridors after their relative had died, hoping to perhaps get a glimpse of the body as it was wheeled out of the ward. At other times, families chatted to medical staff for updates. Others used technology to say their goodbyes. The Trust bought a quantity of iPads for hospital wards so that people could see and possibly say a few words to their relatives before they died. This came with its challenges, especially when an elderly spouse would be struggling to get to grips with the technology while saying goodbye to his or her partner (by now probably unconscious and unable to respond) for the last time. But at least it was something.

On 9 April, I was working on one of the Covid wards when one of my consultant colleagues asked me for some help. One of the patients, an elderly man, was dying and his wife had been contacted and informed. She was desperate to come in and see him but this couldn't happen. The consultant didn't have FaceTime on her phone, so she asked me if she could borrow mine to arrange a video call. I gave her my phone and the call was placed successfully. Afterwards, the consultant described the scene as very touching, during which the wife could see that her husband was comfortable, in no distress and at peace. She was able to say that she loved him and would always think of him.

The following day I was at home, enjoying some lovely spring sunshine in my garden, when my phone rang. It was a FaceTime call but I didn't recognise the number. When it stopped, I realised it was the number of the elderly lady from the day before. I thought maybe she was calling to try and see her husband again. I sent her a message to say that I wasn't at work, and did she want one of my colleagues at Northwick Park to call her? After a while, she messaged back:

'Very sorry. I thought it was my granddaughter. I was so grateful that you let me use the phone yesterday. Thank you for all you're doing. Have a good day. May God bless you and those you love and keep them safe.'

When I returned to work after my couple of days' Easter break I dealt with a rapid discharge home for an elderly man with advanced prostate cancer. I called his wife – they had been married for more than sixty years – and initially I couldn't make her understand what was going on. I tried to explain to her just how unwell he was, and that I thought he was in the last few days of his life. She seemed to be worried about his catheter being changed, and didn't want him to come home until the new catheter was in place and fully operational. She was telling me that they had struggled so many times to get it changed, it wasn't straightforward, and so the usual procedure that would be done at home had to take place in the hospital – arranging transport, etc. was hard work, so please could we just get it done while he was here? Evidently I was struggling to get the message across and I knew I had to be direct.

'If we delay getting him home any longer, he will die in hospital. He won't make it home at all.'

Silence. Then she became very tearful. 'Oh, I didn't realise how serious this all is,' she said, before asking a barrage of questions about equipment and masks and PPE.

'Can I still hold him?' she asked. It seemed Covid was making us scared of any contact with anyone, even those we lived with and loved the most.

As Randall explained earlier, we recognised early on that our communication skills could be put to good use. Nurses and doctors on the worst-hit wards were struggling to keep up with the barrage of phone calls. As there was no visiting, families were relying on this daily phone contact to keep them updated. Many patients had their own mobile phones and were maintaining contact with their friends, families and loved ones, but even with that, people were still keen to get a 'medical' perspective on how things were. And of course, for those who might not have access to a phone or those too unwell to be using their phone, this daily call from the doctor or nurse became the focus of their day.

Those of us in the team who could go out on to Covid wards would take turns in helping Randall to make the daily calls. Usually we would be on HDU as this is where the sickest patients were and the most anxious relatives were waiting at home for their daily call. Sometimes you could tell that the person you were calling had placed you on loudspeaker for an audience of multiple family members eagerly awaiting today's news. From day one we had learned how unpredictable this disease was so we were always cautious not to give false hopes, only for them to be dashed a few hours or days later. In order to be fully informed when making the calls, we would join the lunchtime handover. We'd listen intently, learning which patients were 'stable' and which ones were not doing so well. It was like a journey to my past nursing life on Dickens ward – talking about oxygen levels, CPAP pressures, arterial blood gases and respiratory rates. The turnover of patients was quite astounding, meaning that we were learning about new patients most days. Many of the patients left for ITU, some as step-downs back to the general wards, and many on the porter's trolley in a body bag.

I was helping with the calls one day in late April. I picked up the phone and dialled the number for a patient's wife, the allocated next of kin. It wouldn't be an easy call; her husband was not doing well. His oxygen requirement was increasing along with his respiratory rate but despite that, the oxygen levels in his blood were getting worse. He was very unstable, deteriorating and waiting to be reviewed by ITU. I took a deep breath, made the call and was surprised when I heard a younger than expected voice answer. This wasn't his wife, it was his daughter – so I asked to speak to her mum. Her next words took me by surprise.

'My mum's in ITU at Northwick Park with Covid.'

Oh my. From her dad's age of fifty-one and her young-sounding voice, I surmised the daughter was in her twenties. I then had to tell her that her dad was not doing well, his breathing was getting worse despite being on maximum oxygen with the CPAP machine and that he was likely to be taken to ITU and ventilated if he didn't start to improve. It was obviously devastating news for her, but she seemed to take it so well. She told me she would let her brother know and would wait to hear further news.

The resilience shown by relatives, loved ones, friends, wives, husbands, whoever we were calling, was amazing. People were even overwhelmingly grateful for their daily call. One family even left a box of chocolates at reception for Randall, as he had kept them updated every day about their father's progress from HDU back to the general ward. It was an incredible time.

Being on HDU meant that we would see and hear emergency situations all around us. The doctors on HDU carried the emergency bleeps that would alert when there was a 'medical emergency team' (MET) call or cardiac arrest call. A few of the HDU team would immediately leave to attend whatever emergency was happening. Intrigue often got the better of me and I would try to find out what was taking place. One day the cardiac arrest call sounded out through the emergency bleep system.

'Cardiac arrest call Eliot ward, cardiac arrest call Eliot ward, D3, that's Delta 3'.

I happened to still be on the ward when a couple of the HDU team arrived back, looking distressed. A thirty-year-old woman had suffered a Covid-related respiratory arrest and was seven days postpartum after having a baby via caesarean section. By getting to her in time, the emergency teams had managed to prevent full cardiac arrest but she was intubated, ventilated and taken to ITU. I didn't hear what happened to her – hopefully she recovered and made it home to her new baby.

The following day I was back on the wards and was asked to support the ward with a family who were really struggling with accepting that their mum, Mrs Patel, was dying. The ward was being bombarded with phone calls and was also struggling to manage her symptoms of breathlessness. She was Covid positive.

I went to see the patient and focused on her symptoms initially before tackling the family. Her death wasn't imminent, although she was in her last days of life. The symptoms were fairly easy to get under control – a small dose of opioid –and this time oxycodone rather than morphine due to her poor kidney function. Oxycodone has the same effect and Mrs Patel looked more comfortable within half an hour. We agreed to monitor how long the effects lasted before deciding the right dose to start a syringe pump. In the meantime, I called her daughter.

From the moment she answered I was hit with question after question. She was anxious beyond words. As we had recognised that her mum was dying, we agreed for her to come and visit and I arranged to meet her as I thought she needed more time than the busy ward nurses could spare. I met her as promised and showed her how to put on the correct PPE. It was actually a really lovely moment to witness – the daughter made a FaceTime call to the rest of the family waiting at home, they were all singing and sending messages of love to their mum/grandma/ aunt. She then made another call to her sister in America, who was saying goodbye to her mum via the wonders of technology – it was all very moving.

When we left the bay and had taken off our PPE, the daughter asked what time she could come back tomorrow and the ward sister, who already thought she had been generous by allowing her to stay for longer than the allocated fifteen minutes, told her that she couldn't come back – this was her one and only visit. At this point, the daughter broke down in tears. She was absolutely devastated. She could still see her mum through the window to the room and was reaching out to her, crying loudly in absolute distress. I felt so very helpless.

Mrs Patel died the following morning and a different ward sister was on duty. The daughter begged her to be able to come in and see her mum's body and was allowed to visit. In one sense, it was lovely that even a pandemic could not hold back compassion, but on the other hand, it was devastating that some patients were dying without seeing their loved ones.

Despite this, I chose to accept that in times of such uncertainty, there will be inconsistencies. Many nurses across the hospital were struggling with the 'no visiting' rule and would often make little allowances where they felt they safely could. After all, there are no second chances when someone is dying. No going back to do it differently next time – *one chance to get it right.*

Chapter 18

Following the chaos which came with the opening days of the Covid crisis, the palliative team had, by mid-April, settled into something that resembled a routine: triaging, arranging discharges, liaising between patients and families, and supporting colleagues exhausted by their time on the front line.

So we had plenty of work to do, and it was highly valid and useful work too. But some of us wanted more. Almost without exception we'd all experienced general and acute nursing before we'd gone into palliative care, and although we'd seen our nursing colleagues who'd been transferred to HDU and ITU looking knackered and in high degrees of emotional distress as a result of their experiences, there was a part of us that whispered, 'I want to know how that feels too.'

Well, that was certainly the case for me. It wasn't an ego thing – I'd certainly seen enough Covid-related death, trauma and exhaustion to last a lifetime. Yet something inside nagged at me to step up and 'do my bit' using all the skills I'd learned since I first qualified. Here was a situation that none of us had experienced, one that was testing every ounce of our knowledge, compassion and physical and mental strength. As a team, palliative care had carved out a vital role and had shown flexibility and adaptability. We had a huge amount to be proud of and there was still a long way to go before any easing of the crisis. On the contrary, mid-April was just about the worst point for the UK, with 1,224 deaths recorded on 21 April, the highest total in a single day since the outbreak began.

Perhaps it was that feeling of helplessness in the face of such horrifying statistics that made me determined to volunteer my services in HDU or ITU as an acute nurse. I spoke to Randall, my boss, outlining the reasons I thought I'd be useful. Quite rightly, he argued that I should keep doing what I was doing. Experienced nurses like Claire, Kerry and myself, he said, were doing a vital job and just because we weren't wearing full PPE and doing twelve-hour shifts in ITU didn't mean that we weren't helping to keep the show running.

I totally got all that. As a service we were very much needed, and we'd more than proved our worth. Even so, precedence was set for volunteering on the most acute wards. Agnieszka Jaworska, a qualified occupational therapist in our team, had been told by her manager that she and the other OTs working at Northwick Park were eligible to volunteer for up to five weeks in ITU as a helper. Below is her account of her experiences within ITU, and I think it's important to allow her to speak fully, because she represents the thousands of volunteers who, although trained in their own field, went selflessly into ITU with little to no experience of an intensive environment and put themselves at risk to help their colleagues.

Agnieszka Jaworska, Occupational Therapist, Palliative Care Team, Northwick Park: *I didn't think about this decision much, to be fair. I never questioned my safety. I just felt this is the right thing to do, and it wasn't so much about helping patients because whatever happens would happen to them anyway. I think it was more for the solidarity of the nurses who had to be there, and was there a better way to show them that people want to help? So to have solidarity was more the reason than actually helping patients, because I couldn't really help them that much.*

Because I've never worked in the intensive care before, I couldn't really say what's normal and what's not normal in terms of their working ways before Covid. I was quite scared about having the full PPE on because I'm usually quite claustrophobic. And it was quite difficult working conditions because it was twelve hours. We worked twelve-hour shifts, day or night. It wasn't encouraged to go to the toilet or to have a drink, to save PPE because you would have to completely undo everything if you go out, even for a second. So no drinking, no toilet. So that was a challenge, but you get used to it. It's amazing what you can actually get used to. I never normally do night shifts, so I think I treated it as a personal challenge for me.

My role was vague at the start because no one initially knew what was going on. It was really difficult to communicate with each other because of the PPE and bleeping noises as well. How it usually works in ITU is

*one-to-one nursing, but quite often it was one ITU
nurse per four to five patients, with other nurses or other
healthcare professionals helping and doing whatever we
were asked to do, replenishing the supplies or repositioning
patients and changing them and things like that. Some days
we were doing one-to-one, which was quite scary because
you were told if there's an alarm bleeping you have to inform
the ITU nurse. But then if the alarm was bleeping with
every patient in the bay there was still only one ITU nurse.
That was really stressful because you can't do much to help.
You're not allowed to touch medications.*

*On some shifts I did very basic things like taking the
rubbish out. The nurses said, 'Whatever you can do, it's
helpful', because it was a crazy, chaotic place. With time,
I even learned to do things I would never dream of doing
or be allowed to do, like taking some blood from the line
or doing the blood gases machine. Obviously things like
holding the [ventilation] tube we were never allowed to
do, but I think the boundaries were quite pushed towards
what you could or couldn't do. Whatever you learned,
then on your next shift you could do. But there was
confusion because some nurses were expecting quite a lot
from you and it was difficult to explain that you cannot
do it, so there was this kind of stress as well. It wasn't
communicated well. Some nurses were even crying before
going onto the shift because they were not from ITU,
so they were extremely scared. Either they'd had a bad
experience already or were scared of what was going to
happen to them, or they were exhausted.*

For me, the scariest thing was when you knew that

patients needed to be attended to now, either because one of the drugs would finish and the nurse had to change it, or they needed suctioning or something like that, and there is actually no one that can physically do it even though you are alerting someone. So that was scary. The dying bit of the experience didn't affect me much. I think maybe because I'm from the palliative care side so dying is nothing new to me, but for some nurses or my colleagues it was a big experience. For me, it was more about comfort, but ITU is all about surviving and it's not comfortable. So I think seeing suffering was the worst.

I remember one patient. We were told that he was dying. He was quite a young chap. He had a mobile phone next to his bed. I was kind of one-to-one with him for some time and the doctor told me just to watch if his family called on his mobile. We knew he had maybe hours left because everything was failing. It's strange to see someone dying on ITU because they're connected to the monitors so you just see numbers changing. He kept receiving messages from his friends and family saying, 'You're going to pull through. We're going to do this or this next year,' but they had no idea that he was actually dying. They were calling him by his nickname like they expected him to read it, so it was just heartbreaking to see that. That's when palliative care is so lovely because we have communication, we discuss things and the patients can do whatever they want.

I was tired at the end of a shift. It was a strange and a very new experience, quite physical because I had a proper marking on my nose from the mask, which was really painful. And obviously things like not being used to doing the shifts. When you do a night shift, obviously you should go to bed before the next night shift, but I couldn't because it was daytime. So then I didn't sleep for that day, then I did the night duty and I found it hard to sleep the following day. Then I had another night shift. Luckily it goes quicker than you think because there are bright lights and monitors and people are moving around, so it's not like you have a night shift sitting in a quiet room. But you can't be sleeping and it's hard to try to sleep during the day. I wouldn't be able to do it for a full-time job.

I have to say that it didn't affect me as emotionally as I thought it might. Perhaps I was running on adrenaline. But I just think that in life you do whatever you are faced with. And maybe there was resilience in the fact that I've got such a lovely team to come back to, and also that I knew there was an end to my five-week rota. I knew it was going to be difficult, so it's not like I really suffered emotionally about that.

I saw the palliative team occasionally but obviously it was difficult because of the twelve-hour shifts. The shifts are quite lonely. You can't talk because of the PPE and anyway, you just need to get on with your job. But also, when you finish, no one's around because you just go home at very strange times. So you can't really offload to anyone then, but when you do meet the team or you have something difficult going on, you just come into the office and say, 'I've had the most horrible experience,' and we all talk about it as and when. Some of the other ITU volunteers don't have teams like mine, so they came back to their teams feeling lonely and that feeling continued. In palliative care we are taught how to build up resilience and how to look after yourself. But maybe this is not the same with other teams.

Looking back, I'm glad I did it. I'm actually quite proud that I survived those things like having the PPE on for twelve hours, which even now feels like 'How did I do it, seriously?' Or the night shifts. It was an amazing experience that I would never even dream of having in other circumstances.

There were challenges. I enjoyed working with the ITU team but some nurses weren't always easy to get on with because they felt that this was not how it was supposed to be, that OTs were helping, because we couldn't help fully. We just couldn't do some things. Some nurses were annoyed about it, but others said, 'Without you, we wouldn't be able to go through this.' And some shifts finished with clapping, so there was this amazing atmosphere of 'We did it.' It was a very positive experience in a funny way.

I went with a view that I do whatever I can, but there are things I cannot do. No one expected them from me. But if you go to ITU as a doctor, even a junior doctor, or an experienced nurse, you are expected to do a lot of things and you feel that responsibility with drugs and things like that. So I think that had a big impact.

I felt proud to be able to help in any way I could, but I didn't have the responsibility that others had. It was more like, 'Tell me what to do and I will do it,' rather than me deciding what I needed to do, as in my usual job. So it wasn't like I was making decisions about patients, which I think the doctors did and maybe there was a difference. If ever volunteers were needed again, I'd do it, definitely. It would be a waste of experience if I didn't.

Whenever we saw Agnieszka in the office we'd quiz her about the experiences she was having in ITU. It sounded extremely demanding, exhausting but, as she said, also very fulfilling. The more I listened to her, the more I wanted to have the same experience. I knew from talking to others, and from making phone calls on their behalf, that what was going on in HDU and ITU was extraordinary.

Mike Dean, Consultant, Anaesthetics and ICU, Northwick Park: *The junior doctors were amazing. Absolutely extraordinary. The people we already had in ICU who knew their way around went from being F2s [Foundation doctor level] to working at registrar levels with nothing in between. And you'd walk round at 3am with an ophthalmologist (an eye specialist), you're having a discussion with them about whether you should prone this patient (i.e. have them lie face down on their front, which is found to be more effective for those struggling with breathing) and you're thinking, They're doing quite well, given that they probably haven't seen a patient lying down for three years. They are bright people, adaptable and resilient. You are in awe of the fact they have picked this up so quickly. They've mastered it within a week or two of getting there. Very impressive.*

When it was going fine, it was going fine, but it was a brittle system because everyone had to work on nothing but Covid and there was a lot of stuff people couldn't do. From things you'd normally assume would be done, suddenly you have to think about every single part of what was going on. For example, someone would have hyperkalaemia [increased potassium levels in the blood], and you had to get them on a

*filter, and they'd say, 'Oh, we've no filters left,' and so you say
we'll treat them medically, and the surgeon can't remember
how to do that. So you have to say, this is how we do X or Y,
and that was difficult. You're using a lot of your brain power
to take an overview of the patients and who might live or
die, or be proned or transferred, and you have to get into the
minutiae of stuff you don't have time for.*

*I was fortunate that nobody flicked their tube out when
they were being proned, but there was a guy who did have
that experience and it was awful. You have to re-intubate
them, which sounds easy, but when you're dealing with it
alongside someone who hasn't done this before, instead of
a team of people who know, you're with people you don't
know. You're asking them for stuff and they don't know the
equipment. When it went wrong, it would go wrong hard
and all of the things you'd normally do didn't apply, so you
have to think through every possible gap. That was difficult.*

More than a few of us wanted to employ the clinical skills we'd
learned as qualified nurses and doctors on one of the Covid
wards. Gilli Erez, our dedicated consultant within the palliative
care team, was one of those.

**Gilli Erez, Consultant, Palliative Care Team,
Northwick Park:** *Yes, I wanted to help out. Not in
intensive care because that's not an environment where I'd
feel most confident in my skills, but I definitely could go
on any of the medical wards and just be a general medic.
I suggested that at some point but it didn't happen. At the
time we weren't busy with our normal business, but we*

weren't sitting there doing nothing. Some staff were ill and others self-isolating, and so every day you didn't actually know who was going to be there. Our team is not big and you'd think, Actually, if you need some of us and you lose me for a month or two, that could be difficult. I think my consultant colleagues were not happy about that. Nobody would have physically stopped me, but they were not encouraging. So I decided, fine, I'll try to find things to do that I will feel I'm helpful. And yes, I found them and they were helpful, if not always satisfying.

I was more than happy with the work myself and the palliative team had been doing up to this point. I also knew that if I didn't have the opportunity to work in either HDU or ITU, I would regret it. Again, I approached Randall, my boss, and this time he agreed. So I booked a bank shift in HDU. Now I could finally join the front line, at least for a few shifts. As ever, my self-doubt was present. Was I being selfish? Was I doing this for personal gains? Was I putting my family at risk? How will I manage the guilt if I catch Covid and then my team is another member down? Oh well, too late now. I would be assigned to HDU on 24 April.

Chapter 19

A warm spring morning. 7.30am, 24 April 2020. Walking towards the hospital from the nearby Tube station, I felt an unusual buzz of anticipation. Since Covid had taken a grip on the country and thousands of NHS staff went from being doctors and nurses into something close to battlefield medics, every day in the war against coronavirus felt unpredictable, scary and sometimes thrilling. Even so, now about six weeks into the crisis we were adapting to this strange 'new normal', along with everyone else in the country.

Today, though, was a different kind of anticipation. I would be working in Northwick Park's high dependency unit, which was full of patients with Covid-19, for the best part of twelve hours. This would be the first time I'd returned to acute medicine for nearly ten years, and on a ward full of extremely sick people needing close and continuous monitoring for any signs of deterioration. Being a senior nurse within the Trust meant that most HDU staff on duty knew me. Today, however, I would be the junior; not Kelly the Palliative Care Nurse, but Kelly the Bank Nurse. I would be guided by them and work according to their way, inviting them to boss me around as needed.

A HDU is based on the same layout as a conventional hospital ward, except it has fewer beds – usually four instead of six. Beside each bed are a cardio-monitor and a machine to regulate and monitor high-flow oxygen. If patients need specific interventions there is more space for machines and medical staff who need access to them. The nurses working in there need to be completely proficient in using CPAP (continuous positive airway pressure) and BiPAP (bilevel positive airway pressure) machines, and managing high-level procedures such as inserting lines straight into arteries and monitoring blood pressure and oxygen levels. In HDU, situations can change rapidly and nurses need to be highly skilled in dealing with such critical developments in a patient's health.

Patients in HDU will generally include those admitted with serious illness – cardiac arrest, perhaps, or chronic asthma and other breathing problems. Age-wise, it's a mixed bag – quite a number of older people but also younger people needing acute treatment, and anyone previously on a general medical ward who may have developed something like sepsis and need more intensive treatment. Most of these patients will be awake, unlike those in ITU, who are likely to be in an induced coma while they are treated, a high-flow oxygen machine working the lungs so the body has a chance to rest and recover.

HDU nurses wear scrubs, as opposed to the regular tunic-and-trousers combination that I and most general medical nurses wear. That day, however, we were all wearing an extra layer of protective clothing. By now, I was used to some level of PPE on the Covid wards – a face shield, mask and goggles – the requirements in HDU were higher. Two people were needed for each 'donning and doffing' session, as they are known. First, you washed and dried your hands and made sure your hair was tied up in a net if it was long. You then put on your goggles and visor, followed by your gloves and an apron. Chlorine wipes used to clean the visor and goggles and the strong bleach made your eyes water and your throat dry up. The apron needed to be tied securely at the back, hence working in pairs. Then you put another set of gloves over your other pair, making sure that the sleeves are tucked in. A pair of polythene protectors are placed over your shoes. Finally, you strapped on the close-fitting face mask that was worn during every minute spent in HDU. As I donned all this gear, immediately feeling the 20-plus degree heat I would be working in, I felt a renewed sense of admiration for the front line staff who had been doing this, day in and day out, for weeks.

We were split into our teams for the day – each bay being allocated two nurses and two HCAs so that there could be two inside the room providing patient care and two outside acting as runners for medications, linen, etc., as well as recording and documenting the patient's vital signs.

Outside every bay there was an hourly record of each person's statistics in the form of a graph. When you completed the observations you'd place a dot on the graph, joining it to the last dot marked on the paper. This gave an indication of how well – or otherwise – someone is doing. If it was going in the right direction you'd be pleased that there was improvement. A trend in the wrong direction, and you'd consider that at some time reasonably soon, you might need to escalate treatment to the ITU team or contact relatives to give them bad news.

It was strange to see very unwell people awake and alert, albeit connected to CPAP or BiPAP machines. Some were looking at their phones, others were reading iPads or books. These were sick people who could very easily take a turn for the worse and be dead within the day, such was the unpredictability of Covid-19. Yet there was an odd air of normality about the scene – another sign that we now lived in a strange new world.

One of the patients in my bay was an elderly gentleman, Mr Singh. He was a widower who lived on his own and although he was in his eighties considered to be reasonably fit and healthy. He was still active and had been doing his own shopping until quite recently. Now, sadly, he was dying.

Mr Singh had been admitted to HDU for a trial of CPAP after contracting Covid, as his oxygen levels were dangerously low, even with high flow oxygen being administered. He had sufficient pre-existing health conditions and a level of frailty that meant he wouldn't be strong enough to go into ITU. But CPAP wasn't enough and he was deemed unfit for ITU treatment, his weakened body not likely to recover enough to ever be successfully taken off a ventilator.

Besides, the process of ventilation is traumatic. If it's deemed necessary, the patient will be given a strong sedative via a cannula. This relaxes all the muscles in the body including the lungs, so effectively, you stop breathing. The ITU team, including senior consultants, anaesthetists and critical care nurses, must now move very quickly. The patient's head is tilted back and the ventilation tube is inserted very carefully down the throat and into the lungs. The machine then starts to do the work of the lungs while the clinicians get to work taking bloods, monitoring heart rate and oxygen levels and generally just allowing the patient's muscles to relax. If the patient shows signs of recovery, which could be days or weeks, eventually the tube is withdrawn when he or she is considered capable of breathing alone. This is known as the 'weaning' process and it can be a slow and complicated business. As a patient you need to have made a strong recovery and be generally resilient before this can happen. Unfortunately, Mr Singh was not in this position.

The Last Days of Life Care Agreement (LDLCA) had been initiated the evening before and Mr Singh's relatives were informed over the phone by the senior doctor who was not able to offer them the opportunity of saying goodbye in person. After a long life within a close-knit family, the best we could offer Mr Singh and his family was a link via the ward iPad. Such hard times, but they understood and had taken that opportunity. They had no choice but to put their trust in us that we would care for his every need while they sat by the phone, waiting for the call to say he had died.

Mr Singh was becoming agitated with the CPAP mask, making feeble attempts to pull it off. I had already been made aware of the care plan details – *'If not tolerating CPAP mask, sedate and remove'*. This would result in death within a few minutes. I made sure he was clean and comfortable, albeit that he was semi-conscious and so weak that he seemed to have nothing left. I wiped over his face with a cool cloth, he was hot and clammy because he was working so hard to breathe. I then gently lifted the mask for a second so I could moisten his lips.

I spoke to the other nurse in my bay and we agreed that she would go and prepare the medications while I stayed with Mr

Singh. She prepared the morphine and midazolam injection, just enough of each drug to reduce the burden of his symptoms of severe breathlessness and agitation. Meanwhile, I made the call to his family to tell them what was about to happen. I spoke to his niece. She sounded upset but resigned to what I was telling her.

'It's fine,' she said. 'I've been expecting this call. Do what you need to do and please ring me again once it's happened.'

Mr Singh was given the sedative and we waited while it took effect. His restlessness abated and now he was calm again. The nurse and I removed his mask together, avoiding eye contact with each other in a strange and surreal moment. Were the other patients in the bay aware of what was happening? Should we have told them and explained what events were unfolding behind the curtain of the man in D3?

After the medications had been given, my co-nurse left and I was alone with Mr Singh. I had offered to stay while she went to prepare the lunchtime meds for our three other patients. The lack of oxygen was taking effect and his breathing had slowed to almost nothing and he was completely unresponsive. There wasn't even a flicker of his eyelids. I held his hand, already cold and changing colour, and for want of anything else I could do, I decided just to talk to him.

There I was, with a man I hadn't met before today, who had been mostly unresponsive in the short time I'd known him and he spoke little English. How could I possibly find the right words to say to him as his life ebbed away?

'I've been talking to your niece,' I said, 'and we've had a nice chat. They all send their love and they've told me they're all thinking of you.'

Through the window I could just about see the shapes of clouds high in the blue sky.

'It's a beautiful day,' I said, 'just perfect. The shapes of the clouds are amazing – changing all the time, but ever so slowly. You're doing really well, Mr Singh. Just keep focusing on your breathing… in… and out… in… and out.'

His eyes flickered for a moment and he started to show weak signs of agitation, including the familiar grimace. As I've previously mentioned, this isn't always a sign of pain but a reaction to the body working a bit harder to breathe.

'There's nothing to be worried about now, no need to fight. Just relax and let go.'

The breath was becoming shallower now as it reached for the last particles of air. There wasn't time to prepare more drugs. Within seconds his life would be over. I imagined his birth so many years ago in a far-off country, and I pictured a little boy, playing in fields and dusty streets with his friends under a sky as blue as the one we had today.

Within a few moments, he died. Although his last few breaths were an exhalation of all the fight and stress he'd been through in the past few days, I can't say it was the settled and peaceful kind of death I was used to seeing. However, he didn't suffer for long, and at least someone was with him at the end. His face was now relaxed. There was no grimace, just a peaceful expression.

Once Mr Singh was checked and his death certified by the duty consultant, I made the call to the next of kin, the niece. The doctor offered but I wanted to do it. I hoped that it might give some comfort to the family to hear from the person who had been with him when he died. Maybe.

Afterwards we washed his body and called for the porters to remove him to the mortuary. For a moment I watched as he was wheeled away. As ever it had been an honour and a spiritual experience to be present with someone at the end of their life.

Following his death I went to see the other patients in the bay. It seemed only right to be honest with them, if they hadn't already guessed. The curtains had been drawn around Mr Singh but he was wheeled out by the porters in a shroud. One man nodded and expressed his sympathies. He was in his fifties and had recovered well enough on CPAP to be stepped down to a medical ward. This was a victory not just for him, but for the resilient ward nurses and doctors who'd battled to keep him going and, in the midst of so much chaos, had some good news to celebrate. He was due to go later that day and although weary from his fight, was pleased to have survived.

'There for the grace of God…' he said, looking at the empty bed across the bay.

Another male patient, Mr Ali, was not doing so well. When I spoke to him about Mr Singh he responded with just a flicker of his eyes. He was only fifty years old and had no significant medical history. He was slightly overweight but not on any medication and had no reason to visit a GP with regularity. Prior to being admitted he hadn't realised how unwell he'd become but the virus had taken hold quickly. When I first encountered him that morning his oxygen levels were low, despite being on the maximum settings on CPAP. His breathing levels were high and he was on CPAP. He was sleeping a lot but managing to do some breathing exercises with the physio and to have a little food and drink at lunchtime. Even so, he was becoming more tired as the day passed and his temperature was rising.

As a precaution his family were called to tell them that things weren't looking too good.

In the early afternoon he asked me if I could help him get to the toilet, situated on the far side of the room. He was having a break from the CPAP on high-flow oxygen. The mask can become very claustrophobic and we aimed to give regular breaks if we felt it safe to do so. I switched the oxygen tubing from the wall to the tank and we set off. He really struggled but he made it. I stayed outside the toilet, wondering if he was OK. Several minutes passed. Finally he emerged, gasping for air.

At that moment I realised I had risked too much and should have offered him a urine bottle at the bedside. In these situations there is always a battle with maintaining independence and dignity. I thought it might be worth the effort to achieve that small level of independence; now I wished I'd erred on the side of caution. With pure determination, hanging onto me with a hot and clammy hand, he made it back to the bed.

I quickly re-attached the oxygen to the wall, making sure it was on maximum. I attached the oxygen saturations monitor and saw the reading – 45 per cent. Immediately I felt a sense of terror rise up in me. Normal oxygen levels should be around 98–99 per cent and we would worry about anything below 90 per cent. Never in my years of nursing had I seen such a low reading for someone who was still up and walking. Very quickly, I put the CPAP mask back on and settled him back on the bed, barely taking my eyes off the monitor. Slowly, the levels came back up, eventually reaching the 90s, and I let out the breath I hadn't realised I was holding. Even so, Mr Ali was still sleepy and barely responsive so my colleague and I decided to alert a consultant. She immediately called the ITU team to come and review him. They took one look at his chart, another at Mr Ali, and realised they would need to intubate him as soon as possible, knowing that no one can maintain a work of breathing level this high for too long.

The ITU senior registrar was young, but calm, collected and clearly very much in control. She acted quickly and efficiently, organising what she needed her team to do while taking it upon herself to call the family. Mr Ali spoke broken English, his first language was Arabic. One of the junior doctors helped to translate the difficult conversation with him, then called his family to explain the situation. The registrar was brutally honest with both Mr Ali and his family, telling him and them that if he wasn't ventilated soon, he would certainly die. She also explained that only 50 per cent of patients who are ventilated will survive – basically his chances of living were now 50/50. Mr Ali's consent was confirmed with a nod of the head.

'Is there anything you would like to say to your family before we put you to sleep?' the doctor added. The undertone was clear, '*You may not survive.*'

But he was now too weak for words. There would be no goodbyes.

Unfortunately Mr Ali's family were not so accepting. He had three children, in their twenties, all of whom had seen the horrific footage from Italy of patients on ventilators and those being nursed in the prone position. Such images were not a pretty sight but they conveyed the truth of how dangerous this virus could be. As soon as they heard the word 'ventilator', they'd consulted Dr Google and knew the survival statistics almost before the doctor had a chance to tell them.

Within the hour they'd arrived at the hospital, despite the

visiting ban, and were outside the ward. The doctor went to meet them and was greeted with a barrage of pleas not to intubate their father. Quickly, this became tearful begging, but the doctor was clearly familiar with the script – she'd had this conversation before and it showed. Kindly, calmly but with extreme clarity, she helped this family to understand that although uncertain, ventilation was the only option left for their father – without it, he would die, and quickly. Given that, there was little choice and the trio finally seemed to get the message. They backed down from their protestations and hovered outside the ward in the hope that they would catch a glimpse of Dad as he left for ITU.

Back on the ward, it was time to get on with the rest of the evening. I wondered if the nurses or doctors ever followed up their patients who left for ITU, looking for closure. I knew I would want to find out about Mr Ali, even if it was the worst news which, given the state he was in, I fully expected it to be.

It was nearing the end of the shift, three of my patients had gone, one male patient remained and another man, in his late forties, had been brought in, currently on CPAP but stable and doing OK. At around 7.30pm, a lady was brought into the bay. She was a Romanian in her eighties and spoke not a word of English. She was in acute respiratory distress, with oxygen levels already low and continuing to fall, and her respiratory rate sky-high.

She was calling out in a very distressed way and although I didn't understand her words, I knew where her distress was coming from. She was in a bay with men. She kept pointing and shouting and then pointing again. She gestured towards the curtains, clearly wanting us to pull them around but we couldn't.

She was really unwell, and almost on the point of hysteria, but she needed to start on CPAP straight away and then be closely monitored, which was not possible with the curtains drawn. In 'normal' times, we would never mix female and male patients in the same bay, but these were far from normal times. If there was a bed with a CPAP machine, the patient would go there, regardless of the gender mix.

None of us could explain any of this to her and she didn't even have a phone that we could use to call her family so they could translate. She was scared and isolated and had no understanding of just how unwell she was. After what seemed like hours, we finally managed to calm her down just enough to fit the CPAP mask. The fight and the distress, plus her acute condition, had totally exhausted her. Even so, I could see the terror in her eyes as the mask was pressed to her face. Her fear was almost contagious and I began to feel somewhat claustrophobic and jittery. As I finished my shift, I could see the nurses were still trying to settle this poor lady. Later, they would attempt to contact her next of kin. It was going to be a long night for the nurses and a terrifying one for the patient.

I was free to go, but not without 'doffing' all my PPE first. Off came the first set of gloves and the apron, to be bundled up and incinerated as soon as possible. Then I was taken to a special taped-off area, where my visor and goggles were removed and cleaned with heavy-duty antibacterial fluid. The shoe coverings were removed and binned. Finally, I could take off my second pair of gloves – very carefully, just in case any microbes of virus were attached to them. Before I left, I looked in the mirror. I still had the deep impression of the mask around my nose and mouth, which wouldn't fade for a few hours ahead. I looked fatigued, and couldn't wait to taste the still-warm air of this gorgeous spring evening.

As I left the ward, I was comforted by the familiar sound of the domestic lady singing to the patients. Francella, a Jamaican woman who brings joy wherever she goes, has worked on HDU for as long as I can remember. Despite the risks to her own health, she donned her PPE without hesitation, singing her beautiful songs as she mopped, scrubbed and polished. Francella was a little ray of sunshine in the middle of a dark storm and for her efforts to keep people's spirits up, she later received a 'Hearts Hero's' award, where the Trust recognises individuals who go above and beyond their duties.

I drove home exhausted but satisfied. I had made a difference today and had been given a glimpse of what the acute ward staff had been through over the previous weeks.

I later found out that Mr Ali was transferred to the Nightingale Hospital before being successfully taken off the ventilator and repatriated to NPH about two weeks later. I can only imagine the relief his family must have felt. The Romanian lady continued to deteriorate, her son was finally reached and she was placed on the Last Days of Life Care Agreement. She died a few days later.

Chapter 20

By May there was a sense that we'd gone past the absolute worst of the pandemic and into a phase in which, if nowhere near 'normal', there was some feeling that the NHS had got a grip on the situation. To paraphrase Winston Churchill, who knew a thing or two about national crises, it wasn't the beginning of the end, but the end of the beginning.

At the end of April we held a minute's silence outside the hospital in honour of all the patients and a number of staff who'd died and so that the Trust's most senior managers could show their gratitude to everyone who had come to work during the crisis, recognising the level of personal sacrifice. It was a wet day – unusual during the pandemic, when most days had been beautiful. Rain or not, we stood outside in solidarity with people we'd worked alongside and some we'd even looked after. For me, the gathering was a very proud and emotional moment, and a time of reflection.

At the end of the silence, we clapped – it started as a slow rhythmic hum, gradually getting louder and louder as people clapped with passion and intensity, an expression of mutual respect and appreciation, with tears flowing down their cheeks but smiles on their faces.

Later that day, I chatted with the ward manager from the respiratory ward, who'd been so unwell with Covid that she'd been admitted to Northwick Park as a patient and had spent more than a week there on high-flow oxygen. She was so ill she thought she was going to die, to the extent that she said her goodbyes to her family. Luckily, she pulled through but weeks later still felt traumatised and was experiencing shortness of breath with overwhelming fatigue. But at least she was back at work, with the colleagues who became her carers.

Then it was back to work as usual, facing the day-to-day challenges the virus had thrown in our paths. Before Covid, I'd often thought about why 'dying' is still such a taboo and why we are so reluctant to talk about it. Coronavirus had made the topic inescapable and certainly many NHS staff had been forced to confront and initiate awkward conversations revolving around the 'D' word. I have to remind myself that I am always going to be much more comfortable with talking about dying than most – it's my job to be OK with confronting worries and concerns from patients, families and staff when it comes to the dreaded topic of 'death'. Yet, there is still a residual feeling that if we talk about death explicitly, somehow that very conversation will make it more likely to happen. It's a completely illogical belief, but one which seems to have a tight grip on people.

A case in point: a man in his mid-nineties was admitted to Northwick Park from a care home in early May. He was diagnosed with Covid, was suffering from dementia and was bedbound. He was given antibiotics, IV fluids and was closely monitored on an acute care of the elderly ward, but it was clear he wasn't improving. Neither was he eating, and we were seeing the signs of deterioration. As there was no visiting, the liaising with the family was done over the phone. The man's son was contacted and it was explained to him as gently as possible that the aggressive treatments and interventions tried so far had not had the desired effect, that despite their best efforts, his father was getting worse. They explained that his father now seemed to be suffering and appeared to be nearing the end of his life. Instead of continuing with treatments that were failing, the focus could be shifted into management of symptoms and an end-of-life care plan that would guarantee him comfort and dignity in his last days.

Then all hell broke loose.

The son accused the consultant making the call of trying to kill his father. 'You've given up on him,' he claimed, going on to suggest that they were starving him to death and didn't care about him. Multiple phone calls were made by senior and junior doctors all trying to convince the son that, in fact, they were trying to do the right thing by him as a human being.

None of this seemed to cut any ice. 'You'd better have your notes in order,' he warned, 'because I'm going to sue the lot of you.'

I could've exploded with anger. How could this kind of behaviour not affect us as practitioners? How could we be expected to do the best for our patients, particularly during the most challenging time in the history of the NHS, when families treated us like this? It was truly hurtful to be accused of neglect, and I wondered how many cases it would take for a doctor or a nurse to throw in the towel and find something less stressful to do instead?

The conversations with the son continued, to the point that he was told that an exception could be made if he wanted to come in to see him and say his goodbyes. But he didn't want to do that. 'No, thanks,' he said, 'that's just putting me at risk.'

Every nurse or doctor in the hospital environment has experienced a 'kicking-off' at one time or another. Very often it's just people letting off frustration-generated steam and it rarely lasts longer than a mistimed outburst. Sometimes, though, it's about a person's own guilt. Perhaps this man felt guilty about placing his dad in a care home, guilty about not being there enough when he'd had the chance, and guilty about not coming to see him in his dying days?

I felt his attitude also reflected badly on the whole palliative care approach. Our mission is to keep people living well until they die. Yet the belief still exists in some that if someone dies, we have 'lost the fight' and if we save them, we have 'won the battle' – even if that means a person is now bedbound, cognitively impaired, fed through a tube. But at least they're still breathing, right?

Other things made me angry. An elderly lady was brought in from a care home with end-stage motor neurone disease. She wasn't able to use her legs and had very little movement in her arms and hands. However, there was nothing wrong with her thinking; that was as clear as day. When I saw her, I was shocked at the state she was in. Her hair was so matted at the back, it had formed dreadlocks and it took me a couple of hours over two days to brush it out, cutting out chunks that were too matted to rescue. Her teeth clearly had not been cleaned for at least a couple of weeks.

I was appalled. *What a sorry sign of our healthcare system*, I thought. I understood that by now, care homes were bearing the brunt of the Covid crisis and were overrun with chronically ill Covid patients, and possibly understaffed to boot, but really, how could anyone excuse the state this poor woman was in? This was *real* neglect, bearing no resemblance to the sort we were being accused of by the son of the elderly man.

> **Diary entry, 14 May 2020:** *The wards are quieter. It's as if someone has pressed 'rewind'. Every few days another ward is cleared of Covid patients. But referrals are increasing, as those who have not died from Covid are battling the symptoms they are left with, and many will die due to poor reserve. Complex patients admitted who have missed planned treatments such as surgery, chemotherapy, radiotherapy because of Covid and are now dying. And there is talk about a second peak. That's too much to think about now. I feel like I haven't dealt with what just happened.*

That last point was an important one. Many of us felt that we'd barely begun to process the effects of the last few weeks. We'd been through something akin to a war situation that none of us were expecting. We often wondered where the next terrorist attack would be, and how we'd respond. We couldn't have predicted this, and as the pace slackened, we started to see emotions coming to the surface as people began to realise what they'd been through. Our department had been having regular ad hoc support sessions at the height of the crisis but it was felt we needed to come together as a team to talk about what had gone on, how we'd reacted to it and what we were feeling now.

Randall, our boss, arranged a debrief session for everyone. It was intense, emotional and often brutally honest. There was sadness for those who'd died and guilt from staff who'd had to self-isolate and not be there when they were needed most.

Randall Jones, Team Leader, Palliative Care Team, Northwick Park: *The debrief was an eye-opener. There was a lot of anger and frustration. Some people considered the Government had mucked it up. They thought some things didn't go right in the Trust, not so much in the team themselves, but I think there was a lot of anger there too. There were a lot of tears – that was just the opportunity to let it all out because they had been so full of adrenaline throughout it all. There is a term 'adrenaline hangover'. Now it was quieter in the hospital and their adrenaline levels had dropped. They were getting back to their normal jobs and it was a bit like, 'What do we do now?'*

So there was that situation going on with them and it was just nice to have this debrief for them to recognise, 'I'm feeling exactly the same way or I've still got similar feelings to that.' I think they've learned new ways of working and are much more supportive of one another. It's a shared experience. I think what they will take forward is that Well, we lived through it.'

Liam Murray, Clinical Nurse Specialist, Palliative Care, Northwick Park: *Having left my previous role as a ward manager, I ventured into the world of palliative care;*

this gave me the opportunity to return to what I loved most about nursing – having patient contact and the ability to spend precious time with patients and those close to them. This luxury was taken away from me and the rest of the team during the Covid-19 crisis.

I felt extreme guilt at times. Due to several health conditions I am regarded as being in the higher risk group, but though not requiring shielding, was rightfully advised to have limited patient contact.

I was given tasks to earn my keep/give me a purpose while also being given the opportunity to watch my colleagues struggle both physically and emotionally every day, knowing full well that I was undeniably adding to their stress levels. I felt like a spare part – unable to support, unable to empathise. All this while waiting for the results of my own Covid test, which has since been confirmed as lost.

I was, and remain, thankful to be part of such an outstanding, professional and caring team, who have each other's back through thick and thin. We have shared lots of good (and not so good) times – as I am sure this book lays testament to. Most of all, I feel blessed. Blessed that I had an amazing wife and three amazing boys, Noah, Samuel and Finn, to go home to every evening, along with my mam and a plethora of family and friends both sides of the Irish Sea at the end of the phone.

Yes, there was a lot of anger, frustration and plenty of tears. We still had staff off sick or shielding and there was a new worry about a second peak and the hospital being full once again. Randall did his best to help people bring out the positives too, and there were many of those. Overwhelmingly, though, there was genuine trauma and stress at what had been witnessed. Some of the nurses looking after patients on ventilators who died said they wondered if they were at fault because they weren't used to using the machinery or hadn't noticed something changing. That seemed to be a common theme among everyone who'd worked on the front line and although it was over-thinking at its best, this kind of 'could do better' guilt still clung to these staff, and to many others in the hospital. People were also scared of letting their barriers down because once they're dropped there is no raising them again. The thought of repeating all this during a second peak was unbearable.

Mike Dean, Consultant, Anaesthetics and ICU, Northwick Park: *I've got this worry that although we never had to make impossible decisions, in the sense we never said, 'We don't have a bed and you can't be ventilated', we did have to make really difficult decisions about who would be appropriate for this level of treatment. But we had to remind ourselves, these were decisions we'd been making for many years and although the circumstances were different, the questions remained the same: 'Is this person likely to survive an ICU admission?' 'What will be the toll on their bodies of the ventilator, the lines, the immobility?' 'Will they ever get back to a quality of life acceptable to them?' 'Will they have the capacity to rehab from the pit they will be in after weeks on ICU?' Early on, we realised there wasn't an effective treatment for this and the stats said that if you're on a ventilator with Covid, it's likely to be two to three weeks. We know better than anyone what two to three weeks on a* *ventilator looks like. You need a certain level of reserve to cope with that. Very early on, we were having conversations with people in their eighties where, in the normal times you'd say, 'You have bronchial pneumonia, we can try antibiotics, ventilate for a couple of days and review,' we couldn't do that with Covid. If people needed ventilating, they would need weeks rather than days of treatment and that caused the goalposts to move massively. Sometimes I felt like we were saying, 'I'm so sorry, but we can't give you a chance.' I'm sure it felt worse because we were having these conversations day in, day out.*

In the early days those were difficult conversations. Our physician colleagues quickly realised we'd moved the bar of ventilation, in that it was recognised that it took so much to survive an ICU admission that for many it was not an option; it was not in their treatment escalation plan, and soon we no longer had to have those discussions. I was grateful at the time but you do worry, 'Who was it we said no to?' or 'Who didn't we even ask the question of?' My parents are in their eighties and a number of times I called them thinking, I will tell them that if they get Covid and they need a ventilator, they won't have it. But I couldn't do it. Luckily, I didn't need to, they've been fine, but there is that sort of 'in the back of the mind' thing of 'Who was it that died that didn't need to?'

In the middle of May, we had a 'Schwartz Round'. This is a forum where staff from all parts of the hospital – clinical and non-clinical – can come together to discuss the emotional and social impacts of working in the NHS. It is named after an

American doctor who died of lung cancer in the 1990s and was very keen on fostering compassion and empathy among caregivers. Schwartz Rounds are held regularly, and obviously it was deemed vital that we have one to deal with the aspects of what we'd so recently experienced, and were still experiencing. The usual format is a panel of three or four who discuss a topic, or topics, and once everyone has spoken, anyone else in the room can chip in their experience or reflection. It's not a forum in which criticism is dished out, or even to fix a problem; it's an opportunity to talk and be heard.

Our 'Covid special' Schwartz Round featured on the panel the hospital's chief nurse, one of the anaesthetic consultants, a HDU nurse and a junior doctor. The discussion was relayed via Zoom to different parts of the hospital, and despite the barrier of technology and screens, the conversation was powerful and hard-hitting. The emotional toll on everyone involved was acknowledged. The chief nurse described how staff felt so alone at the beginning when the crisis hit the hospital, and that even Public Health England couldn't advise on what to do because it was all unknown. They were working until midnight and then back in at 6am the following day, supporting the huge impact of the sudden influx of Covid patients needing ventilators. She then got symptoms and became really unwell at home, infecting her husband, who also became very sick. She told us how panicked she felt when she became breathless, wondering how quickly she might deteriorate. There was also recognition that this thing was far from over, and that staff might need to dig into all their reserves of strength and resilience, if and when a second peak arrived.

For me, the most interesting part of the Schwarz Round was when a nurse said that in times like these, some people cope and others don't. An anaesthetist took this one stage further, observing: 'There are people who look like they cope and others clearly don't, but the ones who look like they cope also need attention and support, because they've seen the worst of this.' I thought these were wise words, and I wondered about all those staff who'd made decisions on the hoof, managed and looked after staff, supported patients and dealt with death on a daily basis. These were the copers – but what would happen to them now?

Randall Jones, Team Leader, Palliative Care Team, Northwick Park: *Following discussions with the psychology team, we agreed to co-facilitate debriefs for nurses who had been redeployed from their normal jobs into intensive care. The most traumatic thing I've ever had to do in all of this was to listen to these nurses as to how traumatised they were by their experience of working in ITU.*

You had nurses who worked in a day surgery unit, dealing with people who would come and get a mole removed and then walk out. Some of these nurses hadn't seen a dead body for twenty years and they were put into ITU, told they were going to be there to help the ITU nurses, and because of the sheer numbers of intensive care patients, by Day Two they were looking after their own patients. Many hadn't seen a ventilator for years, or not at all, but it was a necessary case of 'get on with it'. So there was a lot of trauma.

By now, we all understood that we had been at the epicentre of the UK's experience of coronavirus. It was a surreal position to be in. We'd learned so much about this virus and how to treat it, but that learning came at a hefty price: patient and staff deaths and severe illness, plus the residual 'trauma hangover' many were experiencing. It was no wonder so many of us were wandering the corridors of Northwick Park in a daze.

On Friday, 22 May, I was the designated triage nurse (the person based in the office to process referrals and take all the telephone calls) and it happened to be the busiest day we'd had on triage since the height of the pandemic a few weeks previously. Things were getting back to what passed for normal, with wards gradually emptying of Covid patients and filling again with the non-Covid people who needed urgent treatment for a variety of conditions. It was the usual round of phone calls to wards and families, arranging transport here, there and everywhere. By the end of the day I fully expected to have what we call 'Triage Face' – the look you have when you're about to collapse in a heap. Then we had the weekly Grand Round, a long-established medical tradition of sharing best practice and keeping up to date with procedures. Unsurprisingly, that week's subject was Covid and we had teams from ITU and HDU talking about their experiences. It was also a chance to hear some up-to-the-minute statistics around the hospital's capability; we learned that at Covid's peak there were no less than 63 Covid ITU beds at Northwick Park, the highest number in the country, and there was a need to create 6–8 ITU beds every 24 hours. Enough of our patients needed ventilating to fill a big ITU every three days.

We also learned that patients were transferred to the

temporary Nightingale Hospitals, which had strict criteria to take only the 'straightforward' Covid patients: those with no other significant history, meaning that we had all the complex patients. Despite all of this, they managed not to have to refuse anyone an ITU bed and never had to tell a family that their loved one would die due to a lack of beds.

By all measures this was extraordinary and it made me immensely proud to work at Northwick Park. It has had its detractors, and more than its fair share of bad press over the years. And as staff, we all like to complain about the place now and again. But when Covid struck, we witnessed the absolute best of what the NHS is about, compressed into this hospital's incredible experience on the Covid front line. The teamwork and camaraderie were second to none. We all deserved a pat on the back, but as NHS staff we didn't expect it. We would just keep on keeping on, day after day.

Exhausted from the shift, I went home that evening and fell asleep on the bed. I woke up about thirty minutes later, had dinner and then settled down to watch some TV with Mark. But instead of relaxing, I felt an overwhelming need to get out of the house. I sat quietly, hoping the feeling would pass, but it seemed the walls were closing in and I was becoming more claustrophobic by the second. I needed to leave, right now.

'Mark,' I said, 'I think I need to get out of here for a bit.'

He looked at me quizzically. 'Are you OK?' he asked. 'What's the problem?'

'I don't know,' I said, 'but I need some fresh air. Will you come with me?'

Of anyone, Mark knew how strange and stressful the last few weeks had been, and not just for me. He'd listened while

I'd described the day-to-day life of a hospital practically under siege, and had been 100 per cent supportive and sympathetic. He didn't need to be asked twice.

We got in the car. Mark drove as I sat there, feeling that my head was about to explode. We reached the nearby common, parked the car and found a bench to sit on. Mark began to talk, asking me how my day had gone. I couldn't reply. I was beyond words. Instead, I started to cry and found I could not stop. Mark looked at me in astonishment. I think he thought I was about to tell him we were breaking up.

Of course it wasn't that. The barrier I'd put up when the news broke of a viral tsunami heading our way and the first Covid patients arrived at Northwick Park was finally down. At the beginning of the pandemic I'd been excited, almost. Curious to see what would unfold, thrilled to be part of something so massive. This excitement had mutated into sympathy for those ill and dying, and for the worn-out nurses and medics looking after them. I'd seen the best of humanity and the worst of human suffering. And all the time I'd been running on pure adrenaline, just like so many others, and now I was completely out of juice. Spent, exhausted, running on empty.

'It had to come out, Kelly,' Mark said quietly.

The rest of the weekend I spent doing nothing other than self-care. I didn't phone anyone from work to talk about what had happened. The following Monday, I went into work and, as usual, was handed a list of patients I'd be seeing during my shift. Inwardly, I still felt like collapsing; outwardly, I told myself that I'd get through it. That day I also had my Covid antibody test and just like many others who had the same test, I wondered what the result would be. During lunch I could hear staff talking about it, speculating whether they'd had the virus or not. I assumed that I'd probably had it. It seemed illogical to have worked in a place rammed full of Covid and not to have had a dose. I'd experienced 'symptoms' that I knew weren't really symptoms at all, just psychosomatic reactions to the environment I'd been working in. Perhaps I was one of the emerging cases of people who were asymptomatic but still tested positive. Meanwhile, we were expected to carry on as normal, but sometimes you just can't. You're forced to recognise that you have issues to address.

The following day, my colleague Claire and I met with a Macmillan psychologist, who was part of our wider team. We'd both experienced similar feelings around the difficulties of keeping calm in this crisis while trying not to lose our heads, even when others were losing theirs. We talked about team spirit, and how hard it was when colleagues were away and the team became fragmented and disconnected. We described how it felt to be worried about becoming ill and even dying. The psychologist understood. She'd been working with staff from ITU and all throughout the hospital who'd had their own war stories to tell, their own complex baggage to offload. Even the act of talking this way made me feel better and brighter once again.

The psychologist summed things up in a phrase I have gone on to use many times: 'We've all been through the same storm, but in different boats.'

That same day I received the result of my Covid antibody test. It was negative. I really couldn't believe it – maybe my daily grapefruit had come good after all…

Chapter 21

Diary entry, 6 June 2020: *Patients are feeling the distress at not seeing their family/friends/loved ones. Today I saw a patient on one of the medical wards. Her pain was increasing despite our efforts to symptom manage with analgesia. She said to me, 'Seeing my son and daughter would be better than any of these medicines you keep giving me.' I also heard that a patient with newly diagnosed pancreatic cancer had her 'breaking bad news' consultation with the oncology consultant, Macmillan nurse, and her family, all on FaceTime. We're all noticing that patients are suffering due to lack of physical contact with anyone for weeks.*

The early summer of 2020 brought with it deeply mixed feelings about what had gone on over the past few months. This first wave of Covid was over, but even now there was talk of a second spike, peak or wave. The death toll was shocking, and among those who'd had a bad dose of the virus and survived there were fears over long-term damage to health. Damage of another kind, in terms of the effects of mental stress on patients, staff and the public who'd endured weeks of lockdown, was also coming to the fore. It was a confusing, destabilising time as the fallout from this first wave settled across a dazed and battered country.

The session with the psychologist had, for me at least, helped to clear the air on a few issues. Most of the team was now back in work and once again we were on the wards as palliative care nurses treating non-Covid patients. However, fear and sadness still stalked the corridors, particularly around the lack of access for visitors. All nurses see the value of a friendly visit to a patient, and in palliative care we recognise family involvement and support as integral to what we do. Covid robbed patients of this basic right, but we did our best to facilitate visits where we felt it would be beneficial.

Around this time a man in his thirties was brought in with end-stage lung disease and heart failure brought on by years of heroin smoking. Previously, Pete had been referred for a lung transplant but this was declined because he simply couldn't beat his heroin addiction. On the day he arrived we had a phone call from the community palliative care team to say that he was in A&E and could we see him?

When I got down there I discovered Pete had been placed in a private room on one of the bigger wards. So I went there instead, to find a large group of people talking to the ward sister outside the room. It was the man's family, who were hoping they could see him, but as the ward sister correctly explained there were still restrictions. Only one person from the group could see him, and for just a short time.

The family seemed grateful for the information and wandered off down the corridor. Meanwhile, I went into the room with a consultant to see Pete. I expected it to be a difficult visit; someone so unwell with the added complication of heroin addiction would need to think about the problems of withdrawal and opiate toxicity. I knew his baseline would be poor, and I relayed this to the consultant, but nothing could prepare me for the scene in the room. Pete was lying on the bed, evidently malnourished, skeletal and obviously dying. We knew he'd lived on his own for a long time and the results of that neglect were clear. Recently he'd moved back in with his mum, who'd been doing her best to look after him while he was bedbound. It was a pitiful sight indeed.

Later that day, when his family had been given the bad news, Pete's mother had been told that she could stay with her son. She was really struggling to accept the fact he was dying and her desperation to be with him in his final days, or hours, was there for all to see. Although the fact she was there at all was a bonus in these times, we felt she might benefit from other members of the family being able to visit, so Pete was placed on an end-of-life care plan which gave a little more flexibility and, with permission of the ward sister, would allow the family to come in one by one to say their goodbyes.

Some of the family came, but Pete's mum couldn't be there when they visited. However, she was told that if Pete took a turn for the worse, she'd be called in immediately. The day after this was relayed to her, I came into work to discover that he'd died at 2am. Shortly afterwards, I took a call from a community palliative care nurse who said she'd just come off the phone with Pete's mum. It turned out that despite the promises of the ward sister, no one had made the call to tell her that he had deteriorated further and was likely to die. The first call she said she'd received was shortly after he died and was told that his body was being taken to the mortuary. For its part, the hospital said someone had tried to call before Pete's death but couldn't get a response.

I phoned Pete's mum and she was clearly angry and distressed. After relaying the story to me about how the night nurses had failed to call her, she asked if she might be able to see her son's body in the mortuary and bring one of her other sons who hadn't made it to the ward to say goodbye. It was a big ask – absolutely no visitors had been allowed down there since the Covid outbreak. However, as there'd clearly been some miscommunication somewhere down the line, with tragic results, I hoped the mortuary managers might make an exception. Several phone calls and emails later I had agreement that, yes, the family could visit for a limited period of time.

On the Friday of that week I met the family at the main entrance. Despite saying there would be 'just a few family', about eight of them turned up. Although there was still a lot of upset at what had happened, they were so grateful that we had been able to arrange this final visit. We talked about managing their upset and anger, and how it could be put aside for a while so they could focus on what was about to happen and remember that moment. We walked to the mortuary, and while Kerry and I sat in the waiting room the family were allowed to go in. Pete looked so peaceful, which was a blessing for them all. Sitting in the waiting room, we could hear the family inside the room where Pete was. Although there was plenty of crying, there was also lots of story-telling and even laughter. It was lovely to hear.

After thirty minutes or so the family reappeared. The change in their demeanour was evident; finally, they'd been able to say goodbye and they realised they'd been lucky to have the opportunity to do that. This family's experience brought home the fact that so many people during the Covid period didn't have that opportunity, and I wondered about the seeds of trauma that were sown for such people as a result. Not everyone gets the chance to say goodbye to relatives and friends, but if the opportunity is there, it really should be taken, if only to help with closure at a later stage. For me, one of the saddest aspects of the whole pandemic was the lock-out for visitors. I understood why, and that it was for the right reasons, but it was tragic nonetheless.

All of us who experienced first-hand that terrible onslaught of the Covid pandemic have mixed feelings about it, to say the least. I could never have imagined that the whole team at Northwick Park would come together so strongly in support of each other and our patients, but the battle scars will last a lifetime. And, like a battlefield, people died in distress and fear, and died alone.

Mike Dean, Consultant, Anaesthetics and ICU, Northwick Park: *One of the things that will come out of this is that we will get ongoing psychological support. A lot of reflection has gone on in terms of the clinical aspects, and at an individual level, but the unremitting workload means there isn't much time to sit and come to some conclusions. You have to sort of carry on, and I do worry that will have a long-term impact. I worry that talented people will start saying, 'I don't want to do this anymore. I can't expose myself* *to that again, I need to find something else to do.' Or there will be mental-health issues, lack of resilience, something long-term. I don't know what the solution is, to be honest. As intensivists, we are all relatively pragmatic people; we're not taken to reflective practice and we're a bit more 'crack on, there's work to be done'. So as a group we're not well suited temperamentally to taking stock. But we're all trying to make the best out of it and keep going any way we can.*

My colleague Claire, who spent eight weeks toughing it out on triage, the job no one likes doing much, feels that more open conversations with patients, colleagues and families about death and dying have occurred as a result of the pandemic.

Claire Windsor, Clinical Nurse Specialist, Palliative Care, Northwick Park: *People often say to me, 'I don't know how you do your job. You must be a special kind of person,' but I think looking after the dying is the best part of nursing. It's a real litmus test of how we look after society in general. If you can't do that well, then I think you have to question how you look after any other part of society. For me, it's a privilege to look after people in their final days. Like being a midwife for the soul.*

Death and dying is still taboo in this society. We should try to normalise these conversations and encourage people to talk with their family members and to think themselves about what they would want or what they wouldn't want at the end of their lives. We see so many cases where people have never talked, never been able to voice what they would want, and then they end up with horrific things happening to them – care and treatment that you wouldn't want.

I think Covid has accelerated this, definitely, because it encouraged people to think, 'What would I want or what wouldn't I want? Would I really want ventilation?' I've heard stories of people saying, 'Oh, no, I'm too old for a ventilator. Let's free that up for somebody younger.' It's not usually as black and white as that, but it's encouraged people to consider these difficult issues.

Randall Jones, Team Leader, Palliative Care Team, Northwick Park: *We're about to start a programme called 'Serious Illness Conversations', which is getting non-palliative care specialists to start having conversations earlier in a patient's – I hate the word 'journey', but journey – about what's important to them and what do they want to do? How much treatment would they want to have? Rather than us telling them, we actually start asking them.*

Ironically, one of the aspects of Covid that has been a positive for us was the amount of deaths, because this became a normal conversation for everyone in the nation. Every day we saw on the TV '600 deaths today'. Which got people talking about death and dying. It sounds cruel and awful, but in a way this was good for us. It made it easier for us to have such conversations and when I was ringing families at home, they were asking, 'Are they dying?' Whereas normally you rarely get that open an acknowledgement of the possibility that someone could die. So that's changed palliative care and I think a lot of doctors had a lot of discussions about death and dying. As to whether they did them perfectly or not, that's another matter. But at least they had them.

Among staff, the way the Trust handled the pandemic came in for some criticism. 'Too little, too late, not enough support, not the right PPE', etc. My opinion is that it was brilliant. When events become as serious as they did in February/March 2020, you have to be flexible, be prepared to take serious decisions on the hoof and also make the odd mistake. No doubt mistakes did happen, but because the Trust is under pressure at the best of times they acted very quickly, in my opinion, to establish a command team that made good decisions based on rapidly changing events. The Trust's communications were good – we had an email update every day – and when Covid admissions began to slow, the Trust concentrated a lot on staff well-being, encouraging one-to-one and group discussions. They managed staff anxiety well, fostering a 'be kind' message, which I thought was important because people were feeling and experiencing so many different things. I think a big part of our success in coming together as a team and literally fighting our way through this was due to the general culture and everyday life at Northwick Park. Under-resourced, over-stretched in every way, we are used to dealing with crises on a regular basis – lack of beds, major incidents, etc. – so we have the mentality of just taking whatever is thrown at us.

As a team, we recognised that some of us felt differently about the response to the outbreak than others. I was very much in the 'let's do this!' camp and, as I've mentioned, I found it hard at first to accept that others might be more cautious, but as time went on and I saw the full effect of Covid on patients, I could understand why there was such worry. I wouldn't have done anything different, but perhaps I'd have been more tolerant of differing points of view. As for the perception of our team within the hospital itself... I'm pretty sure we've always had a good reputation but as a team we'd all agree that we've had many moments when staff from other departments haven't really got what we're trying to do in terms of palliative and end-of-life care. I hope that people continue to be braver when approaching difficult conversations and start to talk more openly about dying. I am more passionate than ever about not avoiding these conversations and feel by doing so, we are denying people the chance to live the life they choose – not the one we dictate – in their final weeks and months of life. How do they know their time is coming if we don't tell them?

Claire Windsor, Clinical Nurse Specialist, Palliative Care, Northwick Park: *I think in a way it's brought some of us closer together. I think we have a strong bond in our team anyway, but it is interesting to see how different people respond to crises. There is still the uncertainty of what the future brings. Things are constantly changing. Do we need to self-isolate? Do we not? Do we have to wear masks and how long for? We're having to separate in the office, and when there were only a few of us turning up each day, we didn't have to think about that. It was unsettling when most people were back to work and there was too many of us to fit in our office, with social distancing, and people had to find desks somewhere else. And that just really brought home to me how much of a close-knit team we are.*

There are times in the office when the anxiety and the stress is palpable, but the vast majority of times it's good-natured. We have fun, we sing, and we laugh. We can really be ourselves. We can offload. And when we weren't allowed to do that, when we had to separate, which was so hard to do, it really brought home to me how much I get from my colleagues.

Has the pandemic given us a better standing within the hospital? I'm not sure. I think the wards that we were able to help with the telephone calls, with the support, I think yes, very much so. I feel we have a particularly good standing in this hospital anyway. I definitely feel respect from colleagues on the wards. I get the feeling that they value our input and our expertise. And there are things that we've been trying to implement in the hospital for quite a while. This was a slow process but when Covid came along, it happened overnight.

Kerry Wloskowicz, Clinical Nurse Specialist, palliative Care, Northwick Park: *I'd like to believe our team had a good reputation prior to Covid. We're very proactive. We do things in the name of good patient care, a bit beyond what we should be doing, but I think Covid has given us a different perspective. When sometimes people hear 'palliative', they hear dying. And it's about educating. If someone is palliative, it doesn't mean they're dying. It means that you're not going to get better from what's happening, but that doesn't mean you're going to die today or tomorrow. We can start talking, having discussions and try to take back that word. It shouldn't be an unhappy word.*

Gilli Erez, Consultant, Palliative Care Team: *I think we have changed skills. We've skilled people up very quickly in hospital in managing routine end-of-life care, which is good. Whether it will last, I don't know, but they know*

*basics probably better than they did. Maybe not always to
the quality that we aspire to, but it's better than the baseline
we had before.*

As for the NHS as a whole, at the time of writing our stock is
sky-high. In the past, respect for it has been patchy, to say the
least, and we've had criticism piled on us from all directions.
Now, though, the NHS is on a pedestal and all of us who work
in it need to keep it there. This will happen when we push hard
to drive up standards then consistently maintain them. It isn't
acceptable to not phone a family when you promised to do so;
not acceptable not to give someone good care because they're
demanding; not acceptable to get angry with patients because
they're agitated. My aim is to be part of a drive to get real care
and compassion back into the NHS, just like it used to be.

**Claire Windsor, Clinical Nurse Specialist, Palliative
Care, Northwick Park:** *I was completely overwhelmed
by the support that we had. I'm not usually a weeping
willow, but there's a banner outside the hospital saying,
'Thank you NHS' and every day I saw it, tears came to
my eyes. The support, the gifts, the clapping every week
and the sustenance that we've had from people has been
overwhelming. And I think we've always had the support
of the community, and the whole Covid crisis has escalated
that. There were so many people out there who genuinely
felt helpless and they wanted to do something to help us –
whether that's feeding us or whatever it may have been.
People desperately wanted to help us.*

Nurses as a whole don't like to talk about money and pay.

We've always said, 'Oh, this is a vocation.' But you know what? It may be a vocation, but it's also a professional career. People work so hard with such great qualifications and hard, hard work, and it just doesn't feel that that's recognised. We've never gone on strike really, and I think in a way, we don't do ourselves any favours because it's almost like we're being held over a barrel because we will always put our patients first.

We just get on with it. We have crises, and every winter there are pressures, there are people in corridors, in A&E, and NHS staff just get on with it because that's what we do.

Claire is right. We do get on with it because that's what we do. Kindness and care is at the heart of the whole palliative ethos and although (at the time of writing) the thought of going through this again is almost overwhelming, if we have to do it we will. We are resourceful, adaptable people; fraught and frazzled sometimes, overworked always, but we've signed up to put the patient at the very heart of everything we do as a health service. That, if nothing else, is a reason to get out of bed every morning, pull on an unflattering uniform and head for the hospital, ready to face whatever the day brings.

Epilogue

January 2021

It's a Sunday morning and I've just finished a bank shift in the high dependency unit (HDU) at Northwick Park. It's been an exhausting night, and an emotionally draining one too. Once again, we are looking after people who, in any other circumstances, simply wouldn't be here. A week or so ago they were looking forward to Christmas, albeit in much reduced circumstances than previous years. Even so, they were out shopping, buying presents and hoping the day itself would be as bright and happy as they could make it. Now, they don't know whether they will live or die, and the odds on their survival are not great.

When I put the finishing touches to the final chapter of this book it was late summer 2020 and some sense of normality had returned to Britain following the Covid outbreak in March. The sun was out, pubs and restaurants were open, people were going on holiday (me included: Cornwall was beautiful) and our kids were even looking forward to returning to school after being away for so long. True, we were still wearing masks to go shopping and sort of keeping a sense of social distancing, but other than that, the view was that the worst was over.

At Northwick Park life had returned to near normal. Covid deaths and even admissions had pretty much flat-lined and although we were grumbling about having to wear masks on the wards (a real bugbear of mine – I hate that patients can't see who they're talking to), all the pressure and horror of those early months had fallen away. There was talk of a second wave and among medical staff it was entirely expected at some stage. But not necessarily within our Trust area. We assumed we'd had the worst of it; back in March we were at the epicentre of the UK outbreak, having to declare a critical incident, and once that first wave had subsided, we considered that those who were likely to get Covid had already had it, with the rest developing herd immunity as a result. There were rumblings of problems up north, particularly in the Manchester and Liverpool areas, but as far as we were concerned, north-west London was in a much better place than it had been for months.

Finally, the palliative care team could get back to what we do best: caring for people with life-limiting conditions and providing compassion, warmth and humanity. We were seeing a lot of sick patients around this time, particularly those who had missed appointments or did not want to come in because of the Covid situation. There was still a wariness about coming into the hospital, which meant we were quieter than usual, plus the fact that visiting was still restricted.

Then, in October, the tier system was introduced and we started to see local lockdowns and restrictions come into force in parts of the country where the virus seemed to be increasing. Yet there was still very little happening at Northwick Park in terms of Covid and I began to wonder why media reports didn't reflect the calm, quiet situation we were seeing at the hospital. It seemed strange that we were once again being placed into restrictions of varying kinds, with the knock-on effect of unemployment, failing businesses, school closures and kids being sent home, increased mental-health issues, suicides, etc. Even though I'd seen first-hand the devastating effects of Covid, I really began to question the sense of imposing blanket restrictions on a population who'd already been through so much.

These feelings stayed with me right through the autumn of 2020, but when, in December, the Government announced that Christmas visiting of relatives would be severely restricted because the infection rate was soaring upwards, I was almost relieved. 'Relieved' is the wrong word, but finally I understood that the top scientists were seeing a much bigger picture ahead, and that what was being proposed was the right thing.

As I write this, daily admissions to Northwick Park with suspected Covid are increasing rapidly. Even though most of us took the advice and stayed at home over Christmas, the pre-lockdown mingling, shopping, etc. is no doubt responsible for this spike, plus the new variant of the virus, which seems to be responsible for rapid transmission. There were two HDU wards and two ITU (intensive care unit) wards, but as of now, one of the HDUs has been converted into an ITU. We usually have eighteen beds in ITU and now there are around forty, filled with people severely ill with Covid, most of whom are on a ventilator, with the rest on CPAP (continuous positive airway pressure) machines.

It's a scary situation. It helps that we have been through this before, so we have the logistics, procedures and plans in place, and that helps to alleviate some of the panic. Despite everything, the hospital is calm, though we're still shocked by how unwell people are and how quickly they're deteriorating. The new drugs that have been used for a while now – dexamethasone and remdesivir – are helping to keep people out of ITU, but it remains to be seen just how many people actually leave ITU once they're in. I needed to go to the hospital mortuary last week and was told by the technician that deaths are definitely increasing by the day.

The vaccine is currently being rolled out for staff at Northwick Park but not everyone has got it yet, even front line people. A walk-in facility was opened for us, along with an online booking system. However, problems quickly arose with this when it turned out some members of staff were walking in for their jab and then using the booking system to obtain jabs for relatives, with the result that some members of the public are now happily inoculated while front line staff still haven't been called. Even in a pandemic, and even within the NHS, selfishness knows no boundaries.

There has also been an issue with a small proportion of nurses refusing to have the jab. Whether this is a cultural thing or a misguided belief in various conspiracy theories I don't know, but it's something we've recently had an issue with. One nurse went so far as to issue a WhatsApp message claiming that staff shortages (of which there have been many) are nothing to do with having symptoms and/or self-isolating, but because they've suffered side effects from the vaccine. Nothing could be further from the truth, of course, and the nurse has been disciplined. In my opinion, the disciplinary action didn't go far enough.

We've all had to endure constant disruption to our working lives. Palliative care is a big team and even before Covid, we were somewhat squashed into our small office. Since the pandemic, orders from above have limited numbers in the office to five, which means that some days six or seven of us must look for another workspace. We have to wear masks all the time, as I've mentioned, except when eating food and even that has come with its hazards. Whole teams have been sent home to self-isolate because they've eaten lunch in the staffroom and one person has subsequently been tested positive. So, staff shortages have been an occupational hazard for a long time and now, as a result of the twice-weekly lateral flow tests that have been introduced, we're seeing the infection rate among us rise again, leading to even more shortages. It's a horrible vicious circle right at the wrong time.

The wards have been labelled 'red', 'amber' and 'green', and a risk assessment has to be done for every member of staff to see which wards they can work on ('red' being the highest risk and 'green' the lowest). For various reasons not all members of staff can access red and amber wards, so we're back to the situation where just a few of us are able to see patients in need.

When we can visit, we almost always find there is far more to do than simply offer comfort. The ward phone is constantly ringing, so we will take a turn answering calls, usually from members of the public checking on relatives. We'll also wash patients, help them eat their food – whatever we can do to assist. Often a ten-minute visit becomes an hour, such is the need for extra staff.

Unlike last time, there is more scope for people to visit their dying relatives now. We had a difficult family meeting last week with the daughter of a Romanian man who is very unlikely to survive. She came in with her husband and was allowed to say her goodbyes, dressed in full PPE. This time, doctors are making it very clear that you enter a Covid ward at your own risk, and that you must accept this before you go in. They were one family among many. Once again, some family members are holding vigils outside wards just to feel closer to their loved ones and because they feel so helpless at home.

In the summer I was accepted for the Oxford/AstraZeneca vaccine trial and was given two jabs of either the vaccine or a placebo – obviously, we didn't know which. A couple of months ago, we were given the opportunity to find out which we'd had and it was a big temptation because if you were in the lucky 50 per cent of those vaccinated, you could expect a certain sense of relief. However, it was for this very reason that I chose not to find out until very recently, knowing that if I were aware I was protected my behaviour might change and cause me to become more complacent as a result.

When I could see how bad things were becoming again at work, and how contagious the new strain was, I decided the time was right to find out my results. I've always been highly conscious that I could bring the virus home and I wanted to find out for my family's sake as well as the patients I was caring for in the hospital. So, I did, and it turned out I'm one of the lucky ones who had the actual vaccine (both doses). I've tried hard not to let it change my behaviour and become complacent, because there are still so many unknowns. When I found out I thought, *Oh, great – now I can take the train to work instead of the hassle of commuting by car* – which proves the point about being complacent! So, I'm sticking to the car until things have calmed down again. As the Government has suggested, I'm acting as though I have the virus.

At home, we're trying to keep as positive as we can. It's winter, of course, so the good weather is absent and the opportunities to get out and about, as we did in spring 2020, are much fewer. It's a difficult time for everyone, but at least there is a glimmer of hope that the vaccine will get us through this. Personally, I think I've changed a lot over the past twelve months. I feel happier and more settled at home; previously, it felt as if I needed to fit everything in when I wasn't at work, and that just relaxing at home was boring. Now I appreciate being home, being together with my family and just doing simple things that make us all relax and reduce our stress levels. Understanding this has done wonders for my mental health and although I say this as someone who can get out of the house and go to work, I am thankful for all the things I previously took for granted. I feel lucky, and I see how fortunate I really am.

The personal cost is different for everyone. For many in the NHS, it's living with the effect of seeing patients die despite the very best efforts, medical and nursing care to keep them alive. Also, it's living with the guilt of taking the virus home and passing it on to loved ones.

For me, it's all of this, plus the guilt of not being there for my child. Leaving Ronnie at home alone or sending him to his friend's house, where a support bubble has been established, is heartbreaking. Livvie helps a great deal and is a wonderful sister to Ronnie – but she is just that, his sister, at a time when he needs his mum. The guilt is overwhelming. I had to make a choice and not only did I choose to keep working, I worked longer hours than I needed to and I worked bank shifts. Has it affected Ronnie? Yes, I think it has. Late one evening when he couldn't sleep, I sat on the edge of his bed and had a heart-to-heart. I asked if it bothered him that I wasn't around much at the moment. 'I can't say that,' he replied, 'because I know your job is the most important possible job.' This is the personal price – the trade-offs we make.

Professionally, I feel (and I hope) that I'm kinder and more considerate to my work colleagues. I am a perfectionist and do things to my own high standards, but I've accepted that it's OK if other people aren't like me. I realise that we all have different strengths, and others have strengths in areas that I don't. Also, I appreciate how difficult life can be for ward staff. I really do think that relations between us in palliative care and staff on the wards have improved vastly over the last year. Everyone smiles and says 'hello' to us, and we feel very much part of 'them', as one big team.

I can't speak for the NHS as a whole, but personally I hope we see positive changes once this is over. However, I'm not entirely optimistic; it won't take long for people to slip back into their old ways, taking months and years to make decisions that could and should be taken far more quickly, plus wasting valuable money on management consultants and the like. I'd love to see huge changes – for example, nursing become more accessible to people who aren't academic and don't want to go through the expense and stress of university. Good nursing does not require a degree. It takes a huge amount of kindness, compassion, courage and a determination to make a difference to people in need.

On a local level, I hope individual NHS Trusts learn to look after their staff better. We've had years and years of underfunding, leading to constant staff shortages and resultant drops in the standard of care we should be providing. NHS staff have got the whole country through this. Now it's the country's turn to look after us, and help us put more staff on the wards. And perhaps the public can learn to be a little more patient with us, too!

Back in HDU, we currently have four male patients in the bay. Two have been 'stepped down' from ITU, meaning they're over the worst and will almost definitely live to see another day. I wish I could say the same for the other two men, but I can't. One is fifty-five and really isn't doing well. Up until a few days ago his daughter, who also has Covid, was in HDU but has now been stepped down. Eventually, she will go home to her mother and brother, who have also been infected.

The father is clearly terrified of what might lie ahead. He cannot take his CPAP mask off for more than a few seconds because his oxygen levels immediately drop. He can just about manage a few sips of water before the mask has to go back on. I normally look after patients whose death is expected. This man isn't meant to die yet. He hasn't got a horrible cancer, nor has he been in a terrible road traffic accident. His time isn't up. He has simply been in the wrong place at the wrong time and has contracted a virus that may well kill him. I watch over him all night, noticing that he can only maintain his oxygen levels once he's been 'proned' on his front or to the side. I talk to him, trying to offer comfort, but all I see are tears rolling down his cheeks as he struggles to pick up his phone and send a message to his family. His laboured breathing is accompanied by pinging from all the high-tech machinery around his bed, and those of others in the bay. It is a noise I hear constantly –

even when I'm off duty it's going around in my head – and I wonder how this man (or any of these patients) ever manages any kind of normal sleep.

All I can hope is that he pulls through, and that eventually he looks like the patient in the opposite bed, out of ICU and gradually moving away from the danger zone. The relief coming from him is incredible. He smiles constantly and is literally happy about everything, so much so that he's even looking forward to hospital food. Amid all the horror and upset that this virus has wreaked, and is still wreaking, this man is a symbol of hope, and a testament to a health service that has stepped up to the mark in this terrible crisis, saving his and countless other lives. We're not perfect, but we do our best, twenty-four hours a day. In matters of life and death, that is as much as all of us can hope for.

KELLY CRITCHER
LONDON, APRIL 2021

Acknowledgements

Firstly, thank you to Mark. You have been there for me and stuck by me through more than you imagined.

Thank you to our children: Ellie, you are not always here but you are never far away and always in our thoughts. Livvie, you are a ray of sunshine and you have taught me so much about life and the importance of being happy – thank you. Ronnie, you are brilliant – so strong-minded and stubborn (not sure who you take after!!) but I hope these qualities will take you far in life.

Mum and Dad, thank you for giving me the best possible start in life and the true gift of a happy childhood. Oh, and for bailing us out of Thailand!

Tom Henry, this book is here thanks to your belief in my story. I might write another just to work with you again! And on that note, a big thank you to my editor James Hodgkinson and the team at Bonnier for making my story into an actual book.

My brothers and their families: Andie, Carrie and Millie. My niece and nephews: Morgan, Rhys, Euan, Nate and Zac – reach for the stars.

Mark's family: Christine and Ron, Martin, Kirsty, Laura and Kerrie and all your children and grandchildren. You are all an important part of my life.

My work family: I wouldn't and couldn't have done this without you. Kerry and Claire, we've been together from the start and kept each other strong. Liam, you've kept us laughing. And to those not mentioned in this book but who put up with me every day: Choi, Kelsie, Ian, Nisan, Susan, Charles, Wai-Peng, Charlotte and Rekha – you are my friends, colleagues, and teachers.

To the wonderful junior doctors and consultants who inspire me every day on the busy wards of Northwick Park: you may not be mentioned in this book, but you make a difference to the lives of colleagues and patients every day. Thank you.

To my wider team in cancer services, thank you all. And to Joan, for being the glue that holds us all together.

Will, for being my best life-long friend. We don't see each other often, but I love our time together. Your girls – Rudie, Topsie and Dorrit – are a true credit to you and the time and love dedicated to giving them the best childhood. I'm sure they will have the most wonderful, life-long memories.

My netball family – what would life be without you? A special mention to Denise and Hannah – netball brought us together and keeps us going. The best sport in the world.

Laura and Claire, we give each other the strength to get through the dramas and battles of parenthood and life.

A huge thank you and a world of gratitude to the nurses, healthcare assistants, doctors, AHPs, discharge practitioners, ward clerks, porters, domestic staff, the M&S team, Adam's fruit stall and everyone else who has worked tirelessly and bravely during the past year.

And thank you to India and Sam's families for allowing me to tell their stories. I still meet Mel from time to time and her strength and positivity never ceases to amaze me. After he died, Sam's family set up The Sam Keen Foundation, which to date has raised over half a million pounds.